Statistical Analysis
for Public and
Nonprofit Managers

Statistical Analysis for Public and Nonprofit Managers

Leanna Stiefel

PRAEGER

New York
Westport, Connecticut
London

Library of Congress Cataloging-in-Publication Data

Stiefel, Leanna.
    Statistical analysis for public and nonprofit managers / Leanna
Stiefel.
          p.   cm.
    Includes bibliographical references.
    ISBN 0-275-93301-6 (alk. paper)
    1. Management—Statistical methods.   2. Public administration—
Statistical methods.   3. Corporations, Nonprofit—Management—
Statistical methods.   I. Title.
HD30.215.S75   1990
658.4′033—dc20   89-16131

Library of Congress Catalog Card Number: 89-16131
ISBN: 0-275-93301-6

First published in 1990

Praeger Publishers, One Madison Avenue, New York, NY 10010
A division of Greenwood Press, Inc.

Printed in the United States of America

∞™

The paper used in this book complies with the Permanent
Paper Standard issued by the National Information Standards
Organization (Z39.48-1984).

10 9 8 7 6 5 4 3 2 1

To My Children,
Sara Rachelle Stiefel Schoenfeld
and
Daniel Matthew Stiefel Schoenfeld

Contents

Figures and Tables

TABLES

Preface

An understanding of statistical methods is important for managers of public and nonprofit organizations. In today's complex world, statistics help us understand and manage our not-for-profit organizations. Even if a manager has a staff to perform statistical analyses, intelligent decisions require an ability to evaluate the results. This book is intended for public and nonprofit managers who want to become better users of statistics. It will also be of value to beginning data analysts themselves.

This book emphasizes statistical models that use more than one variable. Simple and multiple regression are explained in detail. Later chapters discuss some of the other techniques that are becoming widely used in the not-for-profit world: logit and probit analysis, time-series models, and simultaneous equation models. The book assumes that the reader has studied statistics at an elementary level. If earlier statistics lessons have been forgotten, the appendices will refresh your knowledge. No math beyond algebra is required; whenever possible, concepts and interpretations are discussed in words rather than symbols.

Throughout the book two kinds of examples are used to make the material relevant. Statistical analyses from reports and professional journals illustrate the use of each technique in practice. These examples appear several times in all chapters except the first and last. In addition, data on the New York City economy, taken from Matthew Drennan's book, *Modeling Metropolitan Economies for Forecasting and Policy Analysis* (New York: New York University Press, 1985) is used in several chapters to illustrate how to perform statistical analyses using a computer. Sample output from the computer is shown. This book should help you understand the statistics used in professional articles and help you interpret results as they appear on computer printouts.

Many individuals contributed to this book. The following colleagues at New York University read and commented on parts of the book: Howard Bloom, Steven Finkler, George Fuller, and Beth Weitzman, all from the Robert F. Wagner Graduate School of Public Service, and William Greene from the Stern School of Business. These people are in no way responsible for the contents but their comments were very valuable. Matthew Drennan, also at New York University's Wagner School of Public Service, generously lent his data base for the computer examples. Robert Berne, Elizabeth Durbin, and Mitchell Moss (Wagner School of Public Service) provided guidance at various times during the project. Chris Hakusa helped set up the computer programs. Harry Barry helped produce the graphs. Numerous students used and commented on drafts of the book in their statistics class at the Wagner School of Public Service; Irene Walter in particular did a thorough job of suggesting editorial changes. My husband, Mel Schoenfeld, made valuable comments on the text. Ramon Burke and Marie Burns were helpful in typing drafts and preparing tables and figures. The Wagner School's Urban Research Center and Health Research Program made available their computer hardware and software without which the graphs and tables could not have been produced.

I am grateful to the Literary Executor of the late Sir Ronald A. Fisher, F.R.S.; to Dr. Frank Yates, F.R.S.; and to the Longman Group Ltd., London, for permission to reprint an abridged version of table III (distribution of t) from their book *Statistical Tables for Biological, Agricultural and Medical Research,* 6th edition (1974). I am also indebted to Biometrika Trustees for allowing me to reproduce material from *Biometrika Tables for Statisticians* and from *Biometrika.*

I enjoyed writing this book; I hope you enjoy reading and using it.

1

Introduction

Public and nonprofit organizations include many of society's most crucial institutions—governments, public and private schools, most hospitals and health-care providers, colleges, universities, museums, and a heterogeneous group of service organizations.[1] Managing these not-for-profits is at least as difficult as managing for-profit companies, and certainly the not-for-profits have no less a need for good quantitative analysis to help in decision making. In fact, in the last two decades, not-for-profit institutions have followed the lead of for-profit enterprises and have increasingly used quantitative methods in making decisions. Multivariate methods, which handle more than two variables, have become especially prevalent. This book is designed to demonstrate how to use multivariate statistics meaningfully in not-for-profit organizations. The book stresses the logic of proofs and limitations of results, rather than the pure mathematics of the statistics. Each chapter contains several real-life illustrations of how the statistical techniques have been used in actual practice.

In this first chapter, the importance of multivariate models is explained; in addition, some basic statistical concepts are reviewed in preparation for more in-depth study of multivariate techniques. In the first two sections, multivariate models are introduced. The following two sections explain types of data and their use with alternative statistical techniques. A concluding section presents examples for managers of uses of multiple regression, the first multivariate technique that will be discussed in detail.

THE IDEA AND IMPORTANCE OF MULTIVARIATE MODELS

Managers of not-for-profit organizations confront numerous problems and decisions that relevant data could help solve. It is usually important to know how things work, on the average, or put another way, what the most likely outcome is. For example, managers in a budget office could use information about the average work force absentee rate in order to budget for overtime and substitute work. A transportation department manager would be interested in the average snowfall during each month in order to plan for snow removal services. A welfare office manager (or IRS personnel manager) would like to know the average number of applicants per day in order to plan staffing and to evaluate the level of service provided. All of these examples involve measures of central tendency—means, medians, or modes. Rather than model a relationship, they describe a situation.

Measures of central tendency help give a general idea of the way operations are proceeding. But, unless some assumptions about relationships are made, decision makers cannot take action on the basis of central tendency measures alone. For example, if a budget office bases daily staffing on average absentee rates, then implicitly it is assumed that absenteeism is the same each day. Rather than make such an assumption, most managers would prefer to explore relationships with their data.[2] Typical relationships can be illustrated by the following questions: Are the number of welfare applications related to the regional unemployment rate? Is swimming pool attendance related to the average daily temperature? Is the average length of stay in a municipal hospital related to the percent of surgery patients? Is the number of visits per family to a health clinic related to the distance the family lives from the clinic? All of these examples involve relationships between one variable and another.

But, even knowledge of simple relationships is inadequate for many decisions. In addition to the question, "Are variables related?" one wants to know:

- How strongly are they related?
- What is the magnitude of the effect of one variable on another?
- Is the relationship spurious? Does a third variable really account for the observed relationship between the first two? For example, absences and month of the year may be related only because a third variable, incidence of respiratory infections, coincides with particular months.
- Are there multiple causes for why a variable takes on one value rather than another value, that is, for the movement of a variable?

The answers to these questions often require a multivariate model. Before further discussion of the meaning of multivariate models, let's first review what is meant by statistics and by model.

The Meaning of Statistics

One meaning of the word statistics, and the one used in common parlance, is summary measures of data (usually central tendency and dispersion measures, such as the average and the standard deviation). This meaning is referred to as *descriptive statistics.* In this text, the interest is also in *inferential statistics*—the use of sample data to make inferences about the population. That is, when there are not data for every member of the population that is to be studied, how can an available sample be used to say something about all members of the population? It will be helpful to keep the idea of inferential statistics in mind as we proceed through the rest of the introduction, even though formal ideas of inference from samples to populations will not appear until Chapter 3.

The Meaning of Model

A model is used as a simplifying device that highlights the most important aspects of the reality. All models make assumptions, which are then used to derive results that help to explain and, possibly, to manipulate reality. Since models are meant to simplify, they should not be evaluated on the basis of how accurately their assumptions describe reality. Rather, they should be evaluated by their end results—How well do they help to explain or to predict? It is generally better to construct a simple model, with few assumptions, than one with many.

In this book, the word model is used in three ways. First, it describes behavioral relationships that managers in not-for-profit organizations may be interested in understanding. For example, in order to statistically analyze staffing patterns in an agency, a model of how employees behave with respect to attendance at work is needed. A simple behavioral model would assume that employees like large blocks of leisure time. One could then predict that if work days are missed for reasons other than illness, the days are more likely to be at either end of a weekend, thus allowing for longer blocks of leisure time. Good statistical work requires that a behavioral model come first. We will see why this is so in later chapters of the book. In fact, one of the secondary objectives of this book is to convince you that thinking about behavioral relationships should precede any use of statistics.

The second use of the word model is as a mathematical representation of behavioral hypotheses. That is, mathematical models use abstract symbols to represent definitions, assumptions, and behavioral relationships. Mathematical models are useful ways to organize thinking. Sometimes, they are able to highlight important relationships that can only be explained at great length in writing.

The third use of the word model refers to the construction of statistical formulas (or estimators). In order to construct a statistical formula, and then use it to say something about a population based on a sample of data, assumptions about whether there is a basic amount of unexplainable randomness, or chance, in the world are necessary. In addition, if it is assumed that there is some unexplainable randomness, then assumptions about how that randomness behaves are required. In other words, *statistical* models must be built to show how a whole series of mathematically represented *behavioral* models about the world can be translated into statements about which inferences from samples to populations can be made.

The meaning of the word model will usually be clear from the context of the discussion. As a guide, the rest of this chapter will refer to model in the behavioral and mathematical senses. Beginning in Chapter 2, the statistical sense of model will dominate.

MORE DETAIL ON MULTIVARIATE MODELS

What is meant by a multivariate model? Why is this kind of model more helpful to not-for-profit managers than univariate or bivariate models? To answer these questions, it is helpful to begin with the more familiar univariate model and to work our way up to the multivariate model.

A univariate model based on one variable is often represented by the letter Y. Such a model most commonly makes use of the mean, median or mode as a statistic.

A bivariate model has a dependent variable, often represented by the letter Y, which is related to one independent variable, usually represented by the letter X. That is:

$$Y = f(X). \tag{1.1}$$

The above expression says that the value of Y is a function of, or depends on, the value of X. In addition to being called a dependent variable, Y is sometimes said to be endogenous or to be a response variable. The values of the X variable determine the values of the Y variable, and the X variable is called alternatively an independent variable, an exogenous variable, or a predictor variable.

A multivariate model has a dependent variable, often represented by the letter Y, which is related to more than one independent variable, usually represented by the letter X with subscripts 1, 2, 3, . . . , K. That is:

$$Y = f(X_1, X_2, X_3, \ldots, X_K). \tag{1.2}$$

The above expression says that the value of Y is a function of, or depends on, the values of K different X's.

As an example of the differences among univariate, bivariate and multivariate models, let's think about the problem of forecasting the average length of stay (ALOS) in days in a particular hospital for the coming year. That is, How long on average do patients stay? This, by the way, is an important question for controlling costs, for projecting occupancy rates, and for assessing one aspect of the adequacy and quality of care. One way to approach the problem is to use the average length of stay from the previous year (or previous five years). This is the univariate model approach. It will only work well if this year is similar to previous years. An alternative approach is to find the relationship between average length of stay and the percentage of patients who undergo a single procedure, such as surgery. The presumption here would be that a higher percent of surgery patients would lead to longer average stays. The average length of stay could then be predicted on the basis of predictions of the percent of surgery patients entering the hospital this year. This second approach uses a bivariate model. Its shortcoming is that it is difficult to choose surgery over other procedures as the one most important independent variable. The third approach (you guessed it) is the multivariate model, where average length of stay is related to numerous independent variables, such as percent of surgery patients, percent of maternity patients, percent of heart patients, percent of patients age 65 and over, or percent of patients with insurance coverage. The multivariate model is likely to lead to more accurate predictions of average length of stay, as long as the independent variables themselves can be accurately forecasted.

We have looked at an example of multivariate versus other models. Let us now try to generalize about why multivariate models are so often needed for decision making in not-for-profit organizations. A great many of the decisions that managers make are based on relationships that come from the social rather than physical or biological sciences. Social scientists cannot usually obtain knowledge of the world through controlled experiments. This is different from the situation of, say, a biologist who wants to know the effect of fertilizer on crop growth. In such a situation, the biologist will make sure that the temperature, amount of water, and other soil nutrients are the same for all crops before varying the amount or kinds of fertilizer and observing crop growth. That is, the other variables will be controlled.

In the social sciences, experiments cannot be conducted in this way. The best that can be done is to randomly assign people to treatment or control groups. There can be no assurance that people are exactly alike. In fact, usually even random assignment is impossible, and the social scientist must take data as they happen naturally or are collected for other purposes.[3] For example, the health planner studying average length of stay and hospital characteristics uses administrative or survey data on existing patients and hospitals. The economist studying the relationship between the unemployment rate and the inflation rate uses data generated by the business cycle.

Because social scientists work with nonexperimental situations, they must statistically control for many variables. Even if the effect of only one independent variable is of interest, it is necessary to control for other independent variables in order to determine the effect of one. Unless all independent variables are uncorrelated among themselves, failure to use a multivariate model will give an inaccurate or biased reading on the influence of the independent variable of concern. The nonexperimental nature of social science data is the primary reason for the importance of the multivariate model for managerial decision making.

CLASSIFICATION OF DATA USED IN MULTIVARIATE MODELS

The use of a multivariate model requires an understanding of the information contained in various kinds of data and the statistical methods appropriate to use with each kind of data. There are three general classifications of data. In order of information contained, from lowest amount of information to highest amount, the three classifications of data are nominal, ordinal, and cardinal.

Nominal data labels nonoverlapping categories, but the numbers used as labels have no meaning. That is, both numbers and single words impart equal information. For example, sex can be represented by the number 1 for female and the number 2 for male, or by the words female and male. This is similarly true with variables such as car ownership or attendance at an event.

Ordinal data, on the other hand, labels and orders from low to high, but provides no information on how much higher or lower one category is than another. For example, satisfaction with a city service could be measured from 1 to 5, with 1 being least and 5 being most satisfied. The same information would be given if the service were ranked from 10 to 90, since the only thing that is important in ordinal data is whether a number is lower or higher than another.

Finally, cardinal data labels, orders, and allows numerical comparisons. A distinction is sometimes made between cardinal data that is interval versus ratio in nature. Interval cardinal data does not have an inherently determined zero. The numbers 2 and 4 provide the same information as the numbers 8 and 10—both are two units apart. The most common example of interval level data is temperature on a Fahrenheit or Centigrade scale, where zero does not mean absence of temperature. Ratio data, on the other hand, does have a naturally defined zero and thus comparisons of fractions or ratios can be made. For example, 2/4 is not equal to 8/10 because 2 and 8 (and 4 and 10) are different units away from zero. Examples of ratio cardinal data are income, average length of hospital stay, number of dental visits, and years of education.

STATISTICAL TECHNIQUES AND THEIR DATA REQUIREMENTS

Different statistical techniques can make use of different levels of measurement. A discussion of this point will provide a convenient way to review (or at least summarize) some statistical techniques with which the reader may already be familiar. The three techniques looked at here are chi-square, analysis of variance, and multiple regression (the latter will be new to most readers). Chi-square can use only nominal data. Analysis of variance can use cardinal data for the dependent variable, but only ordinal data for the independent variables. Chi-square and analysis of variance can be employed with higher level data but, if this is done, some of the information in the data will be lost. Regression can use cardinal data for the dependent as well as the independent variables. If lower level data are chosen for any technique, modifications must *sometimes* be made, especially if the dependent variable is measured in the lower level data.[4] An example of each technique is given below to review and demonstrate the level of measurement in the data.

TABLE 1.1
Example of Type of Data for Chi-Square Analysis

Party Affiliation	Place of Residence		
	City	Suburb	Rural Area
Democratic	% of Sample	% of Sample	% of Sample
Republican	% of Sample	% of Sample	% of Sample
Independent	% of Sample	% of Sample	% of Sample

An Example of Chi-Square Analysis

A typical question amenable to chi-square analysis is the following: Is political party affiliation related to place of residence? Political party is measured on a nominal scale (Democrat, Republican, or Independent), and so also is place of residence (city, suburban, or rural). Table 1.1 visually represents a structure for data that would be collected to answer this question. Each cell in the table would contain the percent of the sample that answered yes to both the particular party affiliation and the place of residence. The chi-square statistic would assess the chances that the percentages across cells are really different from one another.[5] If data on the size of the place of residence were available (cardinal data), these could be converted to ordinal data (for example, small, medium, and large place), and used as if they were nominal data, but some of the information contained in the data would be lost. It would be preferable to use another technique that could take advantage of the added information.

An Example of Analysis of Variance

Analysis of variance (ANOVA) can use cardinal level data for the dependent variable, but only ordinal data for the independent variables. An example of a question that could be tested using ANOVA is whether salaries in a particular organization are related to level of responsibility and pleasantness of job. That is:

Salary = f (responsibility, pleasantness)?

One might be interested in this relationship for a comparable worth study, for example.

TABLE 1.2
Example of Type of Data for ANOVA

Pleasantness of Job	Job Responsibility		
	Much	Medium	Little
Much	Average Salary	Average Salary	Average Salary
Little	Average Salary	Average Salary	Average Salary

Table 1.2 visually represents a structure for data that would be collected to test the statistical significance of the proposed relationship. The dependent variable can be cardinal. The independent variables can be only ordinal or nominal. Cardinal independent variables can be converted to ordinal variables, but with a loss of information. For example, if an additional independent variable, years of education, was added to the above salary relationship, the years could be broken down ordinally to less than 12, 12 to 16, and above 16.

An Example of Multiple Regression

Finally, multiple regression can use cardinal level data for the dependent variable and the independent variables. Nominal or ordinal level data can also be used for independent variables, and sometimes for the dependent one as well. If cardinal level data are converted to ordinal or nominal levels, some information will be lost. An example of multiple regression (previously discussed) is the relationship between the average length of stay in a hospital and the demographic and medical characteristics of the patients. That is:

Average Length of Stay = f (% surgery patients, % patients age 65 and over).

$$(1.3)$$

To summarize, a statistical technique can always be used with higher than the required level of data, but sometimes some of the information in the data will be lost. For example, using cardinal level data for chi-square or the independent variables in ANOVA means that a continuous variable, such as income, will have to be divided. That is, individuals might be grouped according to whether their income falls into a low (0 to $7,499), middle ($7,500 to $29,999), or high ($30,000 and up) group, rather than by the exact income numbers. Multiple regression is most useful when any of the data are cardinal. Chi-square is most useful when the only available data are nominal.

THREE MAIN USES OF MULTIPLE REGRESSION AND SOME SIMPLIFIED EXAMPLES

Multiple regression is one of the most commonly used multivariate statistical techniques. An understanding of multiple regression provides an excellent base for understanding other kinds of multivariate statistics. Multiple regression is presented first in this book and is also the primary focus.

Multiple regression is useful to managers in three different ways—for forecasting or prediction, for hypothesis testing, and for program evaluation. Each of these uses is described and illustrated below.

Multiple Regression and Forecasting

Managers often find it useful to forecast ahead in order to plan effectively their organization's operations. This is especially true when putting together a budget that must request resources for a future period, based on services that are expected to be provided.

As an illustration of the forecasting function of multiple regression, let's return to the average length of stay example looked at earlier. We previously saw that average length of stay could be modeled as a multiple regression equation, such as:

$$\text{ALOS} = B_0 + B_1X_1 + B_2X_2 + B_3X_3 + B_4X_4 + \ldots + B_KX_K. \tag{1.4}$$

The B's are fixed parameters, or constants, and more will be said about them in later chapters. The X's represent variables, such as the percent of surgery patients. If the values of the B's were known, they could be used, for example, to predict average length of stay in a metropolitan hospital. It is the job of the multiple regression statistical technique to provide good estimates of the B's. For now, in order to see why good estimates are important, let's use some made-up numbers for the B parameters and see how the equation could be used.

Suppose the equation with just two independent variables looks as follows for a single metropolitan hospital:

$$\text{ALOS} = 3 + .25\,(\%\text{ surgery patients}) + .10\,(\%\text{ patients age 65 and over}). \tag{1.5}$$

Then, if for next year it is forecast that 20% of the patients will received surgery and 30% of the patients will be age 65 and over, the predicted average length of stay would be calculated from equation (1.5) as follows:[6] ALOS = 3 + .25(20)

+.10(30) = 3 + 5 + 3 = 11 (= 11 days). The units of the intercept and slope coefficients in equation (1.5) and its solution are sometimes not clear to readers who have not previously used regression analysis. In general, the units of each coefficient are equal to the units of the dependent variable divided by the units of the independent variable. The end result is that the number calculated from an equation is in the units of the dependent variable. In the ALOS example, the units of the dependent variable (ALOS) are days. The units of the coefficient .25 are days/%. The units of the coefficient .10 are days/%. The units of intercept, 3, are just days (or technically days/1.0). Thus in the solution above, the units work out as follows:

$$ALOS \text{ (days)} = 3 \text{ (days)} + .25 \text{ (days/\%)} (20\%) + .10 \text{ (days/\%)} (30\%)$$
$$= 11 \text{ days.}$$

The units of each coefficient will automatically adjust themselves to equal the units of the dependent variable divided by the units of the independent variable. In all equations that follow in the text, the units of the coefficients will *not* be explicitly stated but instead they will be assumed to adjust.

So multiple regression can be used to forecast and usually more accurately than from last year's mean. But to use multiple regression this way, the values of the independent variables must be forecasted as well. There are a variety of ways to forecast the future values of independent variables such as by use of expert judgment and by use of past trends. Chapters 4 and 8 return to the discussion of forecasting independent variables.

Multiple Regression and Hypothesis Testing

Managers are often interested in the effect that one particular variable has on another—that is, Does the variable of concern have any effect at all and, if so, How large is the effect? These questions are examples of the hypothesis testing function of regression analysis.

An example of a hypothesis that multiple regression can be used to test is that an individual's earnings are related to the individual's years of education. To test this hypothesis, one needs first to construct a model of the earnings process, being especially mindful to control for the effect of variables other than years of education. Obvious control variables would include ability, sex, years of experience, and kind and quality of education. Suppose, as a simplified example, the following relationship is estimated using multiple regression.

Earnings per year = 500 + 700 (years of education)
$$+ 25 \text{ (ability score)} + 300 \text{ (male).} \qquad (1.6)$$

What does this equation mean? One question it answers is, What is the effect of years of education on earnings? If the coefficient on years of education (700) is accurately estimated, then each additional year of education the individual has adds an average of $700 to earnings per year. The coefficients report the effect of changes—a change of 1 in the independent variable X results in B change in the dependent variable Y. An additional year of schooling results in $700 more in earnings per year; an additional point on an ability test results in $25 more in earnings per year; males receive $300 more than females per year.

But, to believe the coefficients, their accuracy as estimates of the population coefficients needs to be known. In particular, it is usually important to know the chances of each coefficient actually being zero. If a coefficient is actually zero, then the independent variable has no effect at all on the dependent variable. A common hypothesis to test is that each coefficient is equal to zero. Then, if the hypothesis is rejected, more confidence is placed in the estimated coefficient value.

By the way, a regression equation estimated for one purpose (such as hypothesis testing) can be used for other purposes as well (such as prediction). For example, the above earnings equation can also be used for prediction. Suppose an individual has finished high school (12 years of education), has an ability score of 100, and is a male (scored as a 1). Then, using equation (1.6), the earnings of this individual would be predicted to be $11,700 per year.

$$\text{Earnings} = 500 + 700(12) + 25(100) + 300(1)$$
$$= 500 + 8400 + 2500 + 300 = 11,700 \ (= \$11,700).$$

Multiple Regression and Program Evaluation

A third use of multiple regression is as a statistical tool in program evaluation. Not-for-profit managers are often concerned about whether a particular program does what is intended. As examples:

- Do job training programs result in employment for trainees?
- Do antilitter laws result in cleaner streets?
- Does Head Start improve learning?

Multiple regression is often the statistical technique used in such evaluations.

Suppose one wishes to evaluate the effectiveness of job training with respect to the increase in the number of weeks worked per year. If there were available a sample of trainees and nontrainees,[6] who had been followed one or two years after training, the following kind of model could be used:

$$(\text{Weeks worked after training} - \text{weeks worked before training}) = B_0$$
$$+ B_1 (\text{in program}) + B_2 (\text{change in unemployment in area}) + B_3 (\text{education}). \qquad (1.7)$$

The variables for change in unemployment in an area and education are controls to help create an unbiased estimate of the program effect. One would want to see if B_1 is greater than zero. That is, if an individual is in the program, does the number of weeks worked increase more than for an individual not in the program? The sign, size, and accuracy of B_1 are important.

CONCLUSIONS

The purpose of this chapter has been to motivate you to want to understand more about multivariate statistical techniques. In the next chapter, we begin the study of multivariate statistical techniques with the bivariate or simple regression model. This will enable you to understand the regression model in its simplest form. From there, it will not be difficult to generalize to a several variable model and, eventually, to other multivariate techniques as well.

SUMMARY OF CHAPTER 1

1. Multivariate models will usually be more helpful to managers than central tendency measures or bivariate models.

2. Descriptive statistics (summary measures of data) differ from inferential statistics (the use of a sample to say something about a population).

3. The term model, which means an abstract representation of reality, is used in the following three ways in this text: to describe behavioral relationships; to represent behavioral relationships mathematically; and to construct statistical estimators.

4. Multivariate models include a dependent (or endogenous or response) variable, often represented by the letter Y, and independent (or exogenous or predictor) variables, often represented by the letters X with subscripts $1, 2, \ldots, K$.

5. Multivariate models are needed for decisions based on social science knowledge because social scientists usually work with nonexperimental data where they must statistically control to avoid biases.

6. Three classifications of data, based on their levels of measurement are: nominal (labels categories), ordinal (labels and orders, low to high), and cardinal (labels, orders, and allows interval and ratio comparisons).

7. Different statistical techniques can make use of different levels of measurement. Chi-square can make use only of nominal data. Analysis of variance can use cardinal data for the dependent variable, but only ordinal data for the independent variables. Regression can make use of cardinal data for the dependent as well as the independent variables.

8. Three ways regression can be useful to managers are for forecasting, for hypothesis testing, and for program evaluation.

2

The Bivariate or Simple Regression Model

This chapter provides the background for estimating bivariate regression coefficients. Bivariate regression is commonly referred to as simple regression and the two terms are used interchangeably. While the bivariate model is simplistic in many cases, it is the easiest multivariate model to understand, and its results generalize readily to models with more than two variables. The first section of the chapter discusses the meaning of bivariate regression. Section two distinguishes between stochastic and deterministic models, and section three discusses the difference between populations and samples. Section four shows how the formulas used to obtain regression coefficients are established, and section five explains the meaning and importance of the R^2 statistic that accompanies the regression model.

THE MEANING OF THE TERM BIVARIATE REGRESSION

For now, the term bivariate regression model will refer to a simple linear relationship between one dependent variable, Y, and one independent variable, X. That is:

$$Y_t = B_0 + B_1 X_t. \tag{2.1}$$

Y_t and X_t are the tth observation (or case) of the Y and X variables, and B_0 and B_1 are parameters or constants. Specifically, B_0 is the intercept and B_1 is the slope of the line represented by the bivariate equation. The relationship is assumed to be a simple linear one, where unit changes in the independent variable X result in constant, B_1, changes in the dependent variable Y.

The use of the subscript t is one of the common ways to represent individual cases of a given variable. An alternative is to use the subscript i, for example X_i. Subscripts run over all observations in a sample. Generally, when using the

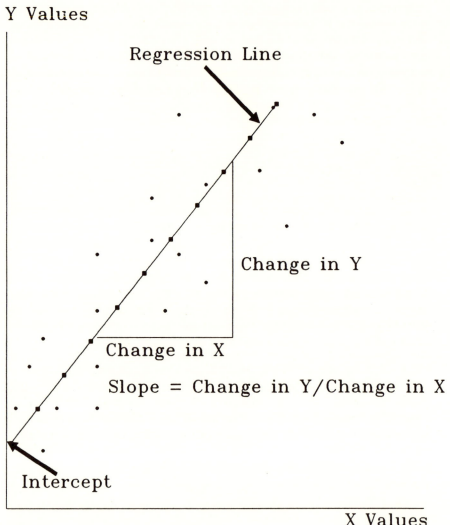

FIG. 2.1 Scattergram for a bivariate regression

t subscript, the sample size would be represented by capital T and one would say that t goes from 1 (the first observation) through T (the last observation). If the i subscript is used, then the sample size is generally denoted by lowercase n, and the observations go from 1 to n. In this book, the t subscript (not the i subscript) will be used.

A scattergram of data that could be used to estimate a bivariate regression is shown in Figure 2.1. The data in this figure are meant to represent all the observations on X and Y in a hypothetical example. The bivariate regression model of the relationship is, then, a straight line that best fits the observations. B_0 is the intercept, or the place where the line cuts the Y axis, and B_1 is the slope. The slope is represented in Figure 2.1 as "Change in Y/Change in X." Change in Y could be represented as $Y_t - Y_{t-1}$ or one observation of Y minus the previous observation of Y. Likewise change in X could be represented as $X_t - X_{t-1}$.

For example, suppose the dollar value of per capita retail clothing sales per year in a municipality is modeled as a function of per capita personal income per year. Presumably, clothing sales increase when income increases. Such a model might be used by a municipal budget office to project expected collections of sales tax revenue on clothing purchases. Symbolically, let Y_t equal the dollar value of per capita retail clothing sales per year, and X_t equal the per capita personal income for the year. A hypothetical regression equation might then look as follows, where the numbers for the intercept and slope would have been obtained from statistical formulas that will be presented later in this chapter:

$$Y_t = 500 + .10X_t. \tag{2.2}$$

B_0, the intercept, equals 500. If X_t, per capita income, equals 0, the per capita clothing sales per year are \$500. B_1, the slope, equals .10. For every additional dollar of per capita income, per capita clothing sales increase \$.10; put in a more meaningful way, for every additional \$100 of per capita income, per capita clothing sales increase \$10 per year.

If per capita income is \$500, then, using equation (2.2), per capita clothing sales are \$550: $Y_t = 500 + .10(500) = 500 + 50 = 550$ (= \$550). In this case, per capita clothing sales exceed per capita income, hardly a realistic situation.

If per capita income increases to \$5000, a somewhat more realistic result occurs, since then per capita clothing sales are \$1,000: $Y_t = 500 + .10(5000) = 500 + 500 = 1000$ (= \$1000). In this model, behavior can be described by a two variable linear model. A "real-life" example of an estimated simple regression is given in Example 2.1.

EXAMPLE 2.1 REGRESSION AND THE DISTRIBUTION OF SCHOOL RESOURCES

In 1976, Anita Summers and Barbara Wolfe published results of a study on the distribution of school resources in 1970–71 among Philadelphia schools.[1] The purpose of the study was to provide very detailed information on how a large variety of resources (such as expenditures per pupil on basic skills, or year in which the school was built) were related to the way black and low income students were distributed among Philadelphia schools. In part, Summers and Wolfe wished to see if resources that most people would think of as compensatory were distributed in greater proportion to black and low income students. To carry out the study, resources per school were regressed on percent of black students per school (or percent of students from low income families). A few of the seventy-six different results are:[2]

- Instructional salary
cost per pupil   = 437.7 + .3719 (percent of black students)
- Instructional salary
cost per pupil   = 428.9 + .5798 (percent low income students)
- Expenditures per pupil
on basic skills,
grades 1–3 (dollars)   = 357.24 + .2261 (percent of black students)
- Expenditures per pupil
on basic skills,
grades 1–3 (dollars)   = 345.54 + .4271 (percent low income students)
- Average score of
teachers on national
teacher's examination   = 596.23 − .1552 (percent of black students)
- Average score of
teachers on national
teacher's examination   = 550.63 − .9410 (percent low income students)

Questions:

a. Do the six regressions reported here provide evidence of nondiscriminatory distribution of resources?
b. (i) What is the difference in instructional salary cost for pupils in a school with no black students and in a school with 100% black students? (ii) What is the difference for teacher's examination scores?
c. What should the citizens of Philadelphia do with these results?
d. Can the results be generalized to other cities?

Discussion:

a. Instructional salary costs and expenditures on basic skills, grades 1 to 3, are distributed in favor of black and low income students (the slope coefficient for each regression is positive). Scores on the national teacher's exam are distributed inversely, however, since every percentage increase in black students (low income students) results in a .16 point (.94) *decline* in the exam score.
b. (i) [437.7 + .3719(100) − 437.7 − .3719(0)] = 37.19 (= $37.19). (ii) −15.52 (= −15.52 points).
c. The "evidence" from the regression results is but one of many inputs into a political process that decides what, if anything, to do about redistributing resources. Occasionally, the court system will make a ruling on the distribution of resources if a state or a federal constitution or law is not adhered to.

d. No, since pretty clearly the study was meant to represent the Philadelphia experience only. Managers and analysts in other large urban cities might suspect similar distributions in their own cities and choose to initiate a study on the basis of the results of this one.

The goal of this chapter is to explain how to obtain the numbers that were hypothetically filled in above. That is, the most statistically accurate line is desired, based on the cases or observations. This means good estimates of the intercept (B_0) and the slope (B_1) are needed. But, before ways to estimate the intercept and slope are developed, a few important distinctions should be made, in particular between stochastic and deterministic relationships and between populations and samples.

DETERMINISTIC VERSUS STOCHASTIC RELATIONSHIPS

Thus far, the linear model has been discussed as if it were deterministic. This means that if a specific value of the X variable is known, then the value of the Y variable can be exactly determined or predicted. That is, there is no error in the model. $Y_t = B_0 + B_1 X_t$ is a deterministic model. There is a one-to-one correspondence between values of X and values of Y.

Deterministic relationships are fine for modeling purposes, but they do not represent the real world of social science relationships. The graph drawn in Figure 2.1 does not really depict a deterministic relationship. Some points are on the line, but many are not. A deterministic relationship would show all points to be on the line. In terms of the per capita clothing sales example, described by the equation $Y_t = 500 + .10X_t$, a deterministic relationship would require, for example, that every year that per capita income increases by $100, per capita clothing sales for the year increase by *exactly* $10.

The more realistic relationship is a stochastic one. Stochastic relationships are impacted by randomness, which requires the recognition of likely errors. Values of X determine values of Y only on average; exact values of Y are not always obtained. A stochastic relationship is written as follows:

$$Y_t = B_0 + B_1 X_t + E_t. \tag{2.3}$$

The E_t, or error, is the stochastic part of the relationship, and its value is greater or less than zero for all points that do not fall exactly on the line.

Why are social science relationships better represented by stochastic than by deterministic relationships? There are three basic reasons. First, human behavior cannot ever be exactly predicted. A social scientist who deals primarily with the study of human interactions must allow for some randomness. For example, while the average relationship between dollars spent on housing and income levels may be known, some people with identical incomes will spend much more on housing than expected, and some will spend less. If individual behavior is to be predicted, the statistical model will have to include an error term.

Second, in addition to the innate randomness of human behavior, the best of models will leave out variables important in determining the behavior of the dependent variable. This is true even in a multivariate model, due to the lack of knowledge about all the determining variables, and because all good models abstract some from reality. These left-out variables will all be included in the error term. Hopefully, the left-out variables are random and unrelated to the included variables, in which case the estimates of the intercept and slopes will still have good statistical qualities.

Finally, models will inevitably contain errors because some of the variables are incorrectly measured. This can occur either because the right variable cannot be accurately conceptualized or because the wrong number is entered into the regression calculations. In either case, the error term will represent the measurement errors.

POPULATIONS VERSUS SAMPLES

The difference between populations and samples is also important to understand before the estimates of the regression coefficients are derived. The population is made up of all the cases or observations to which the model refers. The population model includes the entire universe of observations. Population parameters are, by convention, represented by upper case letters (often capital Greek letters, although in this book capital Roman letters are used). Thus the regression model represented below is a population model.

$$Y_t = B_0 + B_1X_t + E_t. \tag{2.4}$$

A sample, on the other hand, is a subset of cases from the population. The parameters (the intercept and the slope) of the population model are estimated from sample data. The estimated relationship is conventionally represented by lower case letters, as follows:

$$Y_t = b_0 + b_1X_t + e_t. \tag{2.5}$$

The b_0 is the estimated intercept or the sample estimate of B_0. The b_1 is the estimated slope or the sample estimate of B_1. The e_t is the estimated error or the sample estimate of E_t.

It is also conventional to represent sample estimates of population parameters by placing a hat ("∧") over the population parameter. So, for example, the sample estimate of B_0 could be represented as $\hat{B}_0$, the sample estimate of B_1 could be $\hat{B}_1$, and the sample estimate of E could be $\hat{E}$. In this book, when representing sample relationships, the hat notation will be used occasionally, but, by and large, the lower case convention (b_0, b_1, e_t) will be followed.

Note the presumption, even in the population, that the relationship contains an error term. The error term in the population does not result from estimation but rather from the basic stochastic nature of the relationship. In the sample, however, the error term exists for two reasons. First, as in the population, the relationship is stochastic. Second, when the sample relationship is estimated, the intercept and slope coefficients will not necessarily be equal to the population intercept and slope. Therefore, the estimated regression line may inaccurately predict the true value of the population dependent value, Y_t, both because of the stochastic nature of the relationship and also because of the errors in the position of the line. The sample error term, e_t, represents both of these sources of error in the prediction of the true population value of Y_t. The population error, E_t, on the other hand, represents only the stochastic nature of the relationship.

The error in the sample relationship is often called the residual. It is not estimated directly. Only b_0 and b_1 are directly estimated. The residual can be calculated, after b_0 and b_1 are estimated, by subtraction.

$e_t = Y_t - b_0 - b_1X_t$,

or

e_t = observed value of Y_t – estimated value of Y_t. (2.6)

ESTIMATORS FOR THE BIVARIATE REGRESSION MODEL

The bivariate regression model is a statistical model that tells how to use sample data to estimate the parameters (intercept and slope) of the following stochastic population relationship:

$Y_t = B_0 + B_1X_t + E_t$. (2.7)

The goal of the statistical model is to yield good estimates of the values of B_0 and B_1. To do this, formulas, called estimators, are developed for the intercept and the slope.

Figure 2.1 shows a scattergram of the kind of sample data that an analyst or manager will have available. Another way to state the purpose of the bivariate regression model is that it attempts to find the "best" line to fit the scattergram of sample data. How to define "best," and then how to use the definition to derive estimators, are the subject of this section of the chapter. The method used here is that of least squares, the classic regression method. First, the meanings of "best" and "least squares" are discussed. Then the formulas are derived, using the least squares method.

Criteria for the "Best" Line

The straight line that best fits a scattergram of stochastic sample data, such as those shown in Figure 2.1, will never pass through each and every observation in the

Y Values

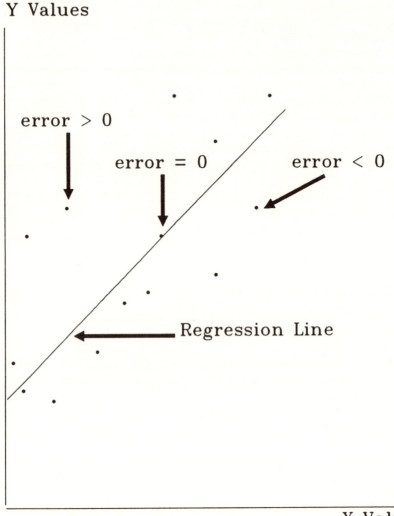

error > 0

error = 0

error < 0

Regression Line

X Values

FIG. 2.2. Regression line and errors

sample. Thus, the line will be a perfect fit only for those sample observations that fall exactly on the line. The line will be in error when predicting all observations that fall off the line. One way to think about the best line is that it should somehow minimize the errors of those observations that fall off the line. The reason we want to minimize the errors is so we can use the estimated line knowing that the true dependent variables will differ from our estimate by the least possible amount. Figure 2.2 shows a possible line to fit a sample of data, as well as the errors associated with that line. Recall that the error (e_t) is the difference between the actual value of the dependent variable in the sample (Y_t) and the value of the dependent variable predicted by the line $(b_0 + b_1X_t)$. In other words, $e_t = Y_t - b_0 - b_1X_t$. Minimizing the errors involves further specifications since there is more than one error involved and somehow all of the errors *together* must be minimized.

One straightforward way to minimize all the errors is to add them up (sum them) and minimize the sum. Using notation, this involves finding b_0 and b_1 to minimize the following:

$$\sum_{t=1}^{T} e_t = \sum_{t=1}^{T} (Y_t - b_0 - b_1X_t). \tag{2.8}$$

(If you do not recall how summation operators [Σ] work, Appendix A provides a review.) The problem with this straightforward criterion is that very large errors might not be adequately taken into account, since a large positive error could be cancelled by a large negative error.

An alternative to the straightforward summing of the errors is to transform them so that positive and negative errors, especially large ones, cannot cancel one another. For example, one could take the absolute value of each error, effectively making negative errors into positive ones. Or the errors could be squared, so that they all are positive *and* the large ones are given more weight than the small ones. The least squares criterion uses the latter method; each error is squared, all errors are added, and the intercept and slope that minimize the summed, squared errors are found. The reason the least squares method is used is that the resulting estimators have good statistical characteristics. These characteristics will be thoroughly discussed in the next chapter. The first order of business is to understand how the formulas for the coefficients can be obtained from a criterion that minimizes the sum of the squared errors around the regression line.

The Ordinary Least Squares Method

The ordinary least squares, or OLS, method finds the intercept (b_0) and slope (b_1) that minimizes the sum of the squared errors. The squared errors can be represented as follows:

$$\sum_{t=1}^{T} e_t^2 = \sum_{t=1}^{T} (Y_t - b_0 - b_1X_t)^2. \tag{2.9}$$

Calculus is used to minimize this sum and two equations result.[3] The two equations are called the normal equations, and they can be solved for the estimators for the regression coefficients. The process of solving the normal equations to obtain the estimators is worth following in detail. The details show that the formulas do not magically appear. Rather, they follow from a criterion (minimize the squared errors) and require manipulation of that criterion through calculus and algebra. The derivation presented here skips the calculus and begins with the normal equations. The two normal equations are presented below. The index ($t = 1$ to T) is dropped from the summation sign and the t subscript is dropped from each variable. This is done here, and frequently throughout the text, to avoid clutter. The reader should remember, however, that any variable refers to a specific value of that variable and any summation operator is summed over specific values of the variable. Normal equations:

$$\Sigma(Y - b_0 - b_1 X) = 0. \tag{2.10}$$
$$\Sigma(Y - b_0 - b_1 X)(X) = 0. \tag{2.11}$$

Beginning with the first normal equation (2.10), one can derive the estimator for the intercept. Commentary on each algebraic manipulation necessary for the derivation is displayed in the left-hand column, and the algebra is displayed in the right-hand column. Recall that the sample size is represented as T.

The first normal equation	$\Sigma(Y - b_0 - b_1 X) = 0.$
Multiplying through with the summation signs	$\Sigma Y - \Sigma b_0 - \Sigma b_1 X = 0.$
Equivalent to above because, for any one sample, b_0 and b_1 are fixed	$\Sigma Y - T b_0 - b_1 \Sigma X = 0.$
Dividing both sides by sample size, T	$\Sigma Y/T - T b_0/T - b_1 \Sigma X/T = 0.$
Representing means in the traditional way	$\bar{Y} - b_0 - b_1 \bar{X} = 0.$
Rearranging	$b_0 = \bar{Y} - b_1 \bar{X}.$

We now have the estimator for the intercept. It says that the estimate for the intercept can be found by taking the mean value of the dependent variable in the sample and subtracting the estimate of the slope times the mean value of the independent variable in the sample. Of course, to use this estimator, the value of the slope is needed.

The estimator for the slope can be found using the second normal equation (2.11). The second estimator is derived below in a similar way; the left-hand column comments on the algebraic manipulations that are displayed in the right-hand column.

The second normal equation	$\Sigma(Y - b_0 - b_1 X)(X) = 0.$
Multiplying through with the summation sign	$\Sigma YX - \Sigma b_0 X - \Sigma b_1 XX = 0.$
Simplifying	$\Sigma YX - b_0 \Sigma X - b_1 \Sigma X^2 = 0.$
Substituting the estimator for b_0	$\Sigma YX - (\bar{Y} - b_1 \bar{X})\Sigma X - b_1 \Sigma X^2 = 0.$

Multiplying through and expanding the terms	$\Sigma YX - \bar{Y}\Sigma X + b_1\bar{X}\Sigma X - b_1\Sigma X^2 = 0.$
Rearranging the terms	$\Sigma XY - \bar{Y}\Sigma X = b_1\Sigma X^2 - b_1\bar{X}\Sigma X.$
Multiplying and dividing by T	$\Sigma XY - T\bar{Y}\Sigma X/T = b_1\Sigma X^2 - Tb_1\bar{X}\Sigma X/T.$
Simplifying	$\Sigma XY - T\bar{Y}\bar{X} = b_1\Sigma X^2 - Tb_1\bar{X}^2.$
Factoring out terms	$\Sigma XY - T\bar{Y}\bar{X} = b_1(\Sigma X^2 - T\bar{X}^2).$
Solving for the slope	$b_1 = (\Sigma XY - T\bar{Y}\bar{X})/(\Sigma X^2 - T\bar{X}^2)$
	$= [\Sigma(X - \bar{X})(Y - \bar{Y})]/\Sigma(X - \bar{X})^2.$

The resultant estimators or formulas are, once again, where $x = X - \bar{X}$ and $y = Y - \bar{Y}$,

$$b_1 = (\Sigma xy)/(\Sigma x^2) \tag{2.12}$$

and

$$b_0 = \bar{Y} - b_1\bar{X}. \tag{2.13}$$

Additional Comments on the Ordinary Least Squares (OLS) Intercept and Slope Estimators

The estimated regression line will not go through all the observations in the sample. This fact leads to two interpretations of the meaning of the estimated line. On the one hand, the line can be seen as the best estimate of the actual values of *individual* dependent variables; sometimes, these estimates will simply contain some errors. On the other hand, the line can be interpreted as estimated *average* values of the dependent variable. For any given value of the independent variable, X, the regression line shows, on average, the value of the dependent variable, Y. This latter interpretation demands less of the regression line, since intuitively it is easier to predict the average value of an occurrence rather than its actual value. Also, if the regression line predicts average values, one might reasonably expect that it would pass through the average (or mean) value of the independent and dependent variables in the sample. Indeed, the regression line does just that: the mean of the sample X and Y values will always fall on the regression line. Either interpretation of the regression line is a valid one; the one chosen depends upon the use to which the estimated line will be put.

A second comment on the regression estimators is that there are many ways to present them. The book shows one way that follows from the algebraic manipulations needed to go from the normal equations to the coefficient estimators. A second convenient way is in terms of variances and covariances. Recall that the sample variance of the X's is written as follows:

$$S_{XX} = \Sigma(X - \bar{X})^2/(T - 1). \tag{2.14}$$

And the sample covariance between X and Y is written as:

$$S_{XY} = \Sigma[(X - \bar{X})(Y - \bar{Y})]/(T - 1). \tag{2.15}$$

The slope estimator can, then, be written as:

$$b_1 = S_{XY}/S_{XX} = \text{Covariance between } X \text{ and } Y/\text{Variance of } X. \tag{2.16}$$

The formulation in terms of covariances and variances will come in handy when the accuracy of individual coefficient estimates is being determined, in Chapter 3.

THE COEFFICIENT OF DETERMINATION OR R^2

One final important statistic that accompanies the regression model is presented in this chapter. The coefficient of determination indicates how well the estimated regression line fits the particular data from which it has been estimated.[4] It is equal to the "explained variation" divided by the "total variation," or the percent of the total variation that is explained or accounted for by the estimated regression line. The coefficient of determination can range between 0 and 1, with higher values indicating higher amounts of explained variation.

Total variation equals $\Sigma(Y_t - \bar{Y})^2$, or the difference between the actual value of each Y and the mean of Y, squared and summed over all observations. This is sometimes called the total sum of squares (TSS).

Explained variation equals $\Sigma(\hat{Y}_t - \bar{Y})^2$, or the difference between the value of each Y predicted from the regression line ($\hat{Y}_t$) and the mean of Y, squared and summed over all observations. This is sometimes called the regression sum of squares (RSS).

Unexplained variation equals $\Sigma(Y_t - \hat{Y}_t)^2$, or the difference between the value of each Y and the value of each Y predicted from the regression line, squared and summed over all observations. This also equals Σe_t^2, or the sum of the squared residuals and is sometimes called the error sum of squares (ESS).

The coefficient of determination is, then, as follows:

$$R^2 = \Sigma(\hat{Y}_t - \bar{Y})^2/\Sigma(Y_t - \bar{Y})^2 = 1 - \Sigma e_t^2/\Sigma(Y_t - \bar{Y})^2; \tag{2.17}$$

or,

$$R^2 = \text{RSS/TSS} = 1 - \text{ESS/TSS}.$$

The explained variation plus the unexplained variation equals the total variation (RSS + ESS = TSS). Thus, the coefficient of determination can be written alternatively as the explained variation divided by the total variation, or as one minus the unexplained variation divided by the total variation.

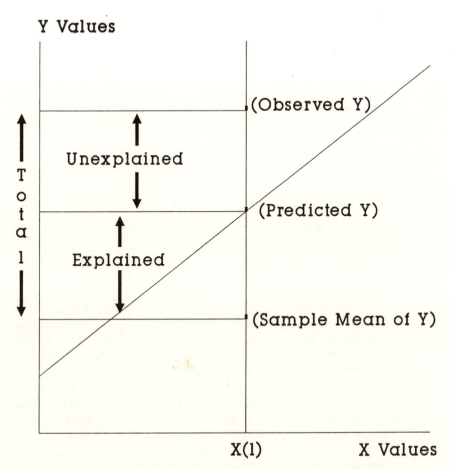

FIG. 2.3. Explained, unexplained and total variation for one observation, $X(1)$

Figure 2.3 shows the elements of explained, unexplained, and total variation for one hypothetical observation. In the case of a bivariate regression model only, the coefficient of determination equals the Pearson correlation coefficient squared; that is $R^2 = r^2$. If you do not recall what the correlation coefficient is, or how it is calculated and interpreted, see Appendix B.

CONCLUSIONS

This chapter has presented the basics of the bivariate or simple regression model. The ordinary least squares (OLS) intercept and slope estimators were derived using the least squares method. There are other ways to derive these same estimators, some of which rely heavily on the assumptions that underlie the regression model. These assumptions have not been stressed here, but they will be thoroughly discussed in Chapter 6. While it is important to understand the assumptions of the regression model, at this point, it is more important to become familiar with the formulas for deriving the coefficients.

The next chapter expands the regression model to the multivariate case. In addition, the characteristics that make the least squares regression estimators good ones are discussed, and ways to perform hypothesis tests on the coefficient estimates are explained.

SUMMARY OF CHAPTER 2

1. The goal of this chapter has been to develop estimators for the slope and the intercept in the bivariate regression model.

2. Deterministic relationships do not contain errors. Statistical estimators are not needed to calculate parameters of deterministic linear bivariate relationships, because all data points fall exactly on only one straight line.

3. Stochastic relationships do contain errors and can be written as follows: $Y_t = B_0 + B_1 X_t + E_t$. Stochastic relationships are realistic for social scientists because human behavior can never be exactly predicted, because some variables will inevitably be left out of social science models, and because there will often be errors in the measurement of the included variables.

5. The population includes all the observations relevant to a particular model, while the sample includes only a subset of the observations. Statistical models are most powerful when applied to samples, where inferences to populations can be made. The sample bivariate regression relationship is written as follows: $Y_t = b_0 + b_1 X_t + e_t$, where b_0 and b_1 are estimates of the population intercept and slope, and e_t is the residual, or estimate of the population error.

6. The slope and intercept estimators are derived using the least squares criterion. This criterion says that the sum of the squared error terms is minimized. Using calculus to minimize the sum of the squared errors leads to the following two normal equations: $\Sigma_{t+1}^{T}(Y_t - b_0 - b_1 X_t) = 0$ and $\Sigma_{t+1}^{T}(Y_t - b_0 - b_1 X_t) X_t = 0$. These two equations are then solved for the intercept and slope estimators (the t subscripts have been dropped): $b_0 = \bar{Y} - b_1 \bar{X}$, and $b_1 = (\Sigma xy)/(\Sigma x^2)$, where $x = X - \bar{X}$, and $y = Y - \bar{Y}$.

7. The coefficient of determination is a useful statistic that accompanies the regression model. It indicates how well the regression line fits the data. It equals the explained variation divided by the total variation or

$$R^2 = \sum_{t=1}^{T}(\hat{Y}_t - \bar{Y})^2 / \sum_{t=1}^{T}(Y_t - \bar{Y})^2.$$

3

The Multiple Regression Model, Part I: Estimators, Statistical Properties, and Significance Tests

Most problems that interest public managers and analysts are inadequately described by two-variable models. Fortunately, the statistical techniques needed to estimate multivariate relationships are fairly straightforward extensions of the simple regression model. In this chapter, the essentials of the multiple regression model are discussed. The first section of the chapter is devoted to an example of a multivariate relationship. The second section develops the estimators for the intercept and the slopes of the multiple regression model. The third section of the chapter presents the statistical characteristics of the least squares estimators, and the fourth section explains significance tests for those estimators. The fifth section examines the output of a popular computer package that can be used to obtain the regression statistics. Ways to judge the importance of individual variables, model building techniques, and the use of the regression model as a forecasting tool are all discussed in the next chapter.

AN EXAMPLE OF THE NEED FOR MULTIVARIATE RELATIONSHIPS

Health managers and analysts are interested in the determinants of the number of annual visits made by families to doctors or dentists. In recent years, the effect of various provisions of health insurance coverage on the number of visits has been a major concern. At other times, interest has centered on the effects of reduced waiting and traveling time. Whatever the management or policy motivation, answers to questions about determinants of variations in the number of annual visits requires a multivariate model. In the mid-1970s, A. G. Holtmann and E.

Odgers Olsen[1] published results of research on annual household visits to the dentist (see Example 3.1 for more details on the actual results). Some of the variables that were hypothesized to determine annual visits were—the dentist's fee, waiting time, traveling time, family income, education of the head of the household, the number of children and the number of adults in the family. (It is a good exercise to try to predict the sign on the coefficient for each of the variables.) If one wishes to estimate the effect of various levels of insurance on dental visits, the coefficient on the fee variable is crucial, since insurance changes the effective fee paid by the patient. But a simple model that relates visits to fee alone is inappropriate, because it does not control for all the other determinants of number of dental visits per year. This shortcoming is particularly crucial if fees are related to family income or number of children (or any other independent variable) because, then, the coefficient on the fee variable is usually biased. Because the two variable regression model cannot be used to adequately model or control, the regression model needs to be generalized to include several independent variables.

EXAMPLE 3.1 THE DEMAND FOR DENTAL VISITS

A. G. Holtmann and E. Odgers Olsen analyzed the demand for dental visits using a sample of data on 923 households taken in 1971–72. One of the equations they estimated was:

Number of annual dental visits per household = −1.462 − .011(price per visit) −.024(minutes of waiting time) −.010(minutes of travel time) + .0012(annual income) + .216(years of education of head of household) + 1.376(number of children) + .958(number of adults).

Questions:

a. What is the unit of analysis in this study?
b. (i) On average, how many more dental visits will be made annually by a family with one child than by a family with no children? (ii) How about a family of four children compared to a family of three children?
c. What is the meaning of a negative intercept?
d. (i) The average price of dental visits in this sample was around $18. How much would the price have to change from $18 in order to encouarge an average of one more yearly visit per household? (ii) Does your result mean the regression is nonsensical?
e. (i) What does the coefficient on "years of education of head of household" tell us? (ii) Does the sign of the coefficient make sense?
f. Should we believe the values of all of these coefficients?

Discussion:

a. Households are the unit of analysis.
b. (i) 1.376 dental visits, the value of the regression coefficient for number of

children. (ii) The same 1.376, since this coefficient shows the difference when one more child is added to the family. Later, we will see how to estimate models where additions of one more can result in different additions to the dependent variable (that is, nonlinear relationships).

c. In many models, such as this one, the intercept is simply an indication of where the model crosses the Y axis and it does not have any meaning that can be interpreted. Specifically, it does not make sense to say that if all the independent variables take on values of zero, then a household will make minus 1.462 visits annually to the dentist.

d. (i) It would have to decline approximately $100, since a decline of $100 would result in $(-.011)(-100) = 1.1$ more visits. (ii) The result does not mean the regression is nonsense. Instead it indicates two things. First, in the realistic range of price decreases and increases, the effect of price on number of visits is not very large (a price decrease of $2 would result in an increase of .022 visits per year). Second, the relationship between price and number of visits may be nonlinear, and again we will see in a future chapter how to deal with nonlinearities.

e. (i) Households with more highly educated heads visit the dentist more often, as indicated by the positive coefficient on the variable "years of education of head of household." (ii) The opposite result might make sense if health status is correlated with education and more highly educated heads of households have families with teeth that need less care. Of course, if health status is an important variable in determining numbers of visits, it should have been included in the model. Leaving it out when it is important will bias the coefficients of the variables most closely related to it. In this case, the coefficient on years of education of head of household may be too low, because a health status variable is omitted.

f. We should not necessarily believe the values of the coefficients because the statistical significance of the coefficients has not been reported. It is possible that the coefficients on some (or all) of the variables could just as likely be zero as what is reported here. Later in this chapter we will learn about statistical significance.

THE THREE VARIABLE REGRESSION MODEL

The estimators for the three variable model, which includes one dependent and two independent variables, will be developed using the ordinary least squares (OLS) method. The mathematics for three variables is uncomplicated and the results easily generalize to any number of independent variables. As was the case for the two variable model, calculus is used to minimize the sum of the squared errors and obtain three normal equations—one for the intercept (b_0) and one for each of the two slopes (b_1 and b_2). The squared errors for the three variable model can be represented as follows:

$$\sum_{t=1}^{T} e_t^2 = \sum_{t=1}^{T} (Y_t - b_0 - b_1 X_{t1} - b_2 X_{t2})^2. \tag{3.1}$$

Using calculus to minimize these errors with respect to b_0, b_1, and b_2, results in the following three normal equations. (The t subscripts are dropped, for convenience, in doing manipulations).

$$\Sigma(Y - b_0 - b_1X_1 - b_2X_2) = 0 \tag{3.2}$$

$$\Sigma(Y - b_0 - b_1X_1 - b_2X_2)(X_1) = 0 \tag{3.3}$$

$$\Sigma(Y - b_0 - b_1X_1 - b_2X_2)(X_2) = 0 \tag{3.4}$$

These three equations can then be solved simultaneously to obtain the estimators for the intercept and two slopes:

$$b_0 = Y - b_1\bar{X}_1 - b_2\bar{X}_2 \tag{3.5}$$

$$b_1 = \frac{(\Sigma x_2^2)(\Sigma x_1 y) - (\Sigma x_1 x_2)(\Sigma x_2 y)}{(\Sigma x_1^2)(\Sigma x_2^2) - (\Sigma x_1 x_2)^2} \tag{3.6}$$

$$b_2 = \frac{(\Sigma x_1^2)(\Sigma x_2 y) - (\Sigma x_1 x_2)(\Sigma x_1 y)}{(\Sigma x_1^2)(\Sigma x_2^2) - (\Sigma x_1 x_2)^2} \tag{3.7}$$

where $x_1 = X_1 - \bar{X}_1$, $x_2 = X_2 - \bar{X}_2$, and $y = Y - \bar{Y}$.

The ordinary least squares method used here to derive intercept and slope estimators can be used for any number of independent variables. The estimators, however, become more and more difficult to write out in simple algebra, and the calculations become more and more difficult to perform by hand. What is important to understand about the derivations is that they are based on a criterion of minimizing squared errors. A computer can be used to obtain the actual numbers for any particular sample, and how this is done is explained in the final section of this chapter.

STATISTICAL CHARACTERISTICS OF THE LEAST SQUARES ESTIMATORS

The least squares estimators have some quite desirable properties that are summarized by saying that the estimators are BLUE—Best, Linear and Unbiased Estimators. These BLUE properties are discussed one by one, beginning with the most intuitive property—unbiasedness.

Unbiasedness

Any particular estimate of a slope or intercept parameter is derived from a sample of data; therefore it may or may not equal the population value of the parameter.

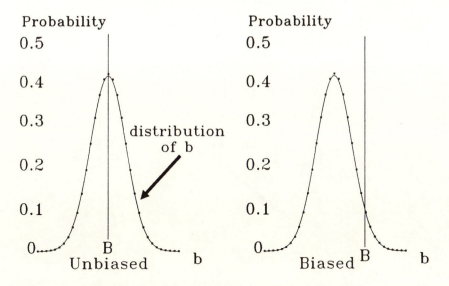

FIG. 3.1. Biased and unbiased slope estimators

One would expect that different samples would yield different estimates. It would be nice if the average value of the estimates derived from all possible samples of the same size were equal to the population intercepts and slopes. We could then say that the estimates based on one sample were *unbiased*, or that the expected value of the intercept or slope estimates equaled the respective population values. Indeed, the least squares estimators do result in unbiased estimates of the intercept and slope parameters; on average, the estimates will be "right." Figure 3.1 illustrates the difference between a biased and an unbiased slope estimator, where the distribution of the sample slope estimates (*b*'s) is normal.

Minimum Variance or Bestness

Unbiasedness says that the distribution of sample estimates is centered on the population parameter, but it does not say anything about how widely dispersed those sample estimates might be around their respective population values. The wider the dispersion, the less likely it is that any particular estimate will exactly equal its population value. So, ideally, an estimator would yield estimated values with small dispersions around the population mean. In fact, the least squares estimators do result in the smallest variance compared to all other possible linear unbiased estimators. This property is called *bestness* or, in general, efficiency.[2] Figure 3.2 illustrates the difference between an unbiased slope estimator that is best and one that is not, again assuming that the distribution of the sample slope estimates is normal.

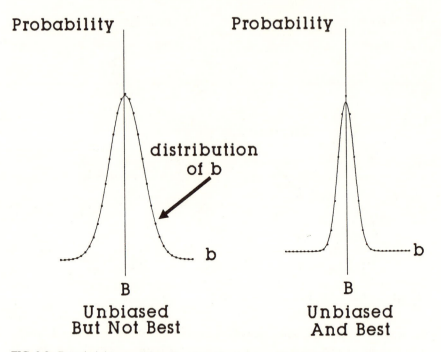

FIG. 3.2. Best (minimum variance) and not best slope estimators

BLUE Estimators Summarized

BLUE estimators are best, linear and unbiased. Best means the estimators have the smallest variance among all linear, unbiased estimators. Linear refers to the nature of the formula (estimator), specifically that the "Y" variable enters the formula in a linear way, without any squared, square root, or other nonlinear terms. Unbiased means that the expected value of the estimate equals the population parameter.[3]

BLUE Properties in More Detail

Although the BLUE properties of the least squares estimators will not be proven here, it is useful, for further understanding, to go over these properties in more detail.

Unbiasedness Again. Let us look further at unbiasedness in the following way. Suppose we take ten samples, each with 50 observations on the X's and the Y's, and calculate ten different values of the slopes (b's), using the least squares estimators. For this exercise, we will assume that the X's can be fixed by the analyst so that, in each of our ten samples, the X values are exactly the same. Then, only the Y values vary across the samples, and this is due to the error terms in the model. The slope estimates will almost surely differ across the ten samples because the Y's will almost always differ, and the estimators involve values of both Y's and X's. The assumption of fixed X's (that is, fixed values of the independent variables) makes the example easier to understand. Relaxation of the assumption does not change the results in ways that are important to this discussion.

Unbiasedness says that, in an experiment similar to the one just described, except that the number of samples includes all possible samples of size 50, the slope estimates that are calculated will average out to the population values of the slopes. Thus, while no one sample would necessarily result in the population parameters, we would expect neither systematic over- or under-estimates. This is a good property because, on average, the estimates are right.

Minimum Variance Again. Minimum variance of the estimators, or bestness, is also desirable. Once it is known that on average the estimate of a slope parameter is equal to its population value (is unbiased), then it is important to ask, How large is the variance of the estimate around the population parameter? The smaller the variance, the closer any sample value of b is likely to be to its population value. The least squares formulas produce estimates with minimum variances, compared to all other possible linear formulas for unbiased estimates.[4]

The values of the independent variables (the X's) are fixed across the samples in our hypothetical experiments with all possible samples, and only the Y values vary. Since the Y's vary because the errors vary, one might guess that the variance of the slopes (b's) will depend in part on the variance of the errors. Although the formulas for the variances of the slope estimates will not be derived, they are given in Chapter 3 notes.[5] The square roots of these variances are called the standard errors of the estimates, and they are used in hypothesis testing and confidence interval formation.

SIGNIFICANCE TESTS AND CONFIDENCE INTERVALS

Any particular least squares estimate of a coefficient may or may not be close to its population value. It would be useful to quantify the likelihood that the sample value of a coefficient occurs "just by chance," or better yet, to quantify the likelihood that a sample value is equal to zero rather than equal to its estimated value. *Significance tests* allow users to state, with specific probabilities, that their estimated sample results are not equal to zero. Another way to quantify the precision of an estimate is with *confidence intervals,* which state that a range of values has a certain probability of containing the true population coefficient.

There is a need for both hypothesis testing and confidence interval formation because sample estimates vary around their true population values. The degree of significance and level of confidence depend on the magnitude of the variance of the estimate. The methods for testing hypotheses and forming confidence intervals are analogous to those used for the sample mean. Readers who do not remember the logic and procedures in the case of the mean may refer to Appendix C. In this section, it is assumed that the basic logic is understood. First, significance tests and confidence intervals for the slope and intercept coefficients are discussed. Then, the R^2 statistic becomes the focus.

Significance Tests for the Slope and the Intercept Coefficients

In order to test hypotheses or construct confidence intervals for the regression coefficients, one must make an assumption about how the estimated slope and intercept coefficients are distributed. The standard regression model assumes that the slopes and intercepts are normally distributed.[6] Knowledge of the distribution of slope and intercept coefficients will permit us to determine the distribution of the various test statistics that are used to evaluate hypotheses.

The most common null hypothesis for the regression coefficients is that they are, one at a time, equal to zero. This may seem odd, since the regression model is generally constructed to reflect what the analyst thinks are reasonable variables to explain the variation in the dependent variable. Regression coefficients of zero imply that the independent variables have no effect on the dependent variable. Actually, the analyst generally hopes that the null hypotheses of zero will be rejected, because then the estimated coefficients can be assumed not to have occurred by chance at the probability level equal to the set significance level. The alternative hypotheses are generally that the coefficients are not equal to zero. Thus, technically, once the null hypotheses are rejected, not much can be said about what the coefficients are. In practice, the estimated regression coefficients are used as if they were the alternative hypotheses. If the hypotheses that the coefficients are equal to zero are rejected, then it is presumed that the estimated model is valid, again at the significance level chosen for the test. This practice can be justified by referring to the BLUE characteristics of the regression estimators. If a coefficient is not equal to zero, then the best guess would be that it is equal to its BLUE estimate.

The most common hypothesis, which we will begin with, is then stated as follows:

$H_0: B = 0$
$H_A: B \neq 0.$

To test this, we must use the estimated b coefficient to form a statistic that allows the use of a distribution that is tabulated in statistical tables for given significance levels. This test statistic, called the t statistic, is distributed according to Student's

t distribution. The statistic is constructed by taking the estimated coefficient, subtracting its population value as hypothesized in the null hypothesis, and dividing by the standard error of the estimated coefficient:

$$t = (b - B_{H_0})/S_b. \tag{3.8}$$

This t statistic has degrees of freedom equal to the sample size (T) minus the number of independent variables plus one ($K + 1$).

Next, the cutoff points (sometimes called critical values) for rejecting the null hypothesis at a given significance level are found. If a 5% significance level is chosen, then the t table is checked to find the cutoff values of t above which, on the positive side, 2.5% of the distribution falls and below which, on the negative side, 2.5% of the distribution falls, assuming the null hypothesis is true. These probabilities can be written as follows:

$$Prob \ [-t_{.025,T-(K+1)} > (b - B_{H_0})/S_b > t_{.025,T-(K+1)}/H_0: B = 0)] = .05,$$

where $t_{.025,T-(K+1)}$ is the cutoff point for a t statistic with $T - (K + 1)$ degrees of freedom. Figure 3.3 shows the cutoff points on a graph.

If the t statistic is greater than the positive cutoff point or less than the negative cutoff point, the null hypothesis ($B = 0$) is rejected.

How Significance Levels are Set. What factors are considered when establishing significance levels? Often an assessment of the costs and the benefits of actions that would be taken on the basis of the statistical results can help determine if the significance level should be set high or low. Setting precise significance levels requires that precise cost and benefit functions be known. Since it is usually not possible to do more than state the costs and benefits in relative terms, this section will only discuss calculations needed for relative determinations.

Suppose, as an example, that two different kinds of policy evaluations are planned. The first is an evaluation of the effectiveness of a state seat belt law in reducing traffic deaths and injuries, and the second is an evaluation of a state bottle law that requires deposits on all bottles and cans in hopes that there will be less litter. How can we reason about which of these should have a lower significance level (that is, higher percentage) for the statistical tests that accompany the evaluation? First, we could explore the social costs of implementing the two policies. Let's *assume* that the *seat belt law* entails *lower social costs*. This might occur if the extra costs that auto companies must undergo to install the belts, plus the extra efforts motorists and passengers must make to wear the belts, are less than the cost of provisions that the bottle companies and grocery stores must make for the bottle return law, plus the efforts that consumers who want their deposits back must make to store and return the bottles. On the other hand, if the *seat belt law* "*works,*" the *benefits* are likely to be *higher* than those of an effective bottle law.

Probability

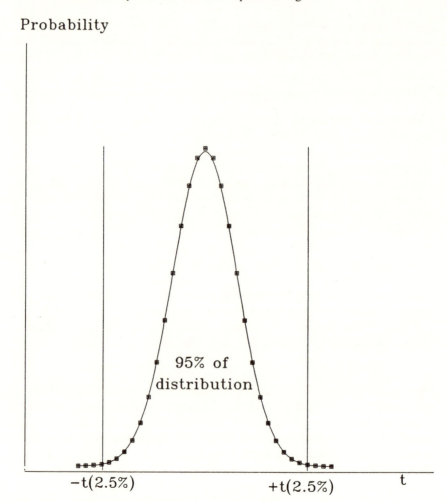

FIG. 3.3. Cutoff points for a two-sided hypothesis test

This is because the value of averting deaths and injuries will add up more quickly to a higher number than will the value of making streets and parks cleaner. Under the circumstances hypothesized, the significance level for the seat belt evaluation should be set lower (that is, at a higher percentage number such as .05 instead of .01), since we would be less chagrined about making a type I error for the seat belt policy (rejecting ineffectiveness and continuing the policy when the policy actually is ineffective) when the costs are relatively lower and the benefits are relatively higher.[7] Appendix C reviews the difference between a type I and a type II error.

A second factor in setting significance levels is the conventional practice of other analysts and researchers. This is particularly valuable when the regression equation is not directly linked to a specific policy, or when the relative costs and benefits are hard to assess. Generally, users of regression look for significance at the 5% or 1% levels, but, if the model is exploratory, then 10% will sometimes be used. In fact, although not absolutely statistically sound, one usually discusses coefficients that are significant at either the 5% or 1% levels and reports the significance level (or corresponding standard error or t value) for all coefficients.

Examples of Hypothesis Testing. Let's return to some specifics of hypothesis testing and look at two examples of tests on slope coefficients. Suppose the following relationship is estimated:

$$Y = -.03 - .61X_1 + 3.25X_2 + 6.19X_3. \tag{3.9}$$
$$\quad (.01)\ (.12)\quad (1.15)\quad (.68)$$

(Standard errors are in parentheses) and $T = 20$; $K = 3$; $R^2 = .80$.

Suppose we want to test the following hypothesis, at the 5% significance level.

$H_0: B_1 = 0.$
$H_A: B_1 \neq 0.$

First, the t statistic is formed: $t = (-.61 - 0)/.12 = -5.08$. Then the cutoff points for a statistic distributed according to Student's t distribution, with 16 (20 − 4) degrees of freedom, is found in the t tables to be 2.120. (See Appendix D, Table D.1, for cutoff points of Student's t distribution.) This allows us to say that the probability of a t statistic being above +2.120 or below −2.120, when the null hypothesis is true, is 5%. Since our t statistic is −5.08, below −2.120, the null hypothesis is rejected, at the 5% significance level.

As a second example, let's test the following one-sided hypothesis test at a 1% significance level:

$H_0: B_3 = 3.$
$H_A: B_3 > 3.$

The t statistic is $(6.19 - 3)/.68 = 4.69$. The cutoff point is 2.583, and the null hypothesis is rejected at the 1% significance level.

Confidence Intervals for the Slope and Intercept Coefficients

Confidence intervals for the coefficients state the probability that a given range of numbers will include the true population coefficient. They can be derived using the same logic as hypothesis testing. For example, suppose we want to establish a 95% confidence interval for the B_2 coefficient in the previous example. If we begin with the basic hypothesis testing equation, we can rearrange it to derive confidence intervals. The basic equation for a 5%, two-sided hypothesis test states that the probability of the t statistic being above the positive cutoff point or below the negative cutoff point, when the null hypothesis is true, is 5%. In equation form, this statement looks as follows:

$$Prob\ [-t_{.025,df} > (b - B)/S_b > +t_{.025,df}] = .05,$$

where B stands for the population parameter when the null hypothesis is true and $t_{.025,df}$ is the cutoff point for the t statistic for a 5%, two-sided test, with "df" (degrees of freedom) equal to a given number.

This probability statement can be rearranged so that a confidence interval instead of a hypothesis test is established. The rearrangement involves some basic knowledge about how inequality operators work; the manipulations should be understandable if the explanation that precedes each step is read.

Step 1: Reverse inequalities so that probability is 95%.

$$Prob\ [-t_{.025,df} < (b - B)/S_b < +t_{.025,df}] = .95.$$

Step 2: Multiply all sides of inequality by S_b.

$$Prob\ [-S_b t_{.025,df} < b - B < S_b t_{.025,df}] = .95.$$

Step 3: Subtract b from all sides of inequalities.

$$Prob\ [-S_b t_{.025,df} - b < -B < S_b t_{.025,df} - b] = .95.$$

Step 4: Multiply all sides of inequality by -1, which reverses the inequality signs. This final step results in a confidence interval:

$$Prob\ [b + S_b t_{.025,df} > B > b - S_b t_{.025,df}] = .95.$$

The confidence interval is, then, $b +/- S_b t_{.025,df}$.

Therefore, the 95% confidence interval for B_2, in the above example, where the 5% cutoff value is 2.120, b is 3.25 and S_b is 1.15, is: 3.25 +/- (1.15)(2.120) = 3.25 +/- (2.438) or .81 to 5.7. These limits would include the true population coefficient for B_2 with 95% probability.

The confidence interval can be used to test hypotheses as well. In the example above, using B_2, the null hypothesis of no effect would be rejected because the confidence interval does not include zero. This can be checked by performing the hypothesis test, where the t statistic is (3.25 − 0)/1.15 = 2.826. Since this statistic is greater than the cutoff value of 2.120, the null hypothesis is indeed rejected.

Significance Tests for R^2

The significance test for R^2 has as its null hypothesis that the population R^2 is zero and as its alternative hypothesis that the population R^2 is greater than zero. This is also a test for the significance of the entire relationship in the sense that if R^2 is zero, the independent variables all together do not explain any of the variation in the dependent variable.[8] The null and alternative hypotheses can be stated as follows:

H_0: $R^2 = 0$.
H_A: $R^2 > 0$.

These hypotheses are tested by forming a statistic from the estimated regression results, determining how that test statistic is distributed, and then obtaining a cutoff value at a predetermined significance level. The test statistic in this case is distributed according to the F distribution. The F distribution is an asymmetric distribution with two different degrees of freedom. Its probabilities for a one-sided test are tabulated in tables, where the degrees of freedom for the numerator are shown along the top of the table (the columns), and the degrees of freedom for the denominator are shown along the side of the table (the rows). The F statistic is written with two subscripts, the first showing the degrees of freedom in the numerator and the second showing the degrees of freedom in the denominator. Each table is generally specified for a single significance level, for example, 5% or 1%. See Appendix D for an F table at the 5% significance level.

The actual F statistic that is formed to test hypotheses about the R^2 is calculated as follows:

$$F_{K, T - (K + 1)} = \left\{ \frac{R^2/K}{(1 - R^2)/[T - (K + 1)]} \right\} = \{R^2/(1 - R^2)\} \{[T - (K + 1)]/K\}$$

where K represents the degrees of freedom in the numerator (and also the number of independent variables in the model), and $[T - (K + 1)]$ represents the degrees of freedom in the denominator (and also the sample size minus the number of independent variables plus one).

Using again the example on hypothesis testing, where R^2 is .80, T is 20 and K is 3, the test to see if R^2 is significant at the 5% level would be performed as follows. Form the F statistic with $3(K)$ and $16[T - (K + 1)]$ degrees of freedom. This F statistic is equal to:

$F = \{.8/(1 - .8)\}\{[20 - (3 + 1)]/3\} = 21.33$.

The 5% cutoff point is 3.24 and thus, since 21.33 is greater than 3.24, the null hypothesis of an R^2 equal to zero is rejected at the 5% level of significance.

If the null hypothesis of a zero R^2 is not rejected, what are the implications for the analysis? The model as specified is an extremely poor predictor of variation in the dependent variable. Unless another model that works better is available, a zero R^2 implies that the mean of the dependent variable (a univariate statistic) will predict (or explain) the variation in the dependent variable as well as the model itself.

Example 3.2 shows a use of multiple regression to help explain efficacy of national science policy and provides an opportunity to practice performing some significance tests and forming some confidence intervals.

EXAMPLE 3.2 REGRESSION, RESEARCH PRODUCTIVITY, AND THE MANAGEMENT OF NATIONAL SCIENCE POLICY

In 1983, Joseph L. C. Cheng and William McKinley published an article that used regression analysis to study the influence of national science policy on the productivity of scientific research units in university settings.[9] The authors stated that science policy was "at least potentially manipulable by individuals concerned with the management of scientific research. . . . Thus, the findings have relevance as a basis for practical recommendations."[10]

Based on literature from organization theory, they argued that research productivity would be influenced by national science policy (in the form of formal guidelines, instructions, and choices of research themes) and the degree of paradigm development (the values, techniques, models, and conventional wisdom of a discipline.) Specifically, they hypothesized that "the influence of national science policy on reseach-unit themes will be positively related to research-unit productivity, but as paradigm development decreases, this relationship will decline significantly and become negative in fields with less developed paradigms."[11]

A sample of data from 288 academic research units in four West European countries (Austria, Belgium, Finland, and Sweden) was used to test the hypothesis. Four academic fields were represented (biology, chemistry, geology, and physics). Research productivity was measured by a weighted index of the number of books and articles published by each unit over the previous three years. National science policy influence was measured by the answers to questions posed to the director of each research unit concerning the percentage of times the research unit's choice of a research theme was influenced by national science policy. The measure of paradigm development was based on previous research that had classified physics and chemistry as highly developed paradigms, biology as a moderately developed paradigm, and geology as a less developed paradigm. Unit size, measured by the number of staff, was entered as a control variable.

The following three regressions show some of the results of the study. (Standard errors are in parentheses.) Intercepts were not reported.

Highly developed paradigm: $T = 169$

Productivity = .058 (national science policy influence)
(.028)

+ .197 (unit size)
(.041)

$R^2 = .13.$

Moderately developed paradigm: $T = 89$

Productivity = .016 (national science policy influence)
(.046)

+ .255 (unit size)
(.092)

$R^2 = .08.$

Less developed paradigm: $T = 30$

Productivity = -.041 (national science policy influence)
(.031)

+ .062 (unit size)
(.074)

$R^2 = .09.$

Questions:

a. (i) Are the coefficients significant at the 5% level? (ii) Do the results support the hypotheses?

b. (i) What is the effect of increasing unit size by one full time staff member in a highly developed paradigm? (ii) in a moderately developed paradigm? in a less developed paradigm?

c. Form a 95% confidence interval for the coefficient on national science policy influence for all three regressions. Are these intervals consistent with the results of the hypothesis tests in (a)?

d. Is the R^2 statistic significant at the 5% level in all three regressions?

e. Do the low R^2's mean that the results should be ignored?

f. (i) What other variables might be entered? (ii) What other regressions might be run?

g. What help might these regressions be in managing national science policy?

Discussion:

a. (i) Significance tests at 5% level: $t_{.05, 166} = 1.960$; $t_{.05, 86} = 2.00$; $t_{.05, 27} = 2.052$.
Highly developed:

$t = .058/.028 = 2.07 > 1.960$, therefore significant at 5% level.

Moderately developed:

$t = .016/.046 = .35 < 2.00$, therefore not significant at 5% level.

Less developed:

$t = .041/.031 = 1.322 < 2.052$, therefore not significant at 5% level.

(ii) Yes, if we use the simple test that the coefficient on national science policy for the highly developed paradigms should be positive and significant and the coefficients for the less developed paradigms should be insignificant.

b. (i) Only the coefficient for the highly developed paradigm is significant at the 5%

level. For the highly developed paradigm, increasing staff by one full time person would increase productivity by .197, on average. (ii) Since the coefficients for the moderately developed and less developed paradigms are insignificant, the best estimate is that increasing unit size for these paradigms would have no effect.

c. Highly developed paradigm:

.058 +/- (1.960)(.028) = (.113; .003).

Moderately developed paradigm:

.016 +/- (2.0)(.046) = (.108; −.076).

Less developed paradigm:

−.041 +/- (2.052)(.031) = (.023; −.185).

The results are consistent with the hypothesis tests, since both the moderate and less developed paradigms have confidence intervals that include zero, and they were both insignificant at the 5% level.

d. F test at 5% level: $F_{2, 166; .05} = 3.0$; $F_{2, 86; .05} = 3.15$; $F_{2, 27; .05} = 3.39$.

Highly developed paradigm:

$F = (.13/.87)(166/2) = 12.40 > 3.0$, so R^2 is significant.

Moderately developed paradigm:

$F = (.08/.92)(86/2) = 3.74 > 3.15$, so R^2 is significant.

Less developed paradigm:

$F = (.09/.91)(27/2) = 1.34 < 3.39$, so R^2 is insignificant.

e. No, since the rest of the variation might be random and not explainable. Also, since the main emphasis here is hypothesis testing, the t statistic is more relevant than the R^2. Finally, since this is a new area for research, a lower R^2 is more acceptable than if the area had been heavily researched already. All things considered, of course, it is better to have a high rather than low R^2.

f. (i) The individual countries might be entered as dummy variables (dummy variables are studied in Chapter 5). (ii) One regression might be run with all the data, entering the paradigm as a dummy or interacting it with the policy influence variable (again, see Chapter 5 for how to interact variables).

g. The regressions themselves are relatively useless because they are so simple-minded. But, combined with the theory that led to their formation, one can come to some conclusions. For example, it would seem that national science policy will be more successful if it concentrates efforts in the highly developed paradigms. In the other paradigms, either there will be no effect, or possibly even a negative effect, since in these areas there is not much consensus on what should be done, or how it should be done. National policy might be better off setting broad general objectives for all but the highly developed paradigms.

USING THE COMPUTER TO OBTAIN REGRESSION STATISTICS

There is little reason for anyone to calculate regression statistics using a calculator. In fact, when the number of observations are above 25 or so, or the number of variables above three, it becomes very tedious and difficult to do the calculations accurately on a calculator. Luckily, there are a wide variety of already programmed regression packages that are available in almost all organizations that have a mainframe computer. In addition, if one has access to a personal computer, many similar packages are available for use on it. Two of the more popular packages available both for mainframe and for personal computers (PC's) are Statistical Package for the Social Sciences and Statistical Analysis System. Both of these are accompanied by good reference manuals, and we will not duplicate the detailed instructions on how to enter data or request statistics. Instead, we will look at the output (or end result) of regression analysis using the SPSS/PC+ system (the PC version of Statistical Package for the Social Sciences),[12] and will carefully go over the meaning of each statistic. While other computer software packages do not display their output in exactly the same way as SPSS/PC+, a knowledge of the SPSS/PC+ format will facilitate the interpretation of output from other packages. SPSS/PC+ output will be presented throughout the text, so that the reader can see how each new technique appears on a computer printout.

Typical SPSS/PC+ output for an estimated multiple regression equation includes summary statistics on the observations, the Pearson correlation matrix of all the variables, the regression slope coefficients and related statistics, and sometimes a scattergram that plots various relationships of interest.

The computer examples illustrated in this text use data and models developed by Matthew Drennan and presented in his book, *Modeling Metropolitan Economies for Forecasting and Policy Analysis.*[13] The equations presented here are part of Drennan's larger model of the New York City economy. The entire model is helpful to city departments and private organizations that need to forecast economic development, business cycles, and tax revenues. The numbers reported are identical or almost identical to the ones in Drennan's book; any differences are due to rounding of the original data. The data are time-series, either 84 quarters (from the first quarter of 1958 to the fourth quarter of 1978), or in some cases, 10 years (from 1975 to 1984).

The equation that will be looked at in this chapter was constructed by Drennan to forecast total income generated within New York City during a quarter. The unit of analysis is the quarter. The dependent variable is total city income, in millions of 1972 dollars, and is labelled CALLY. The four independent variables are: the United States unemployment rate (UUNEMPR), total United States national income in billions of 1972 dollars (UALLY), the ratio of the consumer price index for the region to the consumer price index for the nation (SCPIUS), and city population for the year, in thousands (CPOP). A priori, one would expect UALLY and CPOP to have positive coefficients, and UUNEMPR and SCPIUS to have negative coefficients. Keep in mind that these independent variables are meant to explain city income *in constant dollars* (that is, dollars that are standardized for inflation to their 1972 level).

Figure 3.4 displays the following information—the means and standard deviations for the five variables, the Pearson correlation matrix and the regression output. The means and standard deviations, labelled "Mean" and "Std Devi," can be helpful in a number of ways. First, one can quickly check to make sure that all

SPSS/PC+

	Mean	Std Devi
UUNEMPR	5.537	1.333
CPOP	7722.238	218.093
SCPIUS	1.010	.024
CALLY	45595.301	3185.224
UALLY	803.017	169.178
N of Cases =	84	

Correlation:

	UUNEMPR	CPOP	SCPIUS	CALLY	UALLY
UUNEMPR	1.000	-.517	.167	-.664	.133
CPOP	-.517	1.000	-.277	.215	-.678
SCPIUS	.167	-.277	1.000	.453	.768
CALLY	-.664	.215	.453	1.000	.486
UALLY	.133	-.678	.768	.486	1.000

* * * * MULTIPLE REGRESSION * * * *

Equation Number 1   Dependent Variable .. CALLY

Multiple R	.96738
R Square	.93582
Adjusted R Square	.93258
Standard Error	827.08515

Analysis of Variance

	DF	Sum of Squares	Mean Square
Regression	4	788047524.20415	197011881.05104
Residual	79	54041518.04573	684069.84868

F = 287.99966   Signif F = .0000

Variables in the Equation

Variable	B	SE B	95% Confdnce Intrvl B		Beta
UALLY	24.16005	1.68678	20.80259	27.51751	1.28322
UUNEMPR	-873.09978	104.71910	-1081.53794	-664.66162	-.36543
SCPIUS	-32569.92771	8663.55379	-49814.30062	-15325.55480	-.24174
CPOP	12.11741	1.00475	10.11751	14.11732	.82968
(Constant)	-29640.37027	6362.29863	-42304.20925	-16976.53130	

Variable	T	Sig T
UALLY	14.323	.0000
UUNEMPR	-8.338	.0000
SCPIUS	-3.759	.0003
CPOP	12.060	.0000
(Constant)	-4.659	.0000

FIG. 3.4. Descriptive statistics, correlation matrix, and regression results

the values of the variables are in reasonable ranges; if the means are much larger or smaller than they should be, then the original data needs to be rechecked for errors. Second, one can see the units in which the variables are calculated. For example, percentages can be calculated either as raw percentage numbers, or as decimals. In this example, UUNEMPR is a raw percentage, since the mean is 5.537. The mean would be .05537 (rounded to .056) if decimals had been entered for each observation.

The Pearson correlation matrix, labelled "Correlation," is useful because it shows the strength and the direction of the relationship between variables, two at a time. The matrix repeats itself above and below the diagonal. Thus, there are two ways to locate every correlation. For example, the correlation between CALLY and CPOP (.215) can be found by looking down the CALLY column and across the CPOP row, or down the CPOP column and across the CALLY row. The correlations in the CALLY column are particularly interesting, because they provide information on the bivariate relationship between the dependent and each independent variable. Only UUNEMPR has a negative correlation, but we will see that the correlation coefficients do not definitively tell the signs of the multiple regression coefficients because the signs depend on the effect of each independent variable, controlling for variation in all the other independents. Sometimes, the signs of the simple correlations will differ from the signs of the slopes. From the correlations with CALLY, we can also see that all but CPOP are fairly strongly related.

Figure 3.4 also displays the regression results, labeled MULTIPLE REGRESSION. Two numbers, "Adjusted R Square" (.93285) and "Beta" (the column of four numbers under "Variables in the Equation"), are not explained until Chapter 4. "R Square" (.93582) is the R^2. "Standard Error" (827.08515) is the sum of the square root of the squared residuals divided by their degrees of freedom, or $\sqrt{\Sigma(e_i)^2/[T - (K + 1)]}$. This number is sometimes used to form confidence intervals around the predicted value for Y and its use is explained in Chapter 4.

For the purposes of regression analysis, "F" (= 287.99966) and "Signif F" (= .0000) are the important numbers in the "Analysis of Variance" table. The F is the statistic calculated to test the significance of the entire regression and is equivalent to $\{R^2/(1 - R^2)\}\{[T - (K + 1)]/K\}$, as shown in the text. The significance level shows the lowest level at which the statistic is significant. Of course, a .0000 level makes no sense because it implies that there is no chance that the null hypothesis of no significance is rejected when the null hypothesis is really true. That is, the type I error is presumably zero, making the type II error infinite. (See Appendix C for a description of type I and type II errors.) The .0000 number really means that not enough digits are reported for a number greater than zero to appear. The result should be reported as significant at less than the .01 or .001 level, rather than significant at the 0 level.

The output labeled "Variables in the Equation" shows the regression slope or intercept for each variable (B), the standard error of the estimated slope or intercept (SE B), the 95% confidence intervals ("95% Confdnce Intrvl B"), the Beta coefficients ("Beta") (to be explained in Chapter 4), the calculated t statistic for the two-sided test of no significance of the coefficient (T), and significance of the t statistic ("Sig T"). So, on this one page of computer output, all the statistics that thus far have been painstakingly calculated by hand are available from the computer.

As a final note, observe that while the sign of UUNEMPR is negative like its correlation, the sign of SCPIUS is also negative, unlike its positive correlation, but as one would predict a priori.

CONCLUSIONS

The multiple regression model is a powerful analytical tool when it is combined with a theory of the phenomenon being studied. In addition to calculating intercept and slope coefficients and the R^2, one can also test for statistical significance of the coefficients and of the R^2. The next chapter continues the basic presentation of the multiple regression model. It addresses ways to analyze effects of particular variables, to build models, and to make forecasts of the dependent variable.

SUMMARY OF CHAPTER 3

1. Most problems that interest public managers and analysts are inadequately described by two-variable models, but instead require multivariate ones.

2. The ordinary least squares (OLS) estimators in the multiple regression model are derived by minimizing the sum of the squared errors. The following three normal equations are solved for the estimators (t subscripts and indexes are omitted).

$$\Sigma(Y - b_0 - b_1X_1 - b_2X_2) = 0,$$
$$\Sigma(Y - b_0 - b_1X_1 - b_2X_2)(X_1) = 0,$$
$$\Sigma(Y - b_0 - b_1X_1 - b_2X_2)(X_2) = 0.$$

3. Least squares estimators have some desirable statistical characteristics. The estimators are said to be BLUE or best, linear, and unbiased. This means that among all estimators that are linear functions of the dependent variable, the least squares formulas generate estimates that have an expected value equal to the population value and have the minimum variance.

4. Coefficients can be tested for significance. The most common null hypothesis is that the coefficient is equal to zero. For such a hypothesis, the t statistic is formed $[(b - 0)/S_b]$ and compared to Student's t value for the appropriate degrees of freedom and significance level. Other null hypotheses can be tested as well.

5. Confidence intervals can also be formed. They state the probability that a range of numbers will cover the true population coefficient.

6. Hypotheses concerning the significance of R^2 are tested using an F statistic and the F tables.

4

The Multiple Regression Model, Part II: Importance of Variables, Model Building, and Forecasting

This chapter concludes the development of the basic multiple regression model. The first section discusses ways to judge the importance of individual variables; the second section looks at model building techniques; and the third section develops the regression model as a forecasting tool.

MEASURING THE IMPORTANCE OF INDIVIDUAL VARIABLES

For policy and management purposes, as well as for theoretical or scientific reasons, people are often interested in determining the relative importance of individual variables in a regression equation. That is, after the significance of each variable is determined, the question often arises about which variables have the largest effect, are most important, have the greatest predictive power, and so on. At least six different ways of addressing this problem have been suggested, and in this section each one is described and discussed. The conclusion is that there is no absolutely correct way to determine importance of individual variables; each way has its own shortcomings; several ways make no sense at all. The six alternatives that are discussed are absolute size of regression coefficients, elasticities, beta coefficients, t values, changes in R^2, and cost-effectiveness.

Absolute Size of Regression Coefficients

At first blush, it might seem reasonable to look at the size of the coefficient on all the significant variables. But this will rarely be sensible since the variables are generally not measured in the same units. In Example 3.1 (Chapter 3), where annual dental visits is the dependent variable, the independent variables are price per visit in *dollars, minutes* of waiting time, and *years* of education. The coefficients are for variables that are measured in "apples and oranges" (or at least dollars, minutes and years), and therefore their size cannot meaningfully be compared.

Elasticities

The use of elasticities is one way to "standardize" the regression coefficients. The standardization is done in terms of percentages. Elasticities show the percentage change in the dependent variable in relation to a one percent change in the independent variable. Percentage changes for both the dependent and independent variables are conventionally measured from the mean of each. The formula for calculating an elasticity at the mean is as follows:

Elasticity at the mean = (regression coefficient) $(\bar{X}/\bar{Y})$ = $(b)(\bar{X}/\bar{Y})$.

The conceptual problem with using elasticities is that a percentage measure is not meaningful for all variables. While it is natural to speak about percentage changes in income or price, it is less natural to refer to percentage changes in the portion of the population that is under 5 years old, or in educational levels, for example. In addition, the percentages must be calculated at some specific value of the dependent and independent variables, most usually the means. These specific values may not be relevant for management or policy decisions, especially if the changes will occur far away from the means.

Beta Coefficients

Beta coefficients represent yet another way to standardize the units of the independent variables. This time the standardization is in terms of standard deviations from the means of the independent and dependent variables. The beta coefficients indicate the number of standard deviations that the dependent variable changes (from its mean) when the independent variable changes by one standard deviation (from its mean). The beta coefficients are derived from a regression of the dependent variable, minus its mean, divided by its standard deviation, on each independent variable, minus its mean, divided by its standard deviation. Betas can also be calculated as follows:

Beta Coefficient = (regression coefficient) × (standard deviation of independent variable) ÷ (standard deviation of dependent variable).

Conceptually, the problem with the betas is the same as that with the elasticities; only some variables are naturally discussed in terms of their standard deviations. The natural ones are generally measured ordinally, where a scale has been devised to capture something such as satisfaction or quality of care, and the scale has been tested so that one standard deviation from the mean has a particular signification. Otherwise, standard deviations of variables such as unemployment rates, or surgical discharges, or most other variables measured as continuous cardinal numbers, will be awkward to understand as compared to their raw units. In addition, from a statistical point of view, the betas are problematic because they are sample specific. The larger the sample standard deviation of an independent variable, the larger the beta coefficient. Thus, a user is never sure if a large beta is the result of an underlying population phenomenon or, rather, if it is just idiosyncratic to the particular sample that was used. The use of betas is safer in larger samples, since the sample standard deviations have smaller sampling variances as the sample size increases and thus are more likely to be accurate in larger samples.

The *t* Values

The *t* values are used to test the significance of the null hypotheses that the coefficients on the independent variables are zero. It is sometimes suggested that a larger calculated *t* value implies greater significance and thus more importance. There are both conceptual and statistical problems with this suggestion.

Conceptually, the significance level for a hypothesis test should be established before the test is performed. Then, no matter what the size of the calculated *t* in relationship to the cutoff *t*, the hypothesis is simply rejected or not rejected. Some hypotheses are not "more" rejected than others. In practice, many analysts wait to see what the calculated *t* value is, and then state that the null hypothesis is rejected at the lowest probability possible. In theory, this is not a correct procedure, so by extension it is not correct to use the *t*'s to say that because one variable is "more significant" than another, it is also more important than another.

Statistically, the problem with using the size of a *t* value to judge importance is that the size of a *t* value depends in part on the intercorrelations that one independent variable has with all the others. The higher the intercorrelations, the greater the standard errors of the estimated coefficients. And the greater the standard errors, the lower the *t* values, although not all *t*'s are necessarily lowered the same amount. Thus, use of the size of *t* values will be sample specific, depending on the nature of the intercorrelations among the independent variables.

The Change in R^2

It is tempting to try to find a way to partition the R^2 for the equation into separate parts that represent the contribution of each independent variable to the equation's explanatory power and that would add up to the total R^2. One way of doing this is to add variables one at a time to the regression equation, making sure that the order in which they are added is according to the highest addition to the R^2. For example, the first variable entered into the equation would be the one that results in the highest R^2 for a bivariate relationship; the second variable added would result in the largest change in the R^2 from the level established by the first variable, and so on until all of the independent variables had been entered. The measure of importance would then be how much the R^2 changed when a variable was added. The first entered variable would be the most important, the second entered would be the second most important, and so on.

The problem with this seemingly reasonable procedure is that it again depends on the sample intercorrelations among the independent variables. It does so in such a way that the first entered variable gets the credit not only for its own contribution to the R^2, but also for the contribution of other variables, to the extent that it is correlated with those other variables. And the other variables entered later do not get credit, to the extent of the intercorrelations. Thus, the order in which the variables enter the equation will severely affect the change in R^2 registered for each variable, if there are large intercorrelations. That the order of entry matters is not a good characteristic of an importance measure, but more crucial is that the intercorrelations may be sample specific. It would be far better to use importance measures that represent population values than ones that are contingent on the particular characteristics of a sample.

Cost-effectiveness Assessment

For management or policy purposes, there is a solution to the problem of determining importance, but it involves additional information about the independent variables. Among the independent variables that are significant, it is often possible to specify the ones that are controllable by a manager or policymaker. For example, in a regression meant to explain or predict the collection rate by county of child support payments from absentee fathers whose children are on welfare, an analyst might include variables such as the number of employees assigned to follow these cases, the degree to which the information system on absentee fathers is computerized, the extent of urbanization in the county, and the unemployment rate in the county. Only the first two variables are possibly controllable by managers of the program; the extent of urbanization and the unemployment rate are not controllable. Therefore, from a management perspective, only the first two variables are important. In addition, it might be possible to attach a dollar cost figure to increasing the controllable variables. For example, one could probably determine the cost of an additional full-time employee, as well as the cost of additional computerized information. Once the cost of a unit increase in a controllable independent variable is determined, then the effectiveness of a unit increase, as measured by the regression coefficient, can be compared to the cost. The most important variable, then, would be the one with the highest effectiveness-cost ratio.[1] Example 4.1 uses this kind of reasoning in some of the questions that follow the example.

From a statistical viewpoint, there is no natural, problem-free way to determine the importance of individual regression coefficients. If one of the methods discussed here is used, then the analyst should be well aware of the caveats associated with its use. From a management point of view, it is possible to use a cost-effectiveness technique, although sometimes the costs of obtaining the additional information will be high.

TECHNIQUES TO HELP WITH MODEL BUILDING

Sometimes there is neither good enough theory nor prior empirical work to help an analyst specify exactly which independent variables should be included in a model. Or, the general nature of the variables to include may be clear but it may not be possible to distinguish among several alternative measures of the variables. In such cases, some of the techniques of model building can be helpful. In this section, two of these techniques are discussed—step-wise regression and adjusted R^2.

EXAMPLE 4.1 REGRESSION AND PRODUCTIVITY OF STATE SALES TAX AUDITORS

State tax auditors are hired in large part to make sure state tax laws are obeyed. One measurable benefit to states from their auditors is the amount of unpaid tax money that is recovered. Stuart Greenfield measured the productivity of state auditors with data from 45 states.[2] He regressed the dollar amount (in thousands of dollars) of sales tax revenues recovered due to audits (R) on the number of sales tax auditors (A), the annual salary of entry-level auditors (S), and the state sales tax rate (T). The results of one regression using 1976 data follow: (t statistics in parentheses):

$$R = -25511.20 + 72.47(A) + 1.95(S) + 2384.8(T)$$
$$(11.49) \quad (1.93) \quad (1.98)$$

$R^2 = .84$.

Questions:

a. (i) How much would audit recoveries have increased in 1976, on average, if salaries of auditors increased $1.00 per auditor? (ii) If the number of auditors increased by one?
b. Would you feel confident applying these results to changes over time in one state?
c. In 1976, hiring an additional auditor would have cost $9,789 in salary. Would such an additional staff member be worthwhile?

d. If the $9,789 in salary were used to increase the salaries of current auditors, their salaries would have been increased by $83 per auditor, on average. Would this be worthwhile?

e. Would it be better to spend the $9,789 on an additional auditor or on salary increases?

Discussion:

a. (i) If salary per auditor increased $1.00, audit recoveries would increase $1,950, on average. (ii) If the number of auditors increased by one, audit recoveries would increase by $72,470 on average.

b. Not without checking to make sure that the coefficients were relatively stable over time. It would be better to have a model based on changes and estimated with time-series data if the primary interest were changes over time.

c. Yes, since audit recoveries would increase by $72,470 while costs would increase by only $9,789. However, diminishing returns are likely to set in, so that as more auditors are hired the additional audit recoveries are not likely to be as great as $72,470.

d. Yes, because audit recoveries would increase $(83)(1950) = \$161,850$.

e. From a strict cost effectiveness ratio viewpoint, it would be better to spend the $9,789 on salary increases. However, one would need to look carefully at this. In the cross-section data, differing salaries may mean differing productivity, but raising the salary of starting employees in a particular state may or may not increase productivity.

Stepwise Regression

Stepwise regression is a way to determine which subset of variables, chosen from a larger set, will result in an equation with the highest R^2. The variables are entered into the regression equation one at a time according to how large a change in the R^2 they generate. Each variable entered into the regression remains, and the change in R^2 is calculated for each new variable given the already entered ones.[3] Another way to understand how the best subset of variables is chosen is that choices according to change in R^2 are equivalent to choices according to the size of the F statistic attached to each variable. And choice according to the size of the F statistic is choice according to the significance level of the change in the R^2. Thus, in practice, when stepwise regression is performed on a computer, the analyst may either specify the maximum number of variables that will be included, or indicate the probability level that the F statistic must exceed before no further variables are added, or both.

The value of stepwise regression to the model builder is that a sample of data can be used to help choose the appropriate variables to include. It is desirable to have a high R^2 attached to an equation. The end result of stepwise regression is a model that is the best that can be obtained from a sample. Stepwise regression can also be used when the analyst definitely wishes to include certain variables, but wants the choice among some others to depend on their respective additions to the R^2.

There are problems with the use of stepwise regression in model building. First, the sample has been used to build the model (or, as some say, as a fishing expedition), and that same sample cannot now be used to test the model. The maximum R^2 obtained may or may not be idiosyncratic to that sample; there is no way to know without gathering more data. Specifically, the significance test is not legitimate if the same sample that generated the model is used to test it. Second, if the stepwise regression procedure is asked to choose among a great many variables, it is possible that the final model will have no meaning; it may be impossible to interpret the results except to say that R^2 is maximized. Finally, multivariate statistics are not powerful enough to work well without some kind of theory that constrains, defines, and helps interpret the variables that will be subject to empirical testing. In the end, regression is based on correlations and these may well be spurious. Only some reasoning beyond the statistical results will give a user any confidence that the data have confirmed or rejected some real phenomenon. For all of these reasons, stepwise regression needs to be used with caution. Its best use is probably in very restricted cases where the analyst wishes to choose among a small subset of variables that in theory are all representing a similar phenomenon.

Adjusted R^2

Another aspect of model building is the existence of several different regression equations, all purporting to explain variation in the same dependent variable. The question often arises as to which equation represents the best model. A logical statistic to use in determining the best model is the R^2 for each equation, but several problems exist if the R^2 is used. First the equations that are being compared may have different numbers of independent variables, and the equation with more variables will have at least as high, and usually a higher, R^2. Yet, one characteristic of a good model is a parsimonious use of explanators, since a model is trying to abstract from reality, not describe every facet of it. A second problem is that some equations may have been estimated from larger samples, and generally one would like to give more credence to results that are based on larger sample sizes when an identical population is being studied. The adjusted R^2, often called "R bar squared" and written as $\bar{R}^2$, addresses these two problems.

The adjusted R^2 lowers R^2 as more variables are added to the regression equation and raises R^2 as the sample size increases. It is calculated as follows:

$$\bar{R}^2 = R^2 - \{K/[T - (K + 1)]\}\{1 - R^2\}.$$

The model with the highest $\bar{R}^2$ would presumably be the best.

A problem with the use of $\bar{R}^2$ is that there is no way to statistically test the relationship of one $\bar{R}^2$ to another. All the significance tests for R^2 are based on the null hypothesis that the population R^2 is zero; knowledge about the distribution of the test statistic (the F statistic) is based on the population R^2 being zero. But in the case of $\bar{R}^2$, the tests one would like to do would involve comparisons of nonzero $\bar{R}^2$'s, and there is not a test statistic to perform these tests. In addition, a model should be judged on more than its ability to explain the variation in the dependent variable. Significance of individual coefficients and the policy relevance of individual variables will usually be important as well. Only if the sole purpose of the equation is to forecast values of the dependent variable will $\bar{R}^2$ be a reasonable way to summarize the model.

Example 4.2 describes a regression equation for which it would have been appropriate to use some of the model building techniques just discussed.

EXAMPLE 4.2 REGRESSION AND THE 55 MILE PER HOUR SPEED LIMIT

As part of a National Research Council study of the costs and benefits of the 55-mile per hour speed limit, Charles A. Lave used multiple regression to determine the relationship between fatalities and the speed limit, controlling for accessibility of emergency medical care and driver behavior.[4] Using cross-section data from the states, fatalities per vehicle mile traveled was regressed on average speed, speed variance (measured approximately as one standard deviation of average speed), citations per driver, and hospital access, for six different types of highways. The coefficient on average speed was insignificant in all the equations. The coefficients for the other variables are shown for rural interstate highways. The sample size was 44 states. The intercepts are not reported (t statistics in parentheses).

Fatality Rate =
.190 (speed variance) + .0071 (citations per driver) − 5.290 (hospital access)
(2.6)   (2.8)   (3.7)
$R^2 = .532$.

Questions:

a. For rural interstate highways, what is the interpretation of the coefficient on speed variance, on citations per driver, and on hospital access?

b. Why might average speed have been insignificant, while speed variance was significant, for 6 of the 12 highway types?

c. Do the results mean that the speed limit could be raised and there would be no change in fatalities?

d. (i) What benefits, in addition to fatality reduction, do you think the National Research Council study took into consideration? (ii) What kinds of costs of various speed limits do you think the Council considered? (iii) What kinds of design problems might be encountered in a cross-section study of fatality, such as the one reported here?

Discussion:

a. If speed variance increases by one unit (approximately one standard deviation), fatalities per vehicle mile increase by .190, on average. If citations per driver increase by one, the fatality rate increases by .0071, on average. If hospital access increases by one unit, the fatality rate declines by 5.290.

b. More accidents may be caused when motorists have to slow down significantly and often, than when they all are driving at a fast, but similar, speed.

c. No, because average speed and speed variance may move together, so that increasing the average speed may increase (or decrease) the speed variance.

d. (i) Other benefits considered were reduced numbers and severity of injuries, and savings in fuel. (ii) Costs considered included time spent on the road and enforcement costs. (iii) Those who designed the study had at least two worries: the problem of confounding variables that occurred around the same time as the change in the speed limit (generally changes in driving habits); and the desirability of using time-series data (from before the 55 mile per hour limit to after the limit), in addition to using cross-section data.

FORECASTING WITH A REGRESSION MODEL

A forecast is an estimate of the future value of a dependent variable. Forecasting can be done with the regression model as it has been developed here, as long as the values of the independent variables that are needed for the forecast are known or can be estimated. Generally, one thinks of forecasting with a model that has been estimated with time-series data, but it is equally possible to forecast with a cross-section model.[5] The cross-section forecast asks what the dependent variable would be, given values of the independent variables. Since it is somewhat more natural to think about forecasting into future time periods rather than across the same time period, the rest of this discussion will use the terminology of a time-series forecast; however, everything applies equally to a cross-section forecast.

Forecasts can be unconditional or conditional. In both cases the value of the dependent variable is unknown. In an unconditional forecast, however, the values of the independent variables are known. So, for example, one might forecast enrollment (ENROLL) in a government summer camp program as a function of the enrollment two years previous:

$$(\widehat{ENROLL_t}) = B_0 + B_1 (ENROLL_{t-2}),$$

where $\wedge$ is used to indicate a forecast. Then, in order to forecast enrollment next year, in year $(t + 1)$, one would use last year's enrollment figure $(t - 1)$ as the independent variable. Since last year's enrollment figure is known and does not have to be estimated, next year's enrollment forecast would be unconditional. In general, models such as the enrollment one, where the independent variables take on lagged values, can often result in unconditional forecasts. Also, unconditional forecasts can be generated by models where the independent variables can be determined by managers or policymakers, such as the level of the fare in a model that regresses subway ridership on the fare.

Conditional forecasts are the ones in which the value of the independent variables must be estimated or guessed. For example, if current cash holdings by a municipal government are thought to depend on current interest rates, then forecasts of future cash holdings will require an estimate of the future interest rates. Conditional forecasts will be less accurate than unconditional forecasts because of the additional errors contributed by the estimates of the independent variables.

When making forecasts with a regression model, it is possible, and usually advisable, to form a confidence interval around the forecasted value. The confidence interval will emphasize the degree of imprecision that accompanies the estimate. It will also provide one way of evaluating the model since, if future actual values of the dependent variable fall outside the confidence interval with any regularity, the model will need to be reformulated.

There are at least four possible reasons why a forecast made on the basis of a regression model may be incorrect. First, the population regression model is stochastic and the error term insures that the forecast is often wrong. Although on average the error equals zero, in any one particular case it may be different from zero. Second, the regression coefficients are estimated—they are equal to their population values only on average—and these estimates are a source of error as well. Third, if the forecast is conditional, then the estimates of the independent variables cause errors. Finally, the model may simply be formulated incorrectly. All of these sources of error are summarized in the forecast error, which is the difference between the forecast for a given time period and the actual value of the dependent variable in that time period.

In the rest of this section, the discussion focuses on unconditional forecasts using the least squares estimators. The formation of proper confidence intervals is emphasized—when the population model is known and when it is not.

Forecasts When the Population Model Is Known

If the population model is known and all the assumptions of the ordinary least squares model are met, then the estimate of Y_{t+1} (written $\hat{Y}_{t+1}$), based on a bivariate regression model and given that X_{t+1} is known, would be:

$$\hat{Y}_{t+1} = B_0 + B_1 X_{t+1}.$$

The forecast error would be $\hat{Y}_{t+1} - Y_{t+1} = E_{t+1}$ and its variance would be σ_E^2. Since by assumption, the error in the population model is distributed normally, confidence intervals could be formed using the standard deviation of that error, the cutoff points from the normal distribution, and the estimated $\hat{Y}_{t+1}$. For example, if Y_{t+1} is being estimated, the 99% confidence interval would be written as follows:

$$\text{Prob } [\hat{Y}_{t+1} - (z_{.01})\sigma_E < \hat{Y}_{t+1} < Y_{t+1} + (z_{.01})\sigma_E] = .99,$$

where z_{01} is the 1% cutoff on the normal curve and σ_E is the standard deviation of the population error term. This confidence interval would form a flat band around possible estimates of Y_{t+1}, as shown in Figure 4.1. The purpose of presenting the case of a known population model is to facilitate the comparison of these flat confidence intervals with the more common ones that accompany a model that must be estimated from a sample. More to the point, confidence intervals based on sample data are sometimes misspecified as flat. This occurs when an analyst uses the *estimate* of the error standard deviation (called the standard error of the estimate) in place of the actual population error standard deviation, when forming the confidence interval shown just above. As will be demonstrated, the degree of misspecification is greatest when the forecasted value of the dependent variable lies far away from the sample mean of the dependent variable.

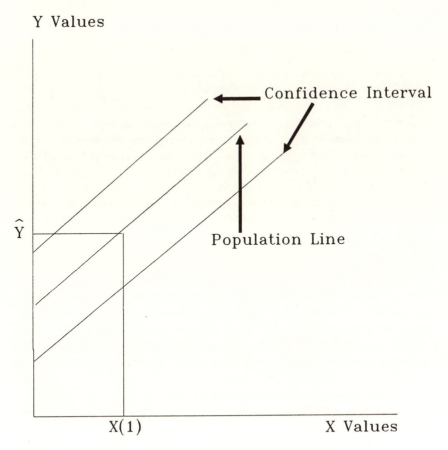

FIG. 4.1. Confidence intervals for known population coefficients

Forecasts When the Population Model Is Not Known

If the least squares estimates are used to forecast, all the statistical assumptions are met, and the model is correctly specified, then there are two sources of error for the forecast. First, the regression model is stochastic so, just as with the population model, there will often be a nonzero random error associated with the forecast. Second, the coefficients of the equation will be estimated and there will be potential errors associated with these estimates. In the bivariate case, the estimate for a value of Y one year in the future, where the model is not lagged, would be: $\hat{Y}_{t+1} = b_0 + b_1 X_{t+1}$. The forecast error (fe) is $e_{t+1} = \hat{Y}_{t+1} - Y_{t+1}$ and the estimated variance of that error (S^2_{fe}) is as follows:

$$S^2_{fe} = S^2_e[1 + 1/T + (X_{t+1} - \bar{X})^2/\Sigma(X_t - \bar{X})^2],$$

where $S^2_e = \Sigma e_t^2/[T - (K + 1)]$.

The square root of this estimated variance (its standard deviation) can be used to form confidence intervals. A 95% confidence interval around Y_{t+1} would be formed as follows:

$$\text{Prob}[\hat{Y}_{t+1} - (t_{.05,df})(S_{fe}) < Y_{t+1} < \hat{Y}_{t+1} + (t_{.05,df})(S_{fe})] = .95.$$

Figure 4.2 shows the shape of this confidence interval for different forecasts of Y_{t+1}. The confidence intervals bow out from the sample mean of X and of Y, which indicates that the accuracy of the forecast diminishes as it is made farther into the future. This is because the values of the independent variables associated with the forecast are probably farther outside the range of experience described by the sample. If the incorrect confidence interval based on the flat bands described for the known population model is used, the error is less important if the forecast is not far into the future.

An Example of Confidence Intervals for Forecasts

Suppose a large city is contemplating raising the fare from eighty-five cents to a dollar per passenger on its subway system, but is concerned about how much ridership will drop off. Weekday peak ridership at the eighty-five cent fare is 1164.2 million annually. The following model has been estimated, relating weekday peak ridership in millions (RIDER) to fare in cents (FARE), using least squares regression. (Standard errors in parentheses.)

$$\widehat{RIDER}_t = 1196.5 - .38(FARE_t),$$
$$\qquad\qquad (249.3) \ (.053)$$

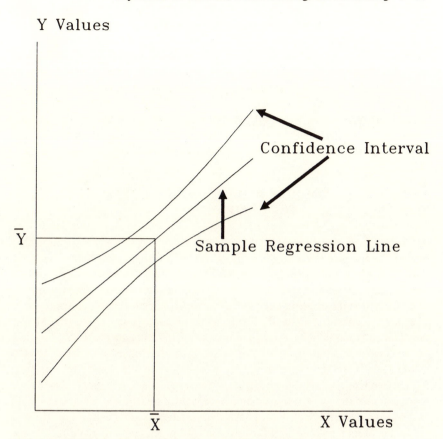

FIG. 4.2. Confidence intervals for unknown population coefficients

where $T = 10$; $R^2 = .73$; $S = \text{SEE} = 4.49$; $\Sigma(X_t - \bar{X})^2 = 4400$; $\bar{X} = 85$; $\bar{Y} = 1203.2$. The forecast for the number of weekday peak riders at the one dollar fare would be:

$$\widehat{\text{Rider}}_{1.00} = 1196.5 - .38(100) = 1158.5.$$

The variance of the forecast error would be:
$$S^2_{\text{fe}} = 20.2[1 + 1/10 + (100 - 85)^2/4400] = 23.25.$$

The square root of this variance (S_{fe}), equals 4.82, and is the standard deviation of the forecast error. A 95% confidence interval would be: $\widehat{\text{RIDER}}_{1.00}$ +/– $[t_{.05,8}][S_{\text{fe}}]$. The value of $t_{.05,8}$ (found from the Student t Table in Appendix D) is 2.306; thus, 1158.5 +/– $(2.306)(4.82) = 1158.5$ +/– $11.11 = 1147.39$ to 1169.61. This says that we are 95% sure that 1147.39 and 1169.61 are boundaries that include the true value of ridership at the one dollar fare. We could use these boundaries to calculate the boundaries of the total revenue at the new fare ($1147.39 millions to $1169.61 millions) compared to the revenue at the old fare [(1164.2)($.85) = $989.57 millions]. Thus, one could state with 95% confidence that the total revenue will be higher under the new fare.

Although the examples so far have used a simple regression model, all the results generalize to the multiple regression model as well. The examples have also been unconditional forecasts, where all the assumptions of the ordinary least squares model hold. Conditional forecasts and estimates that do not meet all the assumptions would have to be somewhat modified.

AN EXAMPLE OF MODEL BUILDING AND STEPWISE REGRESSION USING THE COMPUTER

In Chapter 3, there were 84 quarters of data used to estimate an equation that predicted aggregate income, in millions of 1972 dollars, for New York City (CALLY). Here, the same data are used to illustrate the stepwise method of obtaining a regression equation. The four independent variables from Chapter 3, plus an additional one, are entered into a "forward" stepwise regression procedure. The independent variables are the United States unemployment rate (UUNEMPR); total United States national income in billions of 1972 dollars (UALLY); the ratio of the consumer price index for the region to the consumer price index for the nation (SCPIUS); the New York City population, in thousands, for the year (CPOP); and total city employment, in thousands of jobs (CALLEMP). In Chapter 3, we assumed that we knew what model we wanted to estimate. Here, we will act as if we do not know which of the above five variables would be the more effective predictors of total income. The forward stepwise procedure will be utilized to see which variable enters the equation first and to see if they all enter.

The SPSS/PC+ procedure called forward stepwise regression chooses variables to enter on the basis of the highest partial correlation coefficient. The partial correlation coefficient is the correlation between the dependent variable (CALLY) and each independent variable not yet in the equation, adjusted for the independents already in the equation. This is equivalent to choosing the next variable based on the t-value its coefficient will have when it is entered.

Figure 4.3 shows the output of the stepwise procedure for the first and the last step. UUNEMPR is entered first and SCPIUS is entered last. After each variable is entered, the usual R^2 values, coefficients and t-values are printed. In addition, a table for "Variables Not in the Equation" shows what would happen if each of the listed independent variables were entered next—the Beta coefficient, partial correlation coefficient, t-value, and significance of the t-value. The "Min Toler" column refers to a measure of the interrelationship among the independent variables. If the independents are too interrelated, the next variables will not be entered. The minimum tolerance must exceed .01, which it does for all variables in this equation.

SPSS/PC+

**** M U L T I P L E   R E G R E S S I O N ****

Equation Number 1   Dependent Variable . . CALLY

Beginning Block Number 1. Method: Forward

Variable(s) Entered on Step Number 1.   UUNEMPR

R Square   .44129
F =   64.76688   Signif F = .0000

--------------------- Variables in the Equation ----------------------

Variable	B	SE B	Beta	T	Sig T
UUNEMPR	-1587.16652	197.21776	-.66430	-8.048	.0000
(Constant)	54383.29104	1122.81617		48.435	0000

------------- Variables not in the Equation -------------

Variable	Beta In	Partial	Min Toler	T	Sig T
CPOP	-.17502	-.20042	.73260	-1.841	.0693
SCPIUS	.58034	.76553	.97220	10.709	.0000
UALLY	.58490	.77557	.98235	11.057	.0000
CALLEMP	.07200	.05999	.38794	.541	.5900

Variable(s) Entered on Step Number 5.   SCPIUS

R Square   .96355
F =   412.33671   Signif F = .0000

--------------------- Variables in the Equation ----------------------

Variable	B	SE B	Beta	T	Sig T
UUNEMPR	-379.16532	102.0887	-.15870	-3.714	.0004
UALLY	23.59941	1.28149	1.25344	18.416	.0000
CALLEMP	7.98027	1.03618	.44534	7.702	.0000
CPOP	7.97080	.93310	.54576	8.542	.0000
SCPIUS	-33528.18743	6572.45951	-.24885	-5.101	.0000
(Constant)	-27066.52559	4837.34391		-5.595	.0000

FIG. 4.3. Stepwise regression: first variable (UUNEMPR) and last variable (SCPIUS) to be entered

If we wanted to use the stepwise results to build a model to explain CALLY, then we would be tempted to say that the more important variables are the ones that entered earlier. Again, this interpretation of importance is only workable in two situations. The first is when a group of variables has been identified that makes sense as explanatory variables, but one does not want to include all of them in the equation. In that case, stepwise regression is one reasonable way to choose among the variables. The second situation is when the sole purpose of the regression equation is forecasting and a high R^2 is desired. Then, it is somewhat less important that every variable in the equation be theoretically justified. The example in Figure 4.3 shows that, based on the stepwise results, a different set of four independent variables would be chosen than in the equation in Chapter 3. Specifically, one would include CALLEMP (the fourth variable entered, but not shown in Figure 4.3) and exclude SCPIUS (the fifth variable entered).

CONCLUSIONS

The foundation for the rest of the study of multivariate statistical techniques and their applications is now established. Future chapters show how to make the regression model more flexible, what to do if some assumptions are clearly violated, and how to translate more sophisticated visions or theories of the world into multivariate statistical models. If you understand what has been said until now, you should then have few problems adding sophistication to your use of regression and other multivariate techniques.

SUMMARY OF CHAPTER 4

1. Users of regression are often interested in determining the relative importance of individual variables in a regression equation. Although six different ways of addressing importance have been used by analysts, no one of them is without problems. The six suggestions are absolute size of regression coefficients, elasticities, beta coefficients, t values, changes in R^2, and cost effectiveness. For managers, cost effectiveness is probably the most useful.

2. Stepwise regression and the adjusted R^2 ($\bar{R}^2$) are often used as aids in model building. Stepwise regression is most helpful when the analyst wishes that the choice among several variables, which theoretically represent the same (or similar) phenomenon, be based on statistical considerations alone. It is least useful when the analyst has no theory in mind and simply asks the regression technique to choose several variables so as to maximize R^2. The adjusted R^2 is useful whencomparing two models that have the same dependent variable but differentnumbers of independent variables and different sample sizes.

3. The regression model can be used to forecast values of the dependent variable. It is important to form the appropriate confidence interval around the forecast when the forecast is made far from the means of the sample data.

5

Dummy Variables and Nonlinear and Nonadditive Relationships

This chapter describes ways to increase the versatility of the regression model. Until this point, all the independent variables in the model have been presented as interval or ratio level cardinal variables, whose values potentially go from minus to plus infinity. Now, nominal independent variables, more commonly known as dummy variables, are introduced. In addition, the model developed in previous chapters was strictly linear; a unit increase in an independent variable (X) resulted in an increase or decrease in the dependent variable (Y) that was constant. There were no curved relationships, where a unit increase in X might result in different size increases in Y, depending on whether the value of X was small or large. Now, the model's usefulness will be vastly increased with the introduction of nonlinear relationships that contain exponential, squared or cubed terms. Finally, the model until now has assumed that a unit increase in the independent variable (X) will result in a constant change in the dependent variable (Y), regardless of the values of other independent variables. In contrast, if the change in the dependent variable (Y), occasioned by a unit change in the independent variable (X), varies with one or more other independent variables, then the model is nonadditive or interactive. The first and second parts of this chapter explain what dummy variables are and how to use and interpret them. The third and fourth parts of the chapter explain nonlinear and nonadditive relationships. And the fifth part of the chapter shows computer output for regressions that represent dummy and nonlinear relationships.

DUMMY VARIABLES

Dummy variables are nominal variables whose values fall into one of several categories. For example, a model that is attempting to explain or predict earnings of individual workers might include a variable that describes their sex. Such a variable would take on the values of either male or female and would be called a dummy variable. Or, a regression that estimates the variation in monthly usage of residential water in a community might include variables for the season and could take on the four different values of summer, fall, winter, and spring. As a way to further understand the use and interpretation of dummy variables, the two examples of a sex dummy and seasonal dummies are further developed.

Example of a Sex Dummy Variable Used in a Regression Equation

Equations that predict an individual's earnings are useful for a number of management and policy purposes. Managers have become increasingly interested in whether certain employees are discriminated against in their salaries. Equal rights cases sometimes use evidence from regression equations to demonstrate the existence or lack of existence of such discrimination. In a sexual discrimination case, where a regression equation is used, the evidence pro or con discrimination hinges on the sign, size, and significance of the sex dummy variable. Policy analysts are interested in the same kinds of issues, although the perspective is usually broader than one organization. Analysts often look at economy-wide patterns, sometimes over time. For both managers and analysts, a typical model that explains the variation in individual earnings would include at least the following independent variables—the person's age, education, work experience, and innate ability. In addition, the person's sex, and possibly race, would also be included, if some kind of discrimination is suspected. The logic of using the sex variable to test for sex discrimination is that if all the objective determinants of earnings (such as work experience) have been included in the equation, the sex variable should be insignificant if there is no discrimination. If, however, females are discriminated against, then, even after all objective determinants of earnings have been accounted for, the female dummy variable would have an independent influence.

Illustration Using a Sex Dummy. To illustrate the use of a sex dummy variable in more detail, let's look at a simplified version of an earnings equation, where only the individual's educational level and sex are used to predict variations in yearly earnings. Thus, in this example:

Earnings per year = f (education, sex). $\qquad$ (5.1)

The education variable could be measured cardinally, in years. For the sex variable, it might be tempting to establish two variables, one for males and one for females. Then, if an individual were a male, the male variable would take on the value of one and the female variable would take on the value of zero. On the other hand, if an individual were a female, the female variable would take on the value of one and the male variable would take on the value of zero.

For two hypothetical individuals, where the male had 12 years of education and the female had 14 years of education, the values of the variables would look as follows:

Variables	Education	Male sex dummy	Female sex dummy
Observations			
1. (male)	12	1	0
2. (female)	14	0	1

While the above way of setting up the dummy variables is logical, it will not work statistically. The regression coefficients cannot be calculated when every possible occurrence of the dummy (in this case male and female) has its own variable. In a sense, the equation is overdetermined; technically the dummies and the intercept will be perfectly correlated and this will prevent a solution for the normal equations. Most regression packages will show some kind of error and refuse to calculate coefficient values.

If two sex dummies will not work, what will? The general rule is to establish one *less* dummy variable than there are possible values for the dummy variable. So, for the sex variable, where the possible values are male and female, one dummy variable would be established. It could take on the value of one for female and zero for male (or the reverse; only the interpretation of the coefficient changes). In the above example, the values for the variables for the two individuals would now be as follows:

Variables	Education	Sex Dummy
Observations	12	0
1. male		
2. female	14	1

Hypothetical Example Using a Sex Dummy. To further understand how to interpret the coefficients that would result from an earnings regression with one sex dummy and one cardinal variable for education, let's look at some hypothetical examples. Suppose, first, that an earnings model were estimated with only education level as an independent variable and that no sex dummy were included. Suppose the estimated equation to be as follows:

$$\text{Earnings per year} = 3500 + 1000 \text{ Education}. \tag{5.2}$$

This equation says that, on average, an individual will earn an extra 1,000 dollars for every additional year of education. The intercept, strictly interpreted, says that an individual with zero years of education will, on average, earn \$3,500 per year.

The value of this intercept, as is true for many other estimated intercepts, should not be given much credence. A typical sample is unlikely to include individuals with zero years of education and, in general, setting education equal to zero does not make sense in our society today. The estimated intercept serves the purpose of making the total predicted earnings for most individuals a reasonable number.

The earnings equation as shown without a dummy is no different than those we have examined in previous chapters. Let's see what happens when the dummy variable is added.

The dummy sex variable, coded 1 for female and 0 for male, when added to the equation above, could result in a hypothetical equation with the following parameters.[1]

$$\text{Earnings per year} = 5000 + 1000 \text{ Education} - 3000 \text{ Sex}. \tag{5.3}$$

There are a number of ways to understand the meaning of equation (5.3). One way is to interpret the coefficient on the sex dummy in the same way any other regression coefficient is interpreted. Thus, in this hypothetical case, females, who are coded one, would earn, on average, $3000 less than males, who are coded zero, assuming similar levels of education for both individuals. The coefficient on the dummy is interpreted relative to the left-out, or zero-coded, category.

A second way to understand the regression is to write two equations, one for males and one for females, as follows:

$$\text{Males: Earnings per year} = 5000 + 1000 \text{ Education} \tag{5.4}$$
$$\text{Females: Earnings per year} = 2000 + 1000 \text{ Education}. \tag{5.5}$$

Once again, females with similar education level to males, earn $3,000 less on average, and this shows up in the lower intercept on the female equation.

Finally, the effect of the sex dummy can be seen by graphing the equation as in Figure 5.1. The dummy creates two lines, one for female and one for male. The slopes of the lines remain identical to one another, because thus far the effect of *education* on earnings has been hypothetically the same for females and for males. (In a later section of this chapter, ways to make education's effect differ for males and females will be shown.)

Graphing two lines may suggest estimating two separate regression lines—one for females and one for males. It is possible to do this, but it is generally less desirable than estimating one line. First, each line is estimated with a smaller sample and thus estimation errors are increased. Second, testing to see if the equations are really different is more complicated than if one line is estimated.[2]

Example of Seasonal Dummies Used in a Regression Equation

An example using seasonal dummies will yield further insights into the usefulness of dummy variables because, instead of two possible categories, as with sex, there

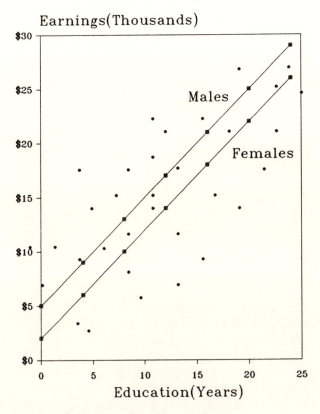

FIG. 5.1. Earnings equation with a sex dummy

are now four categories—summer, fall, winter, and spring. Suppose that it is important to a community to be able to predict the variation in monthly residential water usage, perhaps because of recurrent threats of drought. In addition, suppose the variation is thought to depend primarily on average monthly temperature and season of the year:

Residential water usage per month = f (temperature, season).   (5.6)

The temperature variable would be measured cardinally, on a Fahrenheit or Centigrade scale. The seasonal variables would be nominal or dummies and, following the general rule for dummies, there would be one less variable than there are seasons. Thus, there would be three seasonal dummies. Suppose, in a hypothetical example, the summer season was omitted. Data for four months of water usage might then look as follows:

Variables	Temperature	Fall	Winter	Spring
Observations				
1. (September '86)	72°F	1	0	0
2. (December '86)	40°F	0	1	0
3. (March '87)	58°F	0	0	1
4. (June '87)	79°F	0	0	0

Notice that the observations for the summer season (June) have zero values for all the dummies. Since the three zero values only occur for the summer season, that season will be clearly identified in the data.

Hypothetical Example Using Seasonal Dummies. Let's now see how to interpret the coefficients on seasonal dummies. Suppose the residential water usage equation were estimated as follows (residential water usage measured in billions of gallons):

Residential water usage per month = 15 + .02 temperature

$$- \ 3 \ \text{fall} - 6 \ \text{winter} - 4 \ \text{spring}. \quad (5.7)$$

Each dummy coefficient is interpreted in comparison to the "left-out" summer variable. Thus, fall water usage is 3 billion gallons per month less than summer usage; winter usage is 6 billion gallons less than summer usage; and spring usage is 4 billion gallons less than summer usage. The coefficient on the temperature variable is interpreted the way all cardinal variable coefficients are: for every additional degree of temperature, monthly water usage increases, on average, .02 billion gallons. If winter instead of summer was the left-out season, the equation would adjust and be estimated as: water usage per month = 9 + .02 temperature + 6 summer + 3 fall + 2 spring. The coefficients would then be interpreted relative to the winter season.[3]

Dummy variables can be used when there are two or more categories that a variable may fit. There must always be one less dummy than there are possible values for the variable. The coefficient of each dummy is interpreted in comparison to the left-out dummy. It does not matter which value is chosen for the left-out one, since the coefficients adjust their values appropriately.

TESTING FOR THE SIGNIFICANCE OF DUMMY VARIABLES

If there is only one dummy variable, such as sex, then the appropriate test for the significance of the coefficient is the *t* test. The test is performed exactly the same way as the *t* test for an interval level cardinal variable. The estimated coefficient is divided by its standard error to form a test statistic. That test statistic is compared to the critical *t* value to see whether the coefficient is statistically significant. If the coefficient is not significantly different than zero, then the dummy variable is presumed to have no effect on the dependent variable.

If there is more than one dummy variable, such as the example using seasons, it is often desirable to test the group of dummies simultaneously. The simultaneous test determines if all the coefficients on all the dummies, taken together, differ from zero and, thus, if the concept that the group of dummies represents is significant. It is not the same as testing each coefficient separately. In fact, the group of coefficients may occasionally be significantly different from zero, while one or more individual coefficients may be insignificant. The logic of the group test is that it is the effect of the concept of seasons (for example) that is of interest. If only a single season had been of concern, then only one dummy could have been created by assigning a value of one to that season and a value of zero to all the others.

Test for Several Dummy Coefficients Simultaneously

The significance test for several dummy variables is related to a test that has already been described; namely, the test for the significance of the R^2. The R^2 test was equivalent to testing the significance of the coefficients on *all* the independent variables, and it used the F statistic. Likewise, the test for a group of dummy independent variables, a group smaller than all the independent variables, uses the F statistic.

To see how the group test works, let's establish the following two models. Let the first model be the original model that has all the independent variables, including the dummy variables. Suppose there are K of these variables.

Original model:

$$Y = b_0 + b_1 X_1 + b_2 X_2 + b_3 X_3 + b_4 X_4 + b_5 X_5 + \ldots + b_K X_K. \tag{5.8}$$

Calculated coefficient of determination: R^2_K.

Suppose that the first three variables in the model, X_1, X_2, and X_3, are the dummy variables, and one wants to know if they are significantly different from zero, as a group. Then, a second model that omits those three variables is estimated. The second model has $K - 3$, or, let us say, Z, independent variables; can be called the restricted model; and looks as follows:

Restricted model:

$$Y = b_0 + b_4 X_4 + b_5 X_5 + \ldots + b_K X_K. \tag{5.9}$$

Calculated coefficient of determination: R^2_Z.

The number of coefficients that are simultaneously being tested is $K - Z$, or three in this case. The coefficient of determination (R^2_K) in the original model will always be equal or greater in value than the coefficient of determination in the restricted model (R^2_Z). This is because when variables are added to a model, the explanatory power usually increases; at least it never decreases. The significance test for the group of dummies asks, in effect, if the R^2 in the original model is enough larger than the R^2 in the restricted model to indicate that the group of dummies is significant.

The formal significance test involves the formation of an F test statistic that is compared to a critical value, at a given level of significance. If the F test statistic is greater than the critical value, then the dummies are significantly different than zero. One way to represent the F test statistic is as follows:

$$F = [(R^2_K - R^2_Z)/(1 - R^2_K)]/[(K - Z)/(T - K - 1)]$$

with $K - Z$ degrees of freedom in the numerator and $T - K - 1$ degrees of freedom in the denominator. Looking closely at the first term in this F statistic, the numerator, $R^2_K - R^2_Z$, is the amount that the R^2 increases when dummy variables are included in the equation as compared to when they are not. The denominator, $1 - R^2_K$, is the amount of variation that is not explained when the dummies are present. So, one interpretation of the significance test is to determine if the amount of explanatory power added by the dummies is a high enough percent of the unexplained variation to warrant including the dummies.

If the computer package being used does not produce this F test for a group of variables, then it can be executed by running two regressions. The first regression includes all the dummies and the second regression omits the dummies. Then, the resulting R^2's are used to form the F test statistic, and an F table of critical values at various levels of significance is used to test for significance.

Example of Test for Several Dummy Coefficients

Let's return to the hypothetical example of the residential water usage, equation (5.7). Suppose this equation were estimated with 48 monthly observations. Once again, equation (5.7) is as follows:

Residential water usage = 15 + .02 temperature − 3 fall − 6 winter − 4 spring.
   $R^2 = .85$.

Now, suppose that without the dummies, the equation is as follows:

Residential water usage = 19 + .031 temperature.
   $R^2 = .60$.

In this example, $K = 4$, $Z = 1$, $K - Z = 3$, and $T = 48$.

$F = [(.85 - .60)/(1 - .85)]/[3/(48 - 5)] = 19.11$. The critical F at the 5% level with 3 and 43 degrees of freedom is 2.84. Since 19.11 is greater than 2.84, the seasonal dummies as a group are significant at the 5% level.

The F test for a group of dummy variables can be used to test the significance of any group of variables, dummies or not. An example of the use of dummies in the analysis of hospital lengths of stay is presented in Example 5.1.

NONLINEAR MODELS

There are two types of nonlinear models that are particularly useful for the kinds of problems public managers face—one is the exponential model and the other is the polynomial. Exponential models often depict growth situations, such as when money or populations grow at compound (constant percentage) rates. Alternatively, exponential models can describe relationships when both the dependent and independent variables change by percentages—what economists call elasticity models. Polynomial models describe curves that do not necessarily change by constant percentages. Each type of model is considered in turn.

EXAMPLE 5.1 HOSPITAL LENGTH OF STAY AND ADMINISTRATIVE PRACTICES OF HOSPITALS

Luk Cannoodt and James Knickman studied the determinants of preoperative and postoperative lengths of stay (LOS) in 1978 for 27,384 cases in New Jersey hospitals.[4] While controlling for a large number of procedural, diagnostic and severity of illness variables, the authors' primary focus was upon the effect of independent variables which are under the administrative control of hospitals, such as time and day of admission, type of discharge, and ownership of hospital. Partial results for preoperative LOS are shown in Table 5.1. Not shown are the coefficients on the large number of control variables (approximately 65) and on some of the administrative variables (15).

Questions:

a. (i) Are the reported independent variables all dummy variables? (ii) If so, what is the left-out variable for the two admission time dummies?
b. How would you interpret the effect of the admission time variables?
c. Which variables are statistically significant at the 5% or below level?
d. (i) Why is the adjusted R^2 appropriate here? (ii) What do you think of the size of the reported $\bar{R}^2$?

Discussion:

a. (i) Yes. (ii) For hour of admission, the left-out variable is all times other than between 3 p.m. and 10 p.m. For day of admission, the left-out variable is all days other than Friday or Saturday.

TABLE 5.1

Regression Results for Preoperative Length of Stay (LOS)

Selected Independent Variables	Dependent Variable (Preoperative LOS)	
	Coefficient	t-score
Admission Time		
Between 3 and 10 p.m.	.59	9.3
On Friday or Saturday	.31	5.0
Discharge Status		
To long-term care facility	.08	0.7
To home care agency	-.26	1.5
Left out: routine or to other health institutions		
Hospital Ownership		
For-profit	.39	3.2
Government-owned	.29	1.5
Left out: voluntary not-for-profit		
INTERCEPT	.89	
$\bar{R}^2$	.27	

Source: Luk J. Cannoodt and James R. Knickman, "The Effect of Hospital Characteristics and Organizational Factors on Pre- and Postoperative Lengths of Hospital Stay," *Health Services Research* 19 (1984), Table 2.

b. Ignoring which coefficients are significant, one would interpret the effect of admission time variables as follows: holding all other variables in the equation constant, being admitted between 3 p.m. and 10 p.m., compared to being admitted at any other time, adds slightly more than one-half day (.59 days) to LOS; being admitted on a Friday or Saturday, compared to any other day, adds about one-third day (.31) to preoperative LOS.

c. To determine statistical significance from the information reported above, one must know the two-tailed cutoff for the *t* statistic at the 5% and 1% levels. Since the exact number of independent variables in the entire equation is not given, the degrees of freedom, equal to the sample size minus the number of independent variables minus 1, cannot be determined. Thus the best we can do is to use the *t* statistics for infinite degrees of freedom, which are identical to the statistics for the normal distribution. Most tables of *t* statistics go directly from 120 degrees of freedom to infinite degrees of freedom, since after 120 degrees of freedom, the *t* distribution is nearly identical to the normal distribution; thus there is no problem with our procedure. The two-tailed cutoff for 5% significance is 1.960; for 1%

significance, it is 2.576. Thus, all *but* the following variables are significant at the 1% level: all discharge status variables; and government owned ownership.

d. (i) $\bar{R}^2$ is appropriate because of the large number of independent variables and because variation in the dependent variable, LOS, has been heavily studied by other researchers who might want to compare their equations to those obtained by Knickman and Cannoodt. (ii) While the size of the $\bar{R}^2$ statistic is not high, this is not unusual for individual versus aggregated data. In fact, much lower $\bar{R}^2$'s are commonly reported.

Exponential or Constant Growth Rate Models

Examples of Exponential Models. Constant growth rate models are familiar to anyone who has put money into a savings account and seen it grow at a compound rate. The rate at which the money grows is a constant percentage, called the interest rate, these days usually a rate between 5% and 10%. If no money is removed from the account, then the growth is compounded; the original money put in is added to by the interest earned, and the whole new amount earns interest the next period.

Let's review exactly how compounding works in preparation for using the compound (or exponential) model in a regression problem. Suppose one puts $100 into an account that guarantees 5% interest a year, compounded. After one year, the account will have:

$$\$100 + \$100(.05) = \$100(1.05) = \$105. \tag{5.10}$$

If no money is taken out, the amount at the end of the second year will be:

$$\$105 + \$105(.05) = \$105(1.05) = \$100(1.05)(1.05) = \$100(1.05)^2. \tag{5.11}$$

This process will continue for however many years the money is left in the account. In t years, the money accumulated will be:

$$\text{Money accumulated} = (\$100)(1.05)^t. \tag{5.12}$$

This formulation of the compounding process works for any interest rate and any compounding period, such as a month or a day, as long as the interest rate is specified in months or days as well.[5]

There are times when public managers may wish to use constant growth rate (or compounding) models to help resolve problems. Suppose population projections need to be made into the future and a plotting of historical data indicates the likelihood of a fairly constant growth rate. An equation depicting such a constant (compounded) growth relationship would look as follows:

$$Pop = B_0 B_1^{time} E, \tag{5.13}$$

where B_0 and B_1 are parameters, E is an error term, *Pop* is population, the dependent variable, and *time* is the independent variable.

The equation needs an error term because unlike the compound interest problem, the population growth model is stochastic rather than deterministic. The job of the regression model would be to estimate B_1 (the growth rate) and B_0 (the intercept). B_1 will be estimated as 1 plus the growth rate, as in the compounding problem where 1.05 (1 + .05) was raised to t years. Theoretically B_0 should be the beginning population number, but as with many intercepts, the estimate of this intercept may not be a reasonable number. Instead, the intercept may just "anchor" the regression line to the vertical axis.

Estimating Exponential Models. The compound growth model for population does not look at all like a straight line, so how can it be estimated? The equation must be *transformed* so that it is linear in its new transformation. In the case of the exponential models, logarithms can perform this transformation. If the logarithm of each side of the equation is taken, the following equation results:

$$
\begin{aligned}
\mathrm{Log}_{10}Pop &= \mathrm{Log}_{10}(B_0 B_1^{time} E) \\
&= \mathrm{Log}_{10}B_0 + \mathrm{Log}_{10}B_1^{time} + \mathrm{Log}_{10}E \\
&= \mathrm{Log}_{10}B_0 + time\,\mathrm{Log}_{10}B_1 + \mathrm{Log}_{10}E.
\end{aligned} \tag{5.14}
$$

The base of the logarithm in this example is 10, but any other base, including the often used natural logarithm e (abbreviated as ln), would do as well. Base 10 is familiar to many people, and that is why it is used here. Recall that the logarithm of a product is equal to the sum of the logarithms, and that the logarithm of a variable raised to an exponent is equal to the exponent times the logarithm. The final equation is linear, if one looks at it in the following way. Let $\mathrm{Log}_{10}Pop = Pop'$, $\mathrm{Log}_{10}B_0 = B_0'$ $\mathrm{Log}_{10}B_1 = B_1'$, and $\mathrm{Log}_{10}E = E'$, then:

$$
Pop' = B_0 + B_1'time + E'. \tag{5.15}
$$

To estimate the coefficients, the logarithm of the population variable is taken, and then the logarithm of population is regressed on time (not as a logarithm). The transformation of a variable into its logarithm is easy to do using any standard computer regression package.

Once the equation with logarithm of population as the dependent variable is estimated, it is then necessary to take the transformed coefficients, $\mathrm{Log}_{10}B_0$ and $\mathrm{Log}_{10}B_1$, and obtain the original coefficients, B_0 and B_1. To do this, the antilog of the estimated coefficient is needed, where $B_1 = \text{antilog } \mathrm{Log}_{10}B_1 = \text{antilog } B_1' = 10^{B_1'}$. The antilogs can be obtained from tables of antilogarithms or by using a calculator or a computer. The B_1 coefficient is the more interesting one in this model, since it is equal to the growth rate plus one, or $(r + 1)$.

Hypothesis testing for the transformed model is similar to that for the untransformed one. One uses a t test to see if the transformed coefficient, $\mathrm{Log}_{10}B_1$, is equal to zero. If it is not significantly different from zero, then B_1 is not different from one, since the logarithm of one is zero.[6] A look at the original, untransformed model, equation (5.13), shows that if B_1 is equal to one, then there is no relationship between population and time. That is, if B_1 is equal to one, then the relationship becomes:

$$Pop = B_0 E, \tag{5.16}$$

since one raised to any power is still one. The time variable has dropped out because there is no relationship between population and time, if B_1 is equal to one.[7] Thus, testing to see if the logarithm of B_1 is equal to zero is equivalent to the usual test of no relationship.

Hypothetical Example of an Exponential Growth Model. Suppose the following model is estimated: $Log_{10}Pop = 3 + .025306time$, where *time* is measured in years. The following relationships then hold: $Log_{10}b_0 = 3$, and $Log_{10}b_1 = .025306$. Taking antilogs, we find that $b_0 = 10^3 = 1000$, and $b_1 = 10^{.025306} = 1.06$. If the intercept is meaningful, it implies that population at time zero is 1,000. The coefficient b_1 equal to 1.06 means the yearly compound growth rate is 6% (.06).

Exponential Models—Elasticities

A second kind of exponential model that has been used extensively in public management problems based on economic relationships is the elasticity model. In the elasticity model, both the dependent and the independent variable change by percentages; in the previous growth model, only the dependent variable (population) changed by a percentage, while the independent variable (time) changed by one year units. When both the dependent and independent variables change by percentages, the estimated coefficients yield elasticities.

As an example, suppose a county government owns an airport, and the county manager is interested in initiating a price to be paid by all planes that land at the airport. The manager wishes to price landings so as to break-even financially. While she knows how costs relate to number of landings, she is unsure how price will affect the willingness of plane owners to use the airport. Data from a neighboring county airport are available, and the county manager decides to estimate a simple demand function, where the number of landings per year is a function of the price per landing. Past experience with demand curves leads the manager to think that the functional form might be a curved relationship. The functional form she wishes to try is exponential:

$$Landings = B_0\, Price^{B_1} E. \tag{5.17}$$

Notice the difference between this functional form and the constant growth form shown in equation (5.13). In equation (5.17), the slope coefficient, B_1, is the exponent; in equation (5.13) the independent variable (*time*) is the exponent. Both equations (5.13) and (5.17) are nonlinear but, as with equation (5.13), equation (5.17) can be transformed using logarithms. Taking logarithms of both sides of equation (5.17) yields[8]:

$$\begin{aligned} Log_{10}Landings &= Log_{10}(B_0 Price^{B_1}E) \\ &= Log_{10}B_0 + Log_{10}Price^{B_1} + Log_{10}E \\ &= Log_{10}B_0 + B_1 Log_{10}Price + Log_{10}E. \end{aligned} \quad (5.18)$$

The new equation (5.18) is linear in the logarithms, as can be seen by rewriting it, using $Log_{10}Landings = Y'$, $Log_{10}B_0 = B_0'$, $B_1 = B_1'$, $Log_{10}Price = X'$, and $Log_{10}E = E'$, then:

$$Y' = B_0' + B_1'X_1' + E'.$$

In equation (5.18), B_1 is the critical coefficient because it is the price elasticity of demand. The B_1 coefficient indicates what percent landings will decline when price increases by one percentage point, and the B_1 coefficient is estimated directly from the transformed equation (5.18). Hypothesis tests on B_1 are performed with the familiar t test. (An example of the use of the elasticity model in estimating the efficiency of large government pension plans is presented in Example 5.2.)

Hypothetical Example of Estimated Exponential (Elasticity) Model. Suppose the following values were obtained for a demand equation for *landings:*

$$Log_{10}Landings = 4 + .5Log_{10}Price,$$

where *landings* are measured per year and *price* is measured as dollars per *landing.*This equation means that the following relationships hold: $Log_{10}b_0 = 4$, and $b_1 = .5$. The estimated intercept, b_0, would be $10^4 = 10,000$, implying that at zero *price* there would be 10,000 *landings* per year. This intercept is often not meaningful, but rather is useful to "anchor" the equation to its Y axis. The b_1 coefficient, equal to .5, is the price elasticity. This price elasticity of .5 means that if *price* increases by one percent, *landings* per year will decline by one-half a percent. Demand is inelastic in this hypothetical case.

EXAMPLE 5.2 EFFICIENCY IN ADMINISTERING LARGE STATE AND MUNICIPAL RETIREMENT SYSTEMS

Ralph Pope used regression analysis to study economies of scale in large public pension plans.[9] If economies of scale exist, then costs per unit of output should decline as output increases. In the regression equation, operating cost per participant is the dependent variable and the number of participants (both beneficiaries and others), meant to stand for output of the pension system, is one of the independent variables. Both the dependent and independent variables are transformed into logarithms, so the resulting coefficient on the independent variable (for example, numbers of participants) is an elasticity. If this elasticity is less than one, then economies of scale do exist, since a one percent increase in numbers of participants would result in a less than one percent increase in the cost per participant. A number of control variables were included in the equation. The coefficients on these control variables are shown in the statistics reported in Table 5.2. A sample of 84 pension plans, each with more than 1,000 members, was used for data.

Questions:

a. Which coefficients are statistically significant?
b. What is the specific interpretation of the coefficient on the output variable?
c. What is the interpretation of the dummy wage index variable?
d. Do you think that there are any problems using cross-section data for a study such as this one?
e. What are some of the management and policy implications of this regression?

Discussion:

a. The degrees of freedom are 76 (84 − 7 − 1). The t statistic for 60 degrees of freedom (which is the closest to 76 reported in most tables) is 2.00 at the 5% level and 2.66 at the 1% level. Thus, log of number of participants and log of assets per participant are significant at the 1% level and the wage index dummy is significant at the 5% level.

b. As the number of participants in a state or municipal pension plan increases 1%, the costs per participant increase .700%. Since the costs increase at a lower percentage than the output, there are declining average costs per output unit or positive returns to scale.

c. The reason for including the wage index was to see if the costs of administering pension plans responded to the differing costs of the inputs. A wage index over 100 means that the wage costs for a particular plan are higher than the norm (100). The positive coefficient on the dummy means that for plans where the wage costs are higher than the norm, as compared to plans where the wage costs are at the norm or lower, the costs per participant are higher. Specifically, holding all other variables constant, for a pension plan in an area where the wage index is above 100, the costs per participant will be approximately one tenth of a percent (.096%) higher than in an area where the wage index is 100 or less.

d. Yes, there are always problems using cross-section data when one is studying the behavior of an organization under different conditions, such as when the number of participants differs. Ideally, one would like to look at one organization under changing circumstances. When one uses cross-section data, even with

TABLE 5.2

Regression Results for Operating Expenditures per Participant in Municipal Retirement Systems

Independent Variables	Dependent Variable (Log Operating Expenditures per Participant)	
	Coefficient	t-score
Log of number of participants	.700	16.64
Log of assets per participant	.448	5.15
Log of retired members as % of total	-.007	0.05
Wage index dummy (1 if greater than 100)	.096	2.40
Dummy for in-house investment staff	-.016	-0.42
Dummy for administered under state jurisdiction	.022	0.27
Dummy for administered under city jurisdiction	.0016	0.03
INTERCEPT	.875	
$\bar{R}^2$	.912	
F	123.59	
T	84	

Source: Ralph A. Pope, "Economies of Scale in Large State and Municipal Retirement Systems," *Public Budgeting and Finance* 6 (1986), Table 3.

control variables, one assumes that the different organizations behave in the same way and that the organizational differences are only due to different values of the variables included in the equation. While time-series data on one pension plan would take care of some of these problems, other problems would be created such as autocorrelation possibilities (discussed in Chapter 6) or generalization to other organizations.

e. One implication is that there may be significant cost gains if small pension systems (less than 1,000 members) are combined into larger ones. Another is that the administration of the plan in-house or out, by city, or by state, makes no difference as to costs.

Polynomial Models

Polynomial models describe curves in which the relationship between the dependent and independent variables changes from positive to negative (or vice versa) and perhaps back again a few times. A polynomial can be any degree. The quadratic form (or second degree), in which the highest term is squared and there is one change in direction of the curve, is the most common polynomial. Higher degree polynomials (such as cubics) may fit the data better, but their meaning for a specific problem is often difficult to interpret.

A quadratic polynomial equation looks as follows:

$$Y = B_0 + B_1X_1 + B_2X_1^2. \tag{5.19}$$

Two examples are:

$$Y = 4 + 6X_1 - 2X_1^2 \tag{5.20}$$

and

$$Y = 4 - 3X_1 + 2X_1^2. \tag{5.21}$$

Equation (5.20) has an intercept of 4; that is, the value of Y is 4 when the value of X_1 is zero. In a regression equation, the value of the intercept may or may not make sense, depending on whether it makes sense for the value of X to be zero. The slope of the quadratic line—the way Y changes when X changes by one unit—depends on the coefficients of both X_1 and X_1^2. In general, the slope equals $B_1 + 2B_2$. In the case of equation (5.20) the slope is $6 - 4X_1$. If X_1 equals 1 and changes from 1 to 2, the slope is: $6 - 4(1) = 2$. If X_1 equals 2 and changes from 2 to 3, the slope is $6 - 4(2) = -2$. The slope changes once, in this case, from positive to negative as X_1 increases.

Equation (5.21) has a slope of $-3 + 4X_1$. If X_1 equals 0 and changes to 1, then the slope is: $-3 + 4(0) = -3$. If X_1 equals 1 and changes to 2, then the slope is: $-3 + 4(1) = 1$. Again the curve changes direction once, but this time from negative to positive. In general, a quadratic changes direction only once. The signs of the coefficients in the quadratic determine which way the curve changes and at what value of X it changes.

Polynomials may also be used to estimate models where the data do not show a change of direction in the relationship between Y and X, but only an upward or downward sloping curve. In such a case, only the upward (or downward) sloping part of the polynomial curve is relevant. While such curved relationships may at first appear to be exponential, if the variables are not changing at constant rates, the polynomial will usually provide a more accurate fit to the data. The polynomial form will still imply at least one change in direction of the curve, however, so users of a polynomial regression fit to data which do not change direction will have to be careful not to extrapolate too far beyond the range of their data.

An example of the use of a polynomial regression to inform a public policy issue is provided by the urban studies literature. Urban planners and analysts have long been interested in the relationship between the amount that a city expends per capita and the city's size as measured by population. In particular there has been a debate about whether there is an optimal range for city population, below and above which expenditures per capita are higher than at the optimal. Figure 5.2 shows a graph of city expenditures per capita and population which, if depicting appropriate data, would indicate that a population of around four million is "optimal" in terms of minimizing city expenditures per capita. Generally, a model of city expenditures per capita would include many more independent variables than population. But, for the sake of illustration, suppose a simplified model were estimated with only population and population squared as independent variables,

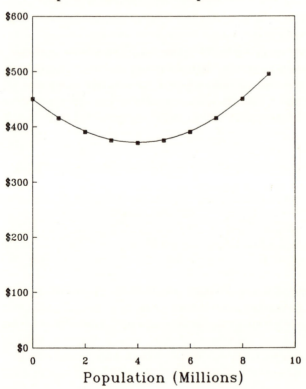

FIG. 5.2. Optimal city size example using a quadratic polynomial

and suppose the following coefficients resulted (where population was measured in millions):

Expenditures per capita = 450− 40(population) + 5(population)^2.   (5.22)

The slope of the expenditure equation with respect to population would be −40 + 10 (population). At a population of 4 million, the slope would be −40 + 10 (4) or 0. With a population of less than 4 million, the slope would be negative and with a population of more than 4 million, the slope would be positive. In this simple illustration, 4 million is the optimal city size because at that size city expenditures per capita are minimized.

NONADDITIVE MODELS

Nonadditive models are those in which changes in the dependent variable depend on changes in a given independent variable as well as on the level of one or more other independent variables. The independent variables do not work singly to influence the dependent variable, as they have up until now. Nonadditive models are sometimes called interactive.

Interactions can occur between a dummy variable and a continuous variable, between two dummy variables or between two continuous variables. Let's begin with the case of an interaction between a dummy and a continuous variable by returning to the example of variations in earnings as a function of sex (dummy variable) and education (continuous variable). The hypothetical equation (5.3) used was:

Earnings per year = 5000 + 1000 education − 3000 sex.

While the intercept of the line differs by 3,000, depending on whether the individual is male or female, the slope with respect to education remains the same (1,000) for both sexes. Now, suppose the effect of a year's change in education differs depending on whether the individual is a male or female; that is, suppose sex and education interact. In particular, let the negative effect on earnings per year of being female diminish as the education level increases. This would mean that women with more years of education experience a smaller earnings gap than women with fewer years of education. Figure 5.3 illustrates how the regression lines would be expected to look. The slope of the female line is steeper than that of the male line; in fact, at some point, the lines would cross, implying that females earned more than males at some high level of education. If this crossover point were outside the range of the data used to estimate the line, however, one would not want to put much credence in an extrapolation.

How does the equation for such interaction effects look? The equation involves not only the additive terms from equation (5.3), but a multiplicative term as well.

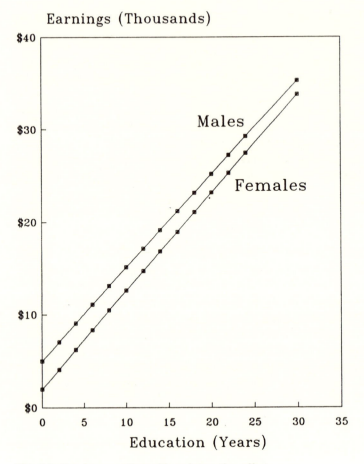

FIG. 5.3. Earnings equation with an interaction effect

In the earnings example, the equation would take the form:

Earnings per year = $b_0 + b_1$ education + b_2 sex + b_3 (education)(sex).   (5.23)

In order to graph the equation as in Figure 5.3, the coefficients would have the following signs: $b_1 > 0$; $b_2 < 0$; $b_3 > 0$. The positive sign on the coefficient of the interactive term, b_3, would make the female line slope more steeply upward. Hypothetically estimated coefficients might be:

Earnings per year = 5005 + 1010 education − 3015 sex
$$+ 50 \text{ (education)(sex)}. \qquad (5.24)$$

Determining the Effect of a Change in an Interactive Variable on a Dependent Variable

Determining the effect of a change in an interactive variable on a dependent variable is somewhat complicated.[10] Returning to equation (5.24) as an example, to find the effect of a year's change in education on earnings, the coefficient on education (1010) and on the interactive term (50) must be utilized. The effect is equal to the coefficient on the education variable (1010) plus the coefficient on the interactive term times the sex variable [(50)(sex)]. In other words, the interactive term contributes its coefficient plus the level of the variable whose effect interacts. In the case of the earnings function in equation (5.24), a year's change in education results in a change in earnings of: 1010 + 50 (sex). Thus, for females, where the value of the sex dummy is one, every additional year of education adds $1,060 to earnings; for males, where the value of the sex dummy is zero, every additional year of education adds only $1,010 to earnings. Since the slope of the line for females is greater than for males, the earnings of females will eventually catch up with males and, as females have more and more years of education, even surpass them.

Determining the effect of sex on earnings is analogous to determining the effect of education on earnings. The coefficient on sex (−3015) is added to the coefficient on the interaction term times the level of education [(50)(education)]. Using the earnings equation (5.24), the effect of being female on earnings is: −3015 + 50(education). The higher the level of education, the more the negative effect on earnings is mitigated.

Testing for Significance of Interactive Terms

The standard *t* test is used to see if the interactive term, by itself, is significantly different from zero. If the coefficient proves to be insignificant, while the other coefficients are significant, then one concludes that the effect of each variable works independently of the level of the other variables. If the total effect of a variable, when it interacts and when it does not, is to be tested, then the *F* test for a group of variables must be used. If the *F* test shows significance, this means that the variable alone *and* interacted has an effect; it does not guarantee that the interactive effect itself is significant.

Interactive Models with Two Dummies and Two Continuous Variables

The final model to be considered is one in which the interactions occur between dummies and between continuous variables. Returning to the earnings model, suppose that in addition to education and sex, race and experience are also independent variables.

Earnings = f(education, sex, race, experience). (5.25)

In addition, suppose that the two continuous variables (education and experience) interact, and that the two dummy variables (race and sex) interact. The complete model would then look as follows:

Earnings = $b_0 + b_1$experience $+ b_2$education $+ b_3$sex $+ b_4$race
$$+ b_5(\text{experience})(\text{education}) + b_6(\text{sex})(\text{race}). \quad (5.26)$$

Assume that sex is coded as before, with female equal to one and male equal to zero, and that race is coded with black equal to one and all other equal to zero.

Why might experience and education interact, and what would be the meaning of the coefficient on the interactive term? It is possible that years of experience is more effective at raising earnings for individuals who have higher rather than lower levels of education. More highly educated individuals may be better able to learn from more experience. If this hypothesis is correct, then b_5, the coefficient on the education and experience interaction term, would be expected to be positive. The positive coefficient would also indicate that more experienced workers gain more from an additional year of education than do less experienced workers.

To find the effect of an additional year of education on earnings, one would add the coefficient on education (b_2) to the coefficient on the interactive term multiplied by the level of experience [$(b_5)(\text{experience})$]. Thus, the effect would be: $b_2 + b_5(\text{experience})$. If both b_2 and b_5 are positive, then an additional year of education increases earnings, but more so the greater the years of experience of a worker.

To find the effect of an additional year of experience on earnings, the coefficient on experience (b_1) would be added to the coefficient on the interactive term multiplied by the years of education [$(b_5)(\text{education})$]. The effect would be: $b_1 + b_5(\text{education})$. With both b_1 and b_5 positive, an additional year of experience would add to earnings, but more for a more highly educated worker.

The interaction between the two dummy variables, sex and race, can be easiest understood through an example. Recall that in this hypothetical example, female is coded one and male zero, and black is coded one and nonblack zero. If the three coefficients on the dummy variables, b_3, b_4, and b_6, are all negative, then the equation says that black women face the most discrimination. Let's see why. To find the effect of any given sex-race combination on earnings, put the appropriate value of the dummy variable after the coefficients and add the values of the coefficients. Since female and black are both coded one, their effect on the earnings of a black female would be:

$$b_3(1) + b_4(1) + b_6(1)(1) = b_3 + b_4 + b_6.$$

The effect of being a black male on earnings would be:

$$b_3(0) + b_4(1) + b_6(0)(1) = b_4.$$

The effect of being a white female would be:

$$b_3(1) + b_4(0) + b_6(1)(0) = b_3.$$

What about white males, where all the dummies are coded zero? White males are the comparison or left-out group, and their effect on earnings is included in the intercept, b_0. If the dummy variables were the only ones in the equation, the intercept would indicate the effect on earnings of being a white male. But, this equation also contains variables for education and experience. The intercept, then, is influenced by variables other than the sex and race dummies. Finding the effect of white males involves either deducing it from the comparisons of other sex-race combinations or rerunning the equation with the sex and race dummies coded differently. Testing for the significance of the variables can be done individually, using the t test, or as group, using the F test.

Example 5.3 shows the use of dummies and interactions in the study of research productivity.

EXAMPLE 5.3 MORE ON REGRESSION, RESEARCH PRODUCTIVITY, AND THE MANAGEMENT OF NATIONAL SCIENCE POLICY

The research of Joseph Cheng and William McKinley on the management of national science policy was described in Example 3.2. In that same research, the authors developed a regression equation that included all scientific paradigms in one model. The basic model used to explain research productivity with two independent variables (national science policy influence and research unit size) was expanded to include (i) dummy variables for the country in which the research unit was located (Finland was excluded), (ii) a variable for paradigm development (1 for high, 0 for medium, and −1 for low), and (iii) a variable that interacted policy influence and paradigm development. The estimated equation for the expanded model is shown in Table 5.3.[11]

Questions:

a. (i) How would you interpret the coefficients on the dummy variables for the countries? (ii) Are they statistically significant?
b. (i) How would you interpret the coefficient for the paradigm development variable? (ii) Is it significant?
c. (i) How would you interpret the coefficient for the interactive variable? (ii) Is it significant?
d. (i) Does this expanded regression equation show anything different than the separate regression equations of Example 3.2? (ii) What is the potential advantage of a regression equation with an interactive variable over several separate regression equations?

TABLE 5.3
Regression Results for Research Unit Productivity

Predictor	Dependent Variable (Research Unit Productivity)	
	Coefficient	Standard Error
Austria (Dummy variable 1)	-.69	.91
Belgium (Dummy variable 2)	.90	.93
Sweden (Dummy variable 3)	-1.85	.86
Unit size	.15	.04
Policy influence	.02	.02
Paradigm development	-.14	.45
(Policy influence) x (Paradigm development)	.06	.02
$\bar{R}^2$	.16	
F	6.61	

Reprinted from Joseph L. C. Cheng and William McKinley, "Toward an Integration of Organization Research and Practice: A Contigency Study of Bureaucratic Control and Performance in Scientific Settings," *Administrative Science Quarterly* 28, 1 (1983): 94, Table 3, by permission of *Administrative Science Quarterly,* copyright © 1983, Cornell University.

Discussion:

a. (i) Holding all other variables constant, compared to Finland, research unit productivity in Austria is .69 published articles lower; in Belgium .90 articles higher; and in Sweden 1.85 articles lower. (ii) All but the Swedish coefficients are insignificant at the 5% level.

b. (i) The index used to represent paradigm development is an ordinal one, so it is best to interpret the coefficient in terms of greater or less. Another set of ordinal numbers would yield a different value, but not sign, for the coefficient. Thus, one can say that the higher the paradigm development, the lower the research productivity, holding all else constant. (ii) The coefficient is not significant at the 5% level.

c. (i) *Ceteris paribus,* the higher the paradigm development, the more science policy will influence research productivity. (ii) This variable is significant at the 1% level.

d. (i) No. The separate regression equations in Example 3.2 showed that research productivity was differently influenced by science policy depending on the paradigm development. The single regression equation in this example shows the same thing. (ii) The potential advantage of using an interactive variable (and thus a single equation) is that the sample size can be larger. Also, there is no perfectly good way to compare coefficients across different regression equations, a problem that does not occur if there is only one equation. The disadvantage of one equation is that if many variables must be interacted, the degrees of freedom may decline, and even with the larger sample size, significance may be difficult to obtain.

EXAMPLES OF COMPUTER OUTPUT FOR DUMMY VARIABLES AND FOR NONLINEAR RELATIONSHIPS

This chapter has explored several ways to make the linear regression model an accurate representation of the causal behavioral model one is attempting to estimate. Typical computer output for two of those methods, the use of dummy variables and the use of logarithmic transformations, is shown here.

Dummy Variables on a Computer Printout

The quarterly data from Matthew Drennan's book, *Modeling Metropolitan Economies for Forecasting and Policy Analysis,* which has been used in Chapters 3 and 4, is called upon again.[12] This time, however, the dependent variable is income for New York City from a specific sector of the economy—transportation, communication, and public utilities. This variable is measured in millions of 1972 dollars and is labelled CYTC. The independent variables include a dummy variable to represent quarters in which the New York City economy was in a depression (DUMDEP). The dummy variable takes on a value of one for depression quarters (the second quarter of 1969 through the first quarter of 1975) and is equal to zero otherwise. The reason for adding DUMDEP is to see if the model for determining transportation income is different during these quarters. One would hypothesize a negative coefficient for the variable, or a downward shift in the intercept. The other two independent variables are the United States unemployment rate (UUNEMPR) and total United States national income in billions of 1972 dollars (UALLY). Figure 5.4 shows a printout for the regression results and for a significance test for the pair of variables, DUMDEP and UALLY.

Figure 5.4 shows that the coefficient on DUMDEP is not significant at the 10% or lower level. If it were significantly different from zero, however, its coefficient would be interpreted as follows. During depression quarters, as compared to nondepression quarters, quarterly income is $66,174,500 lower, holding constant UUNEMPR and UALLY.

Figure 5.4 also shows the *F* test for the pair of variables (DUMDEP and

SPSS/PC+

**** M U L T I P L E   R E G R E S S I O N ****

Equation Number 1   Dependent Variable.   CYTC

Multiple R   .88479
R Square   .78286
Adjusted R Square   .77471
Standard Error   170.96021

Analysis of Variance

	DF	Sum of Squares	Mean Square
Regression	3	8429730.87771	2809910.29257
Residual	80	2338191.35846	29227.39198

F =   96.13962   Signif F = .0000

------------------ Variables in the Equation ------------------

Variable	B	SE B	Beta	T	Sig T
UUNEMPR	-154.56795	14.46502	-.57210	-10.686	.0000
DUMDEP	-66.17450	45.33663	-.08350	-1.460	.1483
UALLY	1.69092	.12191	.79422	13.870	.0000
(Constant)	4167.24855	113.33032		36.771	.0000

F TEST FOR PAIR OF VARIABLES, DUMDEP AND UALLY

**** M U L T I P L E   R E G R E S S I O N ****

Beginning Block Number 2.   Method: Test   DUMDEP   UALLY

Hypothesis Tests

D	Sum of Squares	RSq Chg	F	Sig F	Source
2	6189156.31315	.57478	105.87938	.0000	DUMDEP UALLY
3	8429730.87771		96.13962	.0000	Regression
80	2338191.35846				Residual
83	10767922.2362				Total

FIG. 5.4. CYTC regression results with dummy variable, DUMDEP

UALLY), as executed by SPSS/PC+. The value of the calculated F is 105.87938 and it is significantly different from zero at less than the .001 level (reported as 0 on the printout). This F statistic is the same as the F statistic that was calculated using the formula following equation (5.9) of the text:

$$F = [(R^2_K - R^2_Z)/(1 - R^2_K)]/[(K - Z)/(T - K - 1)].$$

Logarithmic Transformations on a Computer Printout

The data and model to illustrate logarithmic transformations again come from Matthew Drennan's work on the New York City economy. For this example the time-series is composed of yearly data from 1975 to 1984, and the purpose of the model is to forecast city tax revenue from the sales tax. All the variables, dependent and independent, are transformed into logarithmic form, so the coefficients shown on the printouts should all be interpreted as elasticities. The dependent variable is the log of city sales tax revenue (LTXSALE). The two independent variables are the log of total city income, in millions of 1972 dollars, lagged one year (LCALLYLG), and the log of the GNP implicit price deflator (LUDALL). The printout is shown in Figure 5.5. Only the coefficient on LUDALL is significant. It would be interpreted as follows: a one percent increase in the implicit price

SPSS/PC+

	Mean	Std Dev
LTXSALE	7.013	.271
LUDALL	5.135	.211
LCALLYLG	10.606	.050

N of Cases =   10

Correlation:

	LTXSALE	LUDALL	LCALLYLG
LTXSALE	1.000	.991	.945
LUDALL	.991	1.000	.946
LCALLYLG	.945	.946	1.000

**** MULTIPLE REGRESSION ****

Equation Number 1   Dependent Variable ..   LTXSALE

Multiple R	.99153
R Square	.98312
Adjusted R Square	.97830
Standard Error	.03998

Analysis of Variance

	DF	Sum of Squares	Mean Square
Regression	2	.65185	.32592
Residual	7	.01119	.00160

F =   203.90607   Signif F = .0000

----------------- Variables in the Equation ------------------

Variable	B	SE B	Beta	T	Sig T
LCALLYLG	.33065	.82176	.06115	.402	.6994
LUDALL	1.20143	.19561	.93346	6.142	.0005
(Constant)	-2.66267	7.77144		-.343	.7419

FIG. 5.5. Descriptive statistics, correlation matrix, and regression results: log sales tax revenue (LTXSALE)

deflator results in a 1.201% increase in city sales tax revenues. The equation has a high R^2 of .98312.

A SUMMARY EXAMPLE

Example 5.4, which shows a regression equation explaining earnings of Japanese versus American male workers, combines into one regression many of the options described in this chapter.

EXAMPLE 5.4 THE EFFECT OF JOB TENURE ON EARNINGS FOR JAPANESE AND AMERICAN MALES

Japanese male workers generally remain longer with one employer than do American male workers. In the parlance of labor analysts, the Japanese have longer job tenure. Labor economists have wondered if longer job tenure has an effect on the "earnings profile." That is, when one looks at the effect of an additional year of job tenure on earnings, do American and Japanese workers exhibit the same patterns? This is an interesting theoretical question, since a steeper profile for the Japanese workers would be consistent with the idea that workers are receiving job training that can only be used by the firm providing the training and that it takes a while to see if a worker will fit into a particular firm. Masamori Hashimoto and John Raisian studied the earnings profiles of Japanese and American males.[13] The results of two of their regression equations, used to explain variation in earnings, are shown in Table 5.4. The two equations shown are for large firms. The data are from 1979 for Japanese workers and from 1980 for American workers.

Questions:

a. How will the specification of the dependent variable as the logarithm of earnings affect the interpretation of the regression coefficients?
b. (i) What is the effect of high school completion on earnings of American versus Japanese males? (ii) What is the effect of university completion?
c. (i) What is the effect of an additional year of tenure for American and Japanese males when prior experience is 10 years and current tenure is 5 years? (ii) Why must the amount of prior experience and the number of years on current job be specified? (iii) How about when prior experience is zero and current experience is zero (that is, when a worker is just beginning a first job)?
d. What might be a reasonable way to use the regression equations to specify the average beginning salary for American and for Japanese workers?
e. What might explain the differences in the effects of tenure on earnings?

TABLE 5.4

Regression Results for Earnings Equations: American and Japanese Male Workers

| | Dependent Variable | | | |
| | (Ln. Weekly Earnings) U.S. | | (Ln. Weekly Earnings) Japan | |
Independent Variables	Coefficient	t-score	Coefficient	t-score
Constant	4.791	78.1	4.721	180.8
Experience	0.0372	16.4	0.0210	4.9
Experience Squared	-0.0007	13.0	-0.0003	4.1
Tenure	0.0121	4.3	0.0692	11.7
Tenure Squared	-0.0003	3.6	-0.0013	5.6
Interaction: Experience and Tenure	0.0003	2.3	-0.00001	0.1
Years of School	0.0296	5.0		
School Dummies				
High School	0.1286	4.5	0.1048	5.8
Junior College			0.2822	7.2
University	0.1590	5.6	0.4579	20.8
Union Member	0.0020	0.1		
$\bar{R}^2$	0.279			
T	3750		366	

Note: Tenure is number of years at current firm and experience is number of years of work acquired previous to current firm; R^2 is not reported for Japanese firms because the data were grouped data and the R^2 was not readily available in the computer printout.

Source: Masamori Hashimoto and John Raisian, "Employment Tenure and Earnings Profiles in Japan and the United States," *American Economic Review* 77 (1985), Table 5.

Discussion:

a. The coefficients will show the *percentage* change in earnings as a function of a change of one unit in the independent variable. The coefficients will be in decimal form and must be multiplied by 100 in order to appear as traditional percentages. b. (i) Holding all else constant, completing high school as opposed to having less than a high school education, will result in earnings that are 12.86% higher for American males and 10.48% higher for Japanese males. (ii) Completing a university education will result in earnings that are 15.9% higher for Americans and 45.79% higher for Japanese, as compared to having less than a high school education.

c. (i) The effect on percentage change in earnings of an additional year of tenure for an American male is:

$$.0121 - .0006n + .0003j;$$

the effect on percentage change in earnings of an additional year of tenure for a Japanese male is:

$$.0692 - .0026n - .00001j;$$

where n is years of tenure and j is years of experience.
For Americans with 10 years of experience and 5 years of tenure, an additional year of tenure increases earnings by 1.81%.

$$[.0121 - .0006(5) + .0003(10)] = .0181;$$
$$.0181 \times 100 = 1.81\%.$$

For Japanese with 10 years experience and 5 years tenure, an additional year of tenure increases earnings by 5.61%. (ii) Both of these effects require that n (years of tenure) and j (years of experience) be specified before an actual number can be calculated. Thus, the need to specify experience and tenure arises. (iii) For an American with no experience and no tenure, a year of tenure increases earnings by 1.21%. For a Japanese male in a similar situation, earnings are increased 6.92%.

d. One could take the regression equation, plug in zero values for experience and tenure, plug in the average sample values for all the other variables, and calculate the resultant predicted logarithm of earnings. Then, that logarithm could be converted to earnings. (These numbers, using this method, are 129,663 yen per month and $201.63 per week.)

e. The Japanese workers have a steeper earnings profile with respect to tenure. This might be due to more rigorous screening on the part of Japanese employers to make sure they have the "right" workers, after which they are willing to pay those workers higher increases each year. Or it might indicate that Japanese workers obtain job training that can only be used in the firm where they work (specific training), and employers compensate them for the additional productivity that this specific training brings the firm.

CONCLUSIONS

The use of dummy variables, curved equations, and nonadditive models greatly expands the usefulness of the regression model. At this point, any process that can be reasonably depicted by a single equation can be modeled by an appropriate looking regression line. Analysts are not constrained to straight lines or to simplistic assumptions about how the level of one variable influences the effect of another variable. The regression model is a strong tool. In the next chapter, we discover the caveats and potential problems that may arise when using regression models. Without an understanding of the possible problems, the use of regression analysis can result in misleading and erroneous conclusions.

SUMMARY OF CHAPTER 5

1. Dummy variables are nominal variables whose values fit one of several categories. They may be used in a regression equation to shift the intercept, change the slope, or both.
2. The regression equation must include one less dummy than there are possible values for the dummy. Otherwise, the equation will be overdetermined and none of the coefficients will be calculable.
3. The significance of two or more dummies can be tested simultaneously, using an F test. This test can also determine the significance of any group of variables, dummy or continuous, or a combination.
4. Exponential models are one class of useful nonlinear or curved equations that can be easily estimated with regression analysis. Constant growth rate models depict constant percentage changes in the dependent variable. Elasticity models depict percentage changes in both the dependent and independent variables.
5. Polynomial models are used for curved equations where the dependent and independent variables do not change by percentages. Quadratic polynomials, where the independent variable is raised to the power of two, are most popular. Polynomials can depict curves that change direction from positive to negative or vice versa.
6. Interactive models allow changes in the dependent variable to result from changes and levels of the independent variables. Such models say that the effect of one variable depends on the size or level of one or more other variables.

6

Basic Assumptions and Common Problems in Regression Models

Regression analysis is a strong instrument for examining patterns in data. It is flexible. It can be used with various kinds of curved as well as straight lines and with continuous as well as dichotomous independent variables. It is easy to implement because of the many preprogrammed packages available for personal and mainframe computers. It can, however, be a dangerous instrument if it is used without a theory or without knowledge of the basic statistical assumptions that underlie it. Until now, the emphasis in this book has been twofold. First has been stressed the necessity to have a preformed behavioral hypothesis or theory about how dependent and independent variables are related. It is technically possible to regress any variable on any other; one is even likely to find statistical significance if the sample size is large enough. But many a wrong decision will be made if there is no theoretical justification for the statistical results. Second, considerable space has been devoted to the theory and mechanics of the basic regression model — how to derive estimators and how to make the model accommodate dichotomous independent variables or curved relationships.

This chapter discusses the assumptions that underlie the estimators for the regression model, what goes wrong if the assumptions are not met, and some possible corrections to the model when an assumption is not met. In addition, the common problem of multicollinearity, which is unrelated to the assumptions, is explained. The first section of the chapter addresses what is called homoskedasticity or the "constant variance" assumption. Section two looks at autocorrelation, or violations of the assumption that error terms between observations are uncorrelated. Section three explores the violation of the assumption that the error and independent variables are uncorrelated. Finally, section four explains multicollinearity.

THE ASSUMPTION OF CONSTANT VARIANCE OR HOMOSKEDASTICITY

What Is Homoskedasticity?

Homoskedasticity describes how the error terms should be scattered or distributed around a regression line in an ideal regression model. The word literally means *same variance,* and Figure 6.1 shows a scattergram of how the data should look. Figure 6.2 illustrates heteroskedasticity, which means *differing variances,* or that the variance of the error term differs across the X values. Heteroskedasticity need not always take the particular form shown in Figure 6.2, where the variance

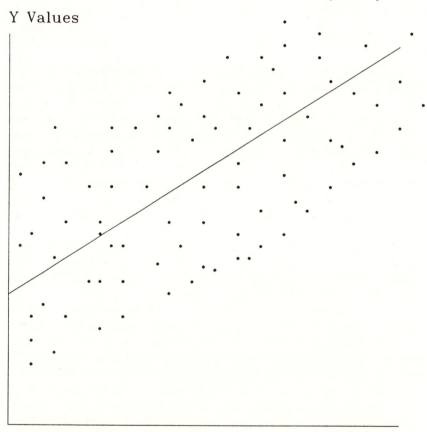

FIG. 6.1. Homoskedastic distribution of errors

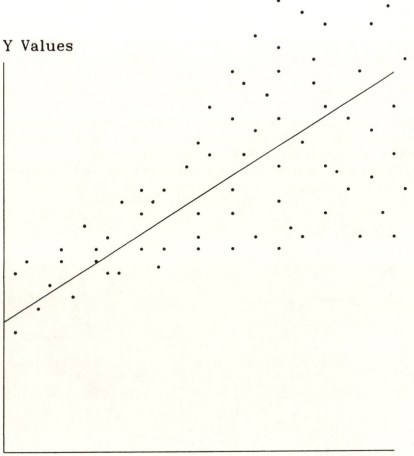

Y Values

X Values

FIG. 6.2. Heteroskedastic distribution of errors

increases as the X values increase; any pattern of nonconstant variances would be heteroskedastic.

What is the importance of the homoskedastic assumption? If it is not met, the standard errors of the regression coefficients are biased; they may be either too small or too large. If they are smaller than they should be, then t statistics that are calculated to test for significance will be too large, and coefficients will be judged significant more often than they should be. If the standard errors are larger than they should be, then significance will be rejected more often than it should be. In either case, the significance tests are inaccurate. On the other hand, the coefficients themselves are still unbiased, so that not all of the BLUE characteristics are affected.

Another way to understand the importance of the assumption is to see how it affects the way one would wish to calculate the regression estimators. When the errors are constantly distributed around the regression line, the least squares method uses the error associated with each X value in a similar way (that is, by squaring it and summing it with other squared errors). But, if the variance of the errors were smaller around some of the X values, it would make sense to give more weight to the observations with smaller variances when calculating regression coefficients. Figure 6.3 shows an extreme case of nonconstant variance for a bivariate regression. In this figure, all observations for independent variables X_3 and X_4 have zero error variances and as such all the corresponding Y values are

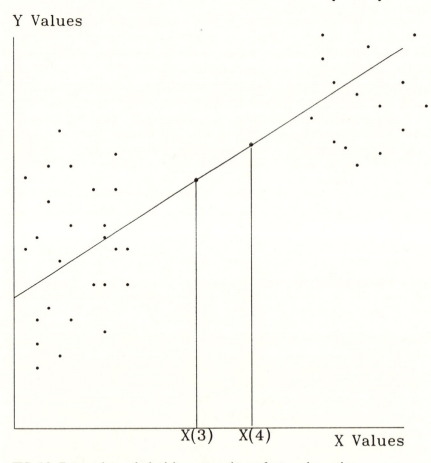

FIG. 6.3. Extreme heteroskedasticity: zero variances for two observations

exactly on the regression line. Since it takes only two points to calculate a bivariate straight line, observations for X_3 and X_4 would be ideal ones to use. The line would be perfectly calculated even though all observations save X_3 and X_4 were ignored. (Note that the presence of many observations off the line indicates the stochastic nature of the population relationship.) In general, one would wish to give more weight to observations with smaller variances.

When Is Heteroskedasticity Present?

How does an analyst know when heteroskedasticity is present? One way is to be alert to those situations when it is likely to occur. In models where the dependent variable is the mean of a group, heteroskedasticity is often present. This is because the group sizes often differ, and the mean of a larger group will generally be measured more accurately (with a smaller variance) than the mean of a smaller group. For example, if the dependent variable is average energy consumption and the independent variable is family size, there may be more families of sizes 2, 3 and 4 than of sizes 1, 5 or 6. Average energy consumption will generally be more accurately measured for the families of sizes 2, 3 and 4.

Other heteroskedastic situations occur because of the nature of the model. Often as the independent variable gets larger (or smaller), there is more possibility of variation in the dependent variable. For example, if one is regressing days spent in formal learning (any kind of schooling, including adult education, college, secondary and elementary school) versus age, one would expect very little variation for young ages and much more variation at older ages. Or, if one is studying the relationship between clothing expenditures and income, one would expect more variation at the higher incomes. At low incomes, most clothing expenditures would be mandatory, but at higher incomes, expenditures would vary more because more discretion is possible.

Checking for Heteroskedasticity

In addition, to thinking about the nature of the data and the model, there are some data manipulations and statistical tests that can be performed to help detect heteroskedasticity. First, the sample residuals from the regression can be plotted. This means that the regression is run and that the residual error terms are calculated. Recall that the residual is the actual value of the dependent variable minus the value that is predicted from the regression equation. These residuals are then plotted against some other variable, generally an independent variable with which they are thought to vary. The residuals can be checked to see if there is a pattern of nonuniformity. Figure 6.4 shows hypothetical residuals that might be calculated from a regression of clothing expenditures on income. The pattern is clearly not uniform.

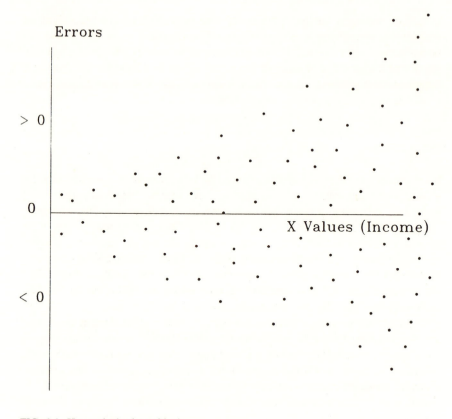

FIG. 6.4. Heteroskedastic residuals

In addition to observing patterns of residuals, there are a few formal tests that cover certain types of heteroskedasticity. All the tests have as their null hypothesis that the variances of the error terms across values of independent variables are identical. The alternative hypotheses differ in detail. Alternative hypotheses that are more restrictive provide more information about how to correct the problem, if it exists. But it is harder to know when the more restrictive hypotheses are warranted. Here, we will examine one of the simpler tests, the Goldfeld-Quandt, as a way to see how the tests work in general.[1]

The Goldfeld-Quandt test is useful if one thinks that the variance of the error term increases or decreases consistently as one of the independent variables increases or decreases. In the case of consistently increasing residuals, the pattern would look as it did in Figure 6.4. To perform the test, the data are ordered by magnitude of the independent variable with which the variance is thought to increase or decrease. Then, some of the middle observation, often one-fifth, are deleted. Separate regressions are run on the observations associated with the low

X values and with the high X values. The residuals for each regression are calculated, squared and summed. Suppose the summed squared residuals for the low X values are denoted SSE_L and the summed squared residuals for the high X values are denoted SSE_H. An F statistic can then be formed by dividing SSE_H by SSE_L ($F = SSE_H/SSE_L$). The statistic has $[T - m - 2(K + 1)]$ degrees of freedom in both the numerator and the denominator, where T is the sample size, m is the number of observations omitted, and K is the number of independent variables. The null hypothesis of constant variances is rejected if the F statistic is greater than its critical value.

Correcting for Heteroskedasticity

The only way to correct for heteroskedasticity is to make an assumption about how the variances of the error terms differ. Generally, such an assumption will be formed in one of two ways. First, either the residuals from a regression that has not yet been corrected for heteroskedasticity will be analyzed to see if there is a pattern, such as the one shown in Figure 6.4, or second, the analyst will have some prior notion, based on theory or experience, of how the variances of the error terms look. Sophisticated methods, called generalized least squares (GLS), are beyond the scope of this book, but a simple version of GLS, called weighted least squares (WLS), can be explained as a way to give the reader a flavor for how the correction works.

When using weighted least squares, the analyst usually assumes that the variance of the error term is linearly related to one of the independent variables. Suppose the regression model is a three variable one:

$$Y = B_0 + B_1 X_1 + B_2 X_2 + E. \tag{6.1}$$

Also, suppose that the variance of the error terms equal a constant times X_1 or:

$$\text{Variance of error} = DX_1, \tag{6.2}$$

where D is a constant.

This assumption about the variance of the error says that as the value of X_1 increases, the variance gets larger. This is the assumption that has been illustrated both in Figure 6.4 and in the example of clothing expenditures regressed on income. To correct for this kind of heteroskedasticity, each observation is weighted by $1/\sqrt{X_1}$, so that the new regression looks as follows:

$$Y/\sqrt{X_1} = B_0/\sqrt{X_1} + B_1 X_1/\sqrt{X_1} + B_2 X_2/\sqrt{X_1} + E/\sqrt{X_1}. \tag{6.3}$$

This new, transformed, regression resolves the heteroskedasticity problem because now the variance of the error term is a constant, equal to D:

Variance $(E/\sqrt{X_1}) = (1/X_1)$(Variance E) $= (1/X_1)(DX_1) = D =$ a constant.   (6.4)

To execute the weighted least square regression, the dependent and independent variables from each observation are divided by $\sqrt{X_1}$ for that observation, and the new transformed variables are regressed. There is no intercept in the transformed model, since B_0 is divided by $\sqrt{X_1}$ (that is, B_0 is the coefficient of the variable $1/\sqrt{X_1}$.) Thus a regression program must be used that forces the intercept to zero. The coefficients of the original equation can be read directly from the transformed one, but it must be remembered that the coefficient of the first transformed variable is the intercept in the original model. Also, the R^2 in the transformed model is not applicable to the original model, since the new R^2 measures the variation in the *weighted* dependent variable, $Y/\sqrt{X_1}$.

THE ASSUMPTION OF ZERO COVARIANCE BETWEEN ERRORS OR ZERO AUTOCORRELATION

What Is Autocorrelation and Why Does It Matter?

Any particular observation in a population may or may not fall exactly on the population regression line; there may be positive or negative errors. The regression model assumes, however, that the error in any one observation is uncorrelated with the error in any other. Thus, if one observation is above the line, it should be impossible to gain any information about whether the next (or any other) one will be above, or below, or on the line. This assumption of lack of correlation between error terms is most likely to be violated in time-series data. When the assumption is violated, the problem is called autocorrelation or, more specifically, serial correlation, when it occurs with time-series data. Autocorrelation is likely to occur with time-series data because something associated with time, such as growth, has not been taken into account and that thing influences several observations. There is a sort of cumulative effect of a left-out time variable.

Autocorrelation can be either positive or negative. An example of positive autocorrelation is shown in Figure 6.5, where a positive error in one time period is followed by several more positive ones in subsequent periods, and a negative error in one time period is followed by negative errors in succeeding periods. Figure 6.5a shows the positive autocorrelation in terms of observed dependent and independent variables. Figure 6.5b shows the same data in residual form, with the residuals plotted against time. Negative autocorrelation is not illustrated. Positive autocorrelation is more common than negative autocorrelation, especially when economic data are involved, because of trends where growth and expansion occur for awhile and then decline and contraction set in for awhile. Negative autocorrelation, while less often present, can occur, particularly if seasonality in the data has not been taken into account. For example, retail clothing sales are

Y Values

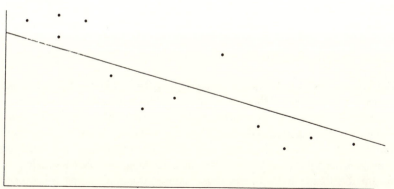

X Values

6.5a Dependent and Independent Variables

Errors

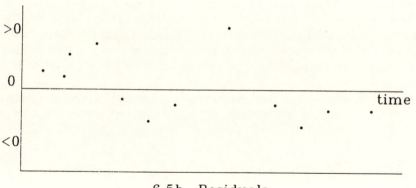

6.5b Residuals

FIG. 6.5. Positive autocorrelation

likely to be high around major holidays, and then fall off, creating an alternating pattern of residuals.

The Consequences of Autocorrelation

Autocorrelation results in biased standard errors for the estimated (sample) regression coefficients. In the more common case of positive autocorrelation, the standard errors are smaller than they should be. Thus, the calculated t statistics are too large and coefficients are judged to be significant more often than they should be. The coefficients themselves are still unbiased; only the standard errors are incorrectly estimated, making those coefficients seem more accurate than they really are.

Identifying Autocorrelation

The first method to use to identify any regression problem is to think about the model and data to see if there is any a priori reason to suspect a problem. After all, one will rarely wish to test blindly for every possible problem, first because of the time and expense, and second because a test can result in a false positive, leading one to corrective action when it is not required. If autocorrelation is suspected, perhaps because time-series data are being used, then a simple first step toward identification is to plot the residuals from an ordinary least squares regression against time (or any other appropriate variable) and to look for patterns. A more or less random distribution of residuals would tend to support the lack of a problem.

In addition to thinking about the model and plotting residuals, there are some other formal statistical tests for autocorrelation. The most widely used is the Durbin-Watson test.[2] That is the one we will consider in detail here. The Durbin-Watson test is used for what is called "first order serial correlation," where the error in one observation is correlated with the error in the very next observation. This is in contrast to higher order correlations, where the error in one observation may be correlated with errors in observations two, three or more time periods away. The Durbin-Watson test uses the estimated correlation coefficient between successive errors, that is between E_t and E_{t-1}. It assumes the following kind of model:

$$E_t = \alpha E_{t-1} + R_t,$$ (6.5)

where R_t meets all the assumptions of the regression model, and α shows how the errors are correlated. If α is equal to zero, there is no autocorrelation. If it is equal to plus or minus one, there is perfect positive or negative correlation. In effect, the Durbin-Watson is testing the following hypothesis:

$H_0: \alpha = 0$

$H_A: \alpha \neq 0.$

The "d" statistic is formed from the residuals of an ordinary least squares regression, as follows:

$$d = \sum_{t=2}^{T}(e_t - e_{t-1})^2 / \sum_{t=1}^{T}e_t^2.$$ (6.6)

This d statistic is approximately equal to: $2(1 - r)$, where r is the correlation coefficient between successive error terms.

The Durbin-Watson d statistic ranges between 0 and 4. If there is no autocorrelation, and r is thus equal to zero, then d equals 2. If there is positive autocorrelation and r is greater than zero, d is less than 2. If there is negative autocorrelation and r is less than zero, d is greater than 2.

The formal statistical test for autocorrelation involves the use of a table showing the distribution of the d statistic for various sample sizes and various numbers of independent variables. In addition, the table gives upper (d_u) and lower (d_l) limits for d. Table D.3, in Appendix D, gives critical values of d for sample sizes ranging from 15 to 100, for two-tailed tests. Once the test statistic d is calculated from the regression residuals, and the d_u and d_l are read from the table, then the outcome of a two-tailed test depends on where the calculated d statistic falls on the following continuum:

positive auto-correla-tion	uncertain	no auto-correla-tion	uncertain	negative auto-correla-tion

| 0 | d_l | | d_u | 2 | $4 - d_u$ | | $4 - d_l$ | | 4 |

Occasionally, the test will give uncertain results, in which case nothing can be said about whether there is or is not a statistically significant correlation between residuals. In some ways, the uncertain outcome is the worst, since then the analyst cannot proceed with corrections but also cannot be sure there is no problem.

As an example of the use of the Durbin-Watson statistic, suppose data from 1968–1982 were used to estimate the following relationship between yearly consumer retail expenditures and personal income:

$$\text{Expenditures} = 4.42 + .88 \text{ Personal Income.} \tag{6.7}$$

$R^2 = .80$; Durbin-Watson (D.W.) = 3.26.

The sample size is 15 and the number of independent variables is one. From the table of critical values for the Durbin-Watson statistic at a 5% significance level (see Table D.3), we note that d_l is .95 and d_u is 1.23. Since the calculated Durbin-Watson of 3.26 is greater than $4 - d_l$ (3.05), the hypothesis of negative autocorrelation is not rejected.

What To Do About Autocorrelation

Any correction for autocorrelation requires some assumption about how error terms are correlated in the population. One simple and common correction that follows directly from the assumptions of the Durbin-Watson test is called differencing. Other more sophisticated corrections, to be used with Generalized Least Squares, are beyond the scope of this text but can be read about in some of the references cited in the bibliographical essay.

The differencing correction assumes that the error terms in the population are linearly related, as in equation (6.5): $E_t = \alpha E_{t-1} + R_t$. Recall that R_t is an error term that meets all the assumptions of the regression model; it exhibits homoskedasticity and no autocorrelation. Differencing, then, works because the regression model holds for all time periods and can be written, in the case of a three variable model, in either of the following two ways:

$$Y_t = B_0 + B_1 X_{t,1} + B_2 X_{t,2} + E_t, \tag{6.8}$$

or

$$Y_{t-1} = B_0 + B_1 X_{t-1, 1} + B_2 X_{t-1,2} + E_{t-1}, \tag{6.9}$$

where t and $t - 1$ are successive time periods.

Equation (6.9), for the $t - 1$ time period, can then be multiplied by α, to yield:

$$\alpha Y_{t-1} = \alpha B_0 + \alpha B_1 X_{t-1,1} + \alpha B_2 X_{t-1,2} + \alpha E_t. \tag{6.10}$$

Finally, equation (6.10) can be subtracted from equation (6.8):

$$(Y_t - \alpha Y_{t-1}) = (B_0 - \alpha B_0) + (B_1 X_{t,1} - \alpha B_1 X_{t-1,1})$$
$$+ (B_2 X_{t,2} - \alpha B_2 X_{t-1,2}) + (E_t - \alpha E_{t-1}). \tag{6.11}$$

The new error term, $(E_t - \alpha E_{t-1})$, is equal to R_t, which meets all the assumptions of the ordinary least squares model. Thus, if α is known or can be estimated, equation (6.11) can be estimated. A convenient assumption is that the value of α is equal to one. In that case, equation (6.11) becomes:

$$(Y_t - Y_{t-1}) = (B_0 - B_0) + (B_1 X_{t,1} - B_1 X_{t-1,1})$$
$$+ (B_2 X_{t,2} - B_2 X_{t-1,2}) + (E_t - E_{t-1}). \tag{6.12}$$

$$\text{or } (Y_t - Y_{t-1}) = B_1(X_{t,1} - X_{t-1,1}) + B_2(X_{t,2} - X_{t-1,2}) + (E_t - E_{t-1}). \tag{6.13}$$

Equation (6.13) is called first differencing. It is easy to execute and to interpret since all the coefficients are the same as in equation (6.8). The intercept, however, will be zero in equation (6.13), so a regression program that forces that result is preferable to an ordinary regression program. If an ordinary regression program is used, then a significance test can be performed to see if the intercept differs from zero.

Differencing can be used when α is not equal to one, but either some a priori way to identify α, or a way to estimate it, must be available. Ways to estimate α from the residuals of the uncorrected regression equation are covered in some of the texts listed in the bibliographical essay and one method is illustrated in Example 6.1.

EXAMPLE 6.1 MODELING THE NEW YORK CITY ECONOMY

Matthew Drennan has developed an econometric model of the New York City economy.[3] The model and data have been used in previous chapters of this book to illustrate the employment of the computer to estimate regression equations. Here, his model illustrates a way to correct for autocorrelation. One of the equations in Drennan's model uses total city income as a dependent variable and is estimated with quarterly data from 1958 through 1978 (84 quarters). The independent variables in the equation are: SCPIUS (ratio of CPI for the region to consumer price index for the nation), CPOP (city population in thousands for the year), UALLY (total U.S. national income in billions of 1972 dollars), and UUNEMPR (U.S. unemployment rate).

The Durbin-Watson statistic in Table 6.1 shows autocorrelation and the following version of differencing was used to correct the equation. The relationship among the errors was assumed to be of the form: $E_t = \alpha E_{t-1} + R_t$. The α coefficient was estimated using the residuals from the OLS equation shown in Table 6.1; that is, for each observation, the predicted value of the dependent variable was subtracted from its actual value to obtain e_t. These residuals were then regressed on themselves, one period lagged, using a computer program that forced the intercept to zero. The resulting a estimate was then used in a differenced equation, where the variables were as follows:

$CALLY'_t = CALLY_t - aCALLY_{t-1}$,
$SCPIUS'_t = SCPIUS_t - aSCPIUS_{t-1}$,
$CPOP'_t = CPOP_t - aCPOP_{t-1}$,
$UALLY'_t = UALLY_t - aUALLY_{t-1}$, and
$UUNEMPR'_t = UUNEMPR_t - aUUNEMPR_{t-1}$.

The estimated coefficients from the new equation, using the differenced variables, are then the appropriate ones because they are corrected for autocorrelation. (Only the intercept must be transformed, but that transformation is not important here). The new equation, corrected for autocorrelation, is shown in Table 6.2.

Questions:

a. For the equation *corrected* for autocorrelation (Table 6.2), how would you interpret the coefficients on the four independent variables?

b. For the original *uncorrected* equation (Table 6.1), demonstrate that the Durbin-Watson coefficient does indeed indicate the presence of autocorrelation.

TABLE 6.1
OLS Regression Results for Total City Income

Independent Variables	Dependent Variable (Total City Income in Millions of 1972$)	
	Coefficient	t-score
Constant	-29,663	
SCPIUS	-32,389	3.7
CPOP	12.10	12.0
UALLY	24.13	14.3
UUNEMPR	-874.8	8.4
$\bar{R}^2$	.932	
D.W.	0.62	
T	84	

Source: Matthew P. Drennan, *Modeling Metropolitan Economies for Forecasting and Policy Analysis* (New York: New York University, 1985), Table 6.4.

c. (i) Is the method for correcting autocorrelation sensible? (ii) What problem might there be with this method?
d. How could one make forecasts with the corrected equation?
e. What uses are there for predictions of the dependent variable shown here?

Discussion:

a. *Ceteris paribus,* when the ratio of regional to national CPI increases one point, total city income (in constant 1972 dollars) decreases $10,899,000,000. Note that a one point increase can be a very large percentage increase, since the variable is a ratio. If the ratio begins at 1 (for example, 100/100) and goes to 2 (for example, 210/105), there has been a 110% increase in the regional CPI.

For all of the following interpretations, it is assumed that all variables, except the one described, are held constant. When city population increases by 1,000, total

TABLE 6.2
Differenced Regression Results for Total City Income

Independent Variables	Dependent Variable (Total City Income in Millions of 1972$) Coefficient
Constant	-12,449
SCPIUS	-10,889
CPOP	7.858
UALLY	16.82
UUNEMPR	-911.5

Source: Matthew P. Drennan, *Modeling Metropolitan Economies for Forecasting and Policy Analysis* (New York: New York University, 1985), Table 6.6

city income increases $7,858,000. When U.S. national income increases by one billion dollars, city income increases by $16,820,000. When the U.S. unemployment rate increases 1 percentage point, total city income decreases $911,500,000.
b. Using a 5% significance test, and the Durbin-Watson statistic for a sample size of 85, the cutoff points are as follows: lower cutoff point = 1.55 and upper cutoff point = 1.75. The calculated Durbin-Watson of 0.62 shows that we cannot reject the existence of positive autocorrelation.
c. (i) Yes, given the information available to the author. (ii) The problem is that using the sample residuals to calculate α is not the same as knowing the true population relationship between the residuals. Therefore, there will be some bias in the corrected coefficients.
d. To make forecasts, one would need forecasts for all the independent variables. The forecasted values of the independent variables would then be plugged into the corrected equation. Forecasts for the independent variables used in this equation are available from public agencies.
e. Among many uses, one could chart recessions and recoveries in the city economy and predict future tax revenues.

THE ASSUMPTION THAT THE ERROR TERM AND THE
INDEPENDENT VARIABLES ARE UNCORRELATED

To meet the assumptions of the ordinary least squares model, the error term must be truly random. This means, in particular, that there can be no correlation between the error and any of the independent variables. If this assumption is not met, then the regression coefficients will be biased.

There are three common situations when the error term and independent variables will be correlated. First, a variable may be left out of the model; this is a form of what is called specification bias. Second, an independent variable may be measured with error; this is called measurement error. Third, the regression equation may be part of a simultaneous equation system; this is called simultaneous equation bias. Each of these situations will be explained here; in addition, simultaneous equation systems will be described in more detail in Chapter 8.

Specification Bias Due to a Left Out Variable

There are a number of reasons why one or more independent variables may be left out of a regression equation. The analyst may simply fail to consider a variable or may use a theory that is deficient and fails to consider the variable. Or, more likely, the analyst may not include a variable because data for it are not obtainable. Either way, the effect is likely to be a correlation between the error and one or more of the remaining independent variables. The variation in the left-out variable will be picked up in the error term. In addition, if the left-out variable and any of the included variables are correlated, then the error term and those independent variables will be correlated. And this correlation between the error term and independent variable(s) will mean the coefficients of the included variables will show their own effects, as well as those of the excluded variables, and thus will be biased.

An example of the left-out variable phenomenon causing bias is the problem of estimating the determinants of elementary school children's educational achievements. Both school variables, such as teachers, supplies, and computers, as well as home variables, such as parental encouragement, books in the home, and parents' educational backgrounds, are likely to influence a child's achievement level. In addition, in the United States, there is likely to be a high correlation between certain home and school variables. This is because public school feeder areas are by and large coincident with neighborhoods, and neighborhoods are homogeneous with respect to socioeconomic characteristics of the families. Parents who are able to provide home inputs that help in high achievement are also likely to fund and manage schools that provide school inputs that encourage high achievement. If a regression equation includes only school inputs as independent variables when trying to explain children's educational achievement, then the coefficients on these school inputs are likely to be too high. They will be picking up the home as well as the school input effects, and they will be biased upward. Technically, the reason will be that the home variables, which are included in the error term, are correlated with the school variables.

A somewhat more technical way to understand the specification bias problem is to compare a true model and a mistakenly estimated model. Suppose the true model is:

$$Y = B_0 + B_1X_1 + B_2X_2 + E. \tag{6.14}$$

Suppose one mistakenly estimates:

$$Y = B'_0 + B'_1X_1 + E'. \tag{6.15}$$

How does the mistaken estimate of the coefficient on $X_1(B'_1)$ compare to the true coefficient on $X_1(B_1)$? It is possibly biased. The direction and sometimes the magnitude of the bias can be specified by the following equation for the expected value of the mistakenly estimated coefficient:

$$\text{Expected Value of } B'_1 = B_1 + a_1B_2, \tag{6.16}$$

where a_1 is the slope coefficient from a regression of X_2 on X_1:

$$X_2 = a_0 + a_1X_1.$$

The expected value of B'_1 equals the true coefficient (B_1) plus the bias (a_1B_2). One can say the following about the bias. First, if X_1 and X_2 are uncorrelated, and therefore a_1 is equal to zero, there will be no bias. This is an interesting result, since it says that there is no necessity, from the point of view of avoiding bias, to run a multiple regression, unless there is *some* correlation between the independent variables. Second, if B_2 and a_1 are both greater (less) than zero, B'_1 will be biased upward—it will be too large. Finally, if B_2 is greater (less) than zero, and a_1 is less (greater) than zero, B'_1 will be biased downward. It is often possible to specify at least the sign of the B_2 and a_1, so that the direction of the bias can be known. For example, when ascertaining the effect of school and home inputs on children's school achievement, the effect of leaving out home inputs can be calculated. Home inputs are likely to have positive effect on achievement, so that B_2 will be positive.[4] In addition, school and home inputs are likely to be positively correlated, so a_1 will be positive. Therefore, the coefficient on school inputs will be biased upward. Generally, only the direction of the bias can be discerned since, if the data were available to regress X_2 on X_1, those same data could be used to correctly specify the equation in the first place. Nevertheless, knowing the direction of the bias can be valuable in decision making.[5]

Measurement Error in the Independent Variable

A second situation that can result in correlation between the error term and the independent variables is when one or more of the independent variables are measured with error. And, of course, this is a common enough situation. Data for the theoretically correct variable cannot always be obtained. Sometimes data for a closely related variable are substituted. At other times, there are simply mistakes in copying data. At any rate, suppose the true independent variable should be X, but the actual variable, measured with error, is $X + V$, where V is a "well-behaved" error, with no heteroskedasticity or autocorrelation. The V term will cause problems, because it will end up in both the independent variable and in the error term. The true model that one wants to estimate is:

$$Y = B_0 + B_1 X + E. \tag{6.18}$$

But the actual variable, X', measured with error, is equal to the true variable plus the error.

$$X' = X + V. \tag{6.19}$$

This means that the model that is estimated is:

$$Y = B_0 + B_1(X' - V) + E$$

or

$$Y = B_0 + B_1 X' - B_1 V + E. \tag{6.20}$$

The new error term will be correlated (have a nonzero covariance) with the independent variable:

$$\text{Covariance } (X', -B_1 V + E) = \text{Covariance } (X + V, -B_1 V + E)$$
$$= (-B)(\text{Variance } V) \neq 0. \tag{6.21}$$

This nonzero covariance will result in a biased coefficient for the independent variable.

Measurement error as a source of bias is particularly problematic because one always suspects there have been some errors in recording the data. However, if the data are carefully collected and entered into the computer, one can presume that such bias will be small. The measurement error that comes from the necessity to use variables that approximate the true variables must usually be lived with until better data can be located.

Simultaneous Equation Bias

A third situation that can result in correlation between the error term and the independent variables is when an equation is part of a system of equations, but the coefficients for the system are not estimated all at the same time. Rather, each equation in the system is estimated individually, or singly. The usual kind of system that causes problems is called a simultaneous system. A simultaneous system is one where the dependent variable in one equation is an *independent* variable in another equation. The most common example is a demand-supply system, where both the quantity and the price of a good or service are simultaneously determined. For example, a city board of education may wish to know what determines the number of teachers willing to work in any one year (the supply of teachers). Partly, the supply will depend on the salary that is offered. But there is also a *demand* for teachers by the school board. The demand depends in part on the salary level because higher salaries will diminish the number of teachers desired by the board. Since the salary in a free market will evolve to a level where the supply of teachers equals the demand for them, both salary and numbers of teachers will be determined simultaneously. This means that, while the supply of teachers depends partly on their salary level, the salary level, in turn, depends partly on the supply of teachers.

To illustrate why simultaneity results in correlation between the error and the independent variables, let's suppose one wants to estimate the first equation in the following pair of simultaneously determined equations. (Y_1 could equal the supply of teachers and Y_2 could equal their salary level, for example).

$$Y_1 = B_0 + B_1Y_2 + B_2X_1 + E_1 \tag{6.22}$$

and

$$Y_2 = A_0 + A_1Y_1 + A_2X_2 + E_2. \tag{6.23}$$

Y_1 and Y_2 are simultaneously determined (sometimes called endogenous variables.) X_1 and X_2 are independent variables that are not simultaneously determined (sometimes called exogenous variables.) E_1 and E_2 are error terms.

Y_2 varies with Y_1; Y_1 varies with E_1. Therefore, Y_2 will vary with E_1 and, in equation (6.22), one of the independent variables (Y_2) will be correlated with the error term (E_1). This in turn will mean that the coefficients in equation (6.22), and equation (6.23) for that matter, will be biased if estimated using OLS on each equation separately.

Luckily, there are ways to correct for simultaneous equation bias. Since the methods are somewhat complicated, they will be left for the last chapter in the text, where simultaneous equations are more thoroughly discussed. In the meantime, it is always a good idea to think about any single equation models to see if some simultaneity is likely to be involved. At least the analyst will then know if coefficients will be biased or not.

MULTICOLLINEARITY

What Is Multicollinearity?

Multicollinearity in a sample is a condition of high correlation among independent variables to the extent that not enough independent information is available to provide reliable, stable coefficient estimates. Perfect collinearity, where variables are correlated plus or minus one, either in pairs or several at a time, results in an inability to calculate any coefficients at all. Multicollinearity will yield estimators that will be BLUE, but a variety of problems often follow.

Multicollinearity results in large variances for the coefficients—that is, the coefficients cannot be accurately estimated. This means that for those variables that are highly correlated, the t statistics will be low and significance will be difficult to establish. In addition, the model is unstable. If the sample size is slightly changed, or a variable is added or deleted, the size, sign, and significance of highly correlated variables may change dramatically.

How Can Multicollinearity Be Recognized?

Multicollinearity is a problem of a "degree." There is no definitive test for it. Its severity is a function of how the regression equation will be used—for prediction or for explanation. The problem is less severe if the model is to be used for prediction and one expects similar correlations among variables in the future. In such a case, it is the predictive value of the entire equation that is important. Multicollinearity is more severe if individual coefficient estimates are important, because the coefficients are likely to have large variances. There are a number of situations where multicollinearity is more likely to occur. There are also some indicators that point to it.

Multicollinearity will often be a problem when the sample size is small, because it is then difficult to get enough independent variation in the variables to permit accurate estimates of coefficients. Likewise, time-series data can result in multicollinearity, when many of the independent variables exhibit similar trends over time. Finally, aggregate data, such as citywide, statewide, or nationwide data on education levels, poverty levels, mortality rates, will often be highly correlated.

There are also several indicators of multicollinearity. However, again, these are only indicators and not tests. Detecting multicollinearity is more of an art than a science, and it is through experience that one gains confidence that one can spot the problem rapidly. A fairly common indicator of multicollinearity is a high R^2, with each independent variable insigificant. This means that the entire equation has a high explanatory value, but that the effect of individual variables cannot be separated. A second indicator is an unstable equation. Here, a smaller sample size or dropping a variable can lead to sizeable changes in the coefficients. A third indicator is the size of the correlations between independent variables, either two at a time, or several at a time. It is easiest to observe the simple Pearson correlation coefficients between variables two at a time. However, these can be deceptive, since the multicollinearity may not show itself this way, but rather may be present in the correlations among several variables. In addition to observing the Pearson correlations, it is wise to look at the R^2's on the regressions of each variable on all others suspected to be correlated. Finally, mulitcollinearity will sometimes occur when the correlations among independent variables are considerably higher than correlations between the independent variables and the dependent variable. It is usually sufficient to observe these correlations two at a time, which means the standard Pearson correlation matrix that is printed from computerized regression packages can be scanned.

What to Do About Multicollinearity

Multicollinearity can be a serious problem, especially if the goal of the analysis is to estimate individual coefficients. In general, the solution to the problem is to acquire more information so as to increase the independent variation of the variables. But more information is not easily available. One source of additional information is a larger sample. However, if a larger sample was easy to obtain, it probably would have been used in the first place. Sometimes, when the multicollinearity is really intractable, it is necessary to await the opportunity (and resources) to use a larger sample, or at least one that is carefully designed to avoid major correlations among independent variables.

A second solution to the multicollinearity problem is to obtain additional information on some of the coefficients, so that they need not be estimated. This information might come from previous research or from theoretical knowledge. For example, suppose one wants to estimate a community's demand equation for trash removal, in anticipation that a government might want to initiate a fee for such a service. Suppose a simplified model postulates that the quantity of trash removal demanded per year is a function of the price per trash bag removed and the average community income, as follows:

$$Q_D = B_0 + B_1 Y + B_2 P + E, \qquad (6.24)$$

where Q_D is number of trash bags removed, Y is average community income, and P is price per trash bag removed.

If the only data set available for estimation is a time-series from a neighboring community that has charged for removal for several years, then multicollinearity could be a problem. Price per trash bag removed and average community income are likely to move upward together over the years. However, if the relationship between average community income and quantity of trash bags demanded is known from previous research, and the coefficient on average community income (B_1) can be approximated, then, rearranging equation (6.24), the following regression can be estimated:

$$Q_D - B_1 Y = B_0 + B_2 P + E'. \qquad (6.25)$$

The new dependent variable combines the original one with average community income times the already known B_1 coefficient. Now there is only one independent variable, P, and the multicollinearity problem is resolved. Of course, the problem with this solution is that it is difficult to obtain an estimate of B_1, and only in cases where there is a lot of previous research will the method be feasible.

In addition to the two reasonable solutions to the multicollinearity problem, there are also several less desirable solutions. One of the most popular ones is to drop some of the collinear variables from the equation. But, if the multicollinearity is serious, then the bias that results from dropping variables will also be serious. While individual coefficients will be more likely to show statistical significance, their values will not be trustworthy because they will be picking up some of the effects of the left-out variables. Trading multicollinearity for bias is not a "good deal," since the only time that multicollinearity causes real problems is when the analyst wishes to use individual coefficient estimates. But this is just the situation when bias from dropping collinear variables is undesirable.

A second less desirable solution is to form a composite variable from those that are collinear. This is only valid if the variables represent the same concept; but in such a case the variables should not all have been included in the original equation. To blindly combine collinear variables will usually result in a misspecified equation, and one is better off living with the problems of multicollinearity.

The best that can usually be done with multicollinearity in the short run is to recognize that it exists and to know and live with its consequences. Over the longer run, better samples, with more independent variation in the variables can be sought.

Example 6.2 illustrates a regression analysis where multicollinearity was spotted at the beginning of the analysis.

EXAMPLE 6.2 FINANCIAL CONDITION OF VOLUNTARY HOSPITALS
IN NEW YORK STATE AND NEW YORK CITY

Charles Brecher and Susan Nesbitt, using data from 1979 to 1981, explored the determinants of financial health of voluntary hospitals in New York State and New York City.[6] The stimulus for their study was the financial stress that many hospitals perceived they were undergoing, and the interest of the state and federal government in possible ways to alleviate the stress. In the early 1980s, the governments did not want to begin any aid programs without some understanding of whether the stress was brought on by poor management or by factors beyond the control of the hospitals. Brecher and Nesbitt used six different measures of financial condition and 18 explanatory variables. The explanatory variables were divided into two categories: environmental characteristics and hospital characteristics. The analysis originally began with 20 explanatory variables, but simple correlations of above .80 between three variables (per capita income, supply of

TABLE 6.3

Regression Results for Return on Assets for New York State Voluntary Hospitals

Independent Variables (Significant)	Dependent Variable (Return on Assets New York State)	
	Coefficient	t-score
Enrivonmental		
Region	-0.039	3.015
Hospital with Specialty Status	0.089	3.553
Aged Population Share	0.004	1.792
Beds per Capita	-5.754	2.777
Hospital		
Percent Blue Cross & Medical Discharges	0.001	2.465
Length of Stay	-0.010	3.156
Occupancy Rate	0.178	3.844
Number of Beds per Capita in County	0.0008	3.131
R^2	.366	
T	208	

Source: Charles Brecher and Susan Nesbitt, "Factors Associated with Variation in Financial Condition Among Voluntary Hospitals," *Health Services Research* 3 (1985), Table 9.

hosptial beds, and supply of physicians) led the authors to drop two (per capita income and physician supply) to avoid multicollinearity. Some of the variables from the New York State equation for "Return on Assets" (net income/total assets) are shown in Table 6.3. Of the eighteen possible variables, only those significant at 10% or better are shown.

Questions:

a. What are the pros and cons of adjusting for multicollinearity as the authors did, by omitting variables with simple correlations above .80?
b. (i) The New York State equation had a lower R^2 and more significant variables than the New York City equation (which is not shown). The New York City

equation had a higher R^2 and fewer significant variables. What might be the reason for these differences? (ii) In this research, which do you think is more important —the R^2 or the number of significant variables?

Discussion:

a. In favor of the authors' solution is that, if this relatively simple test is done before the regression is run, then it might be possible to identify variables that are measuring the same concept and to correct a potential multicollinearity problem without loss of information. A problem arises if the highly correlated variables do not measure the same concept. In such a situation, elimination of one will result in information loss. Also, multicollinearity can occur when several variables are related even though simple correlations may remain below .80.

b. (i) The most probable reason is that New York State had a larger sample size (208 versus 50). This larger sample size cuts down the size of the standard errors. One way to correct for multicollinearity is to obtain a larger sample. (ii) This research was motivated by a desire to find causes of financial stress, which means that significance was more important than explanatory power. In general, significance is more important for hypothesis testing about individual coefficients and explanatory power is more important for forecasting.

AN EXAMPLE OF COMPUTER OUTPUT SHOWING AUTOCORRELATION

This chapter has discussed assumptions of the regular regression model as well as what happens when those assumptions are not met. One of the assumptions, independence of error terms across observations, is often violated in time-series data. The violation is called autocorrelation or serial correlation. Here, Matthew Drennan's model of total New York City income, CALLY, estimated with 84 quarters of data, is again used to illustrate computer output when there is autocorrelation.[7] In addition, differencing to correct that autocorrelation is shown. This computer example shows the calculations that led to the results used in Example 6.2. The regression coefficients reported here differ slightly from those in Example 6.2, due to rounding of data.

Detecting the Presence of Autocorrelation

The model of CALLY presented in Chapter 3 is repeated here, but this time with an eye to determining if autocorrelation is present. The estimated regression, with the four independent variables, UUNEMPR, UALLY, SCPIUS, and CPOP, is shown in the first equation in Figure 6.6. (The first equation in Figure 6.6 is an exact replica of the one in Figure 3.4). Figure 6.7 displays two ways of detecting

SPSS/PC+

* * * * M U L T I P L E   R E G R E S S I O N * * * *

Equation Number 1   Dependent Variable . .   CALLY

R Square   .93582
Adjusted R Square   .93258
Standard Error   827.08515
F =   287.99966   Signif F =   .0000

----------------- Variables in the Equation -----------------

Variable	B	SE B	Beta	T	Sig T
UUNEMPR	-873.09978	104.71910	-.36543	-8.338	.0000
UALLY	24.16005	1.68678	1.28322	14.323	.0000
SCPIUS	-32569.92771	8663.55379	-.24174	-3.759	.0003
CPOP	12.11741	1.00475	.82968	12.060	.0000
(Constant)	-29640.37027	6362.29863		-4.659	.0000

REGRESSION OF RESIDUAL (CLRESID) ON THEIR OWN LAGGED VALUE (LAGRESID)

* * * * MULTIPLE REGRESSION THROUGH THE ORIGIN * * * *

Equation Number 1   Dependent Variable . .   CLRESID

R Square   .45011
Adjusted R Square   .44340
Standard Error   579.24376
F =   67.12043   Signif F = .0000

----------------- Variables in the Equation -----------------

Variable	B	SE B	Beta	T	Sig T
LAGRESID	.65416	.07985	.67090	8.193	.0000

CALLY REGRESSION OF DIFFERENCED VARIABLES
(AFTER ADJUSTMENT FOR AUTOCORRELATION)

Equation Number 1   Dependent Variable . .   DIFCALLY

R Square   .76549
Adjusted R Square .75346
Standard Error   537.62169
F =   63.65116   Signif F = .0000

----------------- Variables in the Equation -----------------

Variable	B	SE B	Beta	T	Sig T
DIFUUNEM	-912.66930	124.17727	-.47419	-7.350	.0000
DIFUALLY	16.81406	2.14674	.91675	7.832	.0000
DIFSCPIU	-10795.32232	11147.95122	-.08357	-.968	.3359
DIFCPOP	7.85991	1.19478	.64046	6.579	.0000
(Constant)	-4342.96444	3406.66414		-1.275	.2061

FIG. 6.6. CALLY equation before adjustment for autocorrelation

autocorrelation—with a casewise plot of residuals and with the Durbin-Watson statistic. The residual is the difference between the actual value of CALLY and the value predicted by the first equation shown in Figure 6.6. The predicted value is determined by using the actual values of each independent variable and calculating the resulting, predicted, Y value. The casewise plot standardizes the residual by subtracting its mean (which is zero by construction) and dividing by its standard

SPSS/PC+

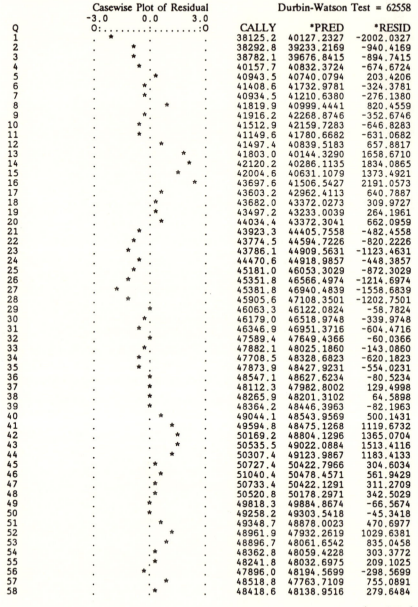

	Casewise Plot of Residual				
	-3.0 0.0 3.0				
Q	0:.........:.........:0	CALLY	*PRED	*RESID	
1	. * .	38125.2	40127.2327	-2002.0327	
2	. * .	38292.8	39233.2169	-940.4169	
3	. * .	38782.1	39676.8415	-894.7415	
4	. * .	40157.7	40832.3724	-674.6724	
5	. * .	40943.5	40740.0794	203.4206	
6	. *. .	41408.6	41732.9781	-324.3781	
7	. *. .	40934.5	41210.6380	-276.1380	
8	. * .	41819.9	40999.4441	820.4559	
9	. *. .	41916.2	42268.8746	-352.6746	
10	. * .	41512.9	42159.7283	-646.8283	
11	. * .	41149.6	41780.6682	-631.0682	
12	. * .	41497.4	40839.5183	657.8817	
13	. *.	41803.0	40144.3290	1658.6710	
14	. *.	42120.2	40286.1135	1834.0865	
15	. * .	42004.6	40631.1079	1373.4921	
16	. * .	43697.6	41506.5427	2191.0573	
17	. *.	43603.2	42962.4113	640.7887	
18	. .*	43682.0	43372.0273	309.9727	
19	. .*	43497.2	43233.0039	264.1961	
20	. .* .	44034.4	43372.3041	662.0959	
21	. * .	43923.3	44405.7558	-482.4558	
22	. * .	43774.5	44594.7226	-820.2226	
23	. * .	43786.1	44909.5631	-1123.4631	
24	. * .	44470.6	44918.9857	-448.3857	
25	. * .	45181.0	46053.3029	-872.3029	
26	. * .	45351.8	46566.4974	-1214.6974	
27	. * .	45381.8	46940.4839	-1558.6839	
28	. * .	45905.6	47108.3501	-1202.7501	
29	. * .	46063.3	46122.0824	-58.7824	
30	. *. .	46179.0	46518.9748	-339.9748	
31	. * .	46346.9	46951.3716	-604.4716	
32	. * .	47589.4	47649.4366	-60.0366	
33	. *. .	47882.1	48025.1860	-143.0860	
34	. *. .	47708.5	48328.6823	-620.1823	
35	. *. .	47873.9	48427.9231	-554.0231	
36	. * .	48547.1	48627.6234	-80.5234	
37	. * .	48112.3	47982.8002	129.4998	
38	. * .	48265.9	48201.3102	64.5898	
39	. * .	48364.2	48446.3963	-82.1963	
40	. .* .	49044.1	48543.9569	500.1431	
41	. * .	49594.8	48475.1268	1119.6732	
42	. * .	50169.2	48804.1296	1365.0704	
43	. * .	50535.5	49022.0884	1513.4116	
44	. * .	50307.4	49123.9867	1183.4133	
45	. .* .	50727.4	50422.7966	304.6034	
46	. .* .	51040.4	50478.4571	561.9429	
47	. .*	50733.4	50422.1291	311.2709	
48	. .*	50520.8	50178.2971	342.5029	
49	. * .	49818.3	49884.8674	-66.5674	
50	. * .	49258.2	49303.5418	-45.3418	
51	. .* .	49348.7	48878.0023	470.6977	
52	. * .	48961.9	47932.2619	1029.6381	
53	. .* .	48896.7	48061.6542	835.0458	
54	. .* .	48362.8	48059.4228	303.3772	
55	. .* .	48241.8	48032.6975	209.1025	
56	. *. .	47896.0	48194.5699	-298.5699	
57	. .* .	48518.8	47763.7109	755.0891	
58	. .* .	48418.6	48138.9516	279.6484	

Durbin-Watson Test = 62558

(continued)

FIG. 6.7. Plot of residuals and Durbin-Watson statistic: CALLY equation before adjustment for autocorrelation

Figure 6.7. (*continued*)

59	. * .	48582.2	48442.2064	139.9936
60	*. .	48704.3	49059.3814	-355.0814
61	. * .	49087.1	47995.3821	1091.7179
62	.* .	48174.4	47943.4841	230.9159
63	* . .	47656.6	48097.1881	-440.5881
64	* . .	47108.6	48133.4281	-1024.8281
65	* .	46056.7	46508.4780	-451.7780
66	* .	45367.4	46619.0036	-1251.6036
67	* .	44905.9	46071.2252	-1165.3252
68	* .	44185.3	44823.2186	-637.9186
69	. * .	42967.0	42131.3229	835.6771
70	. * .	43082.7	41995.8292	1086.8708
71	. * .	43303.0	42794.9404	508.0596
72	*. .	42881.8	43055.5592	-173.7592
73	.* .	43890.4	43733.9263	156.4737
74	* . .	43621.5	44080.8184	-459.3184
75	* .	43932.7	44065.2287	-132.5287
76	* . .	43743.5	44233.9230	-490.4230
77	. * .	44187.3	43620.2525	567.0475
78	* .	44263.8	44334.6190	-70.8190
79	* .	45134.5	45179.8757	-45.3757
80	* . .	44902.8	45753.2858	-850.4858
81	.* .	44957.0	44699.9051	257.0949
82	*. .	45366.6	45663.1200	-296.5200
83	*. .	46015.1	46328.3142	-313.2142
84	* .	45842.4	47031.8547	-1189.4547
Q	0..................0			
	-3.0 0.0 3.0			

deviation. Each plotted value is accompanied by its quarter (Q), the actual value of CALLY, the predicted value (PRED) and the residual (RESID).

Figure 6.7 shows a clear picture of positive autocorrelation. Rather than a random pattern around zero, the residuals curve like a snake, first mostly less than zero, then mostly greater than zero. The Durbin-Watson statistic confirms the impression given by the plot. Its value is .62558. With four independent variables and 84 cases, at the 1% significance level, the lower value of d is approximately 1.41 and the upper value is 1.60 (these values are for a sample size of 85, the closest sample size to 84 available in most standard Durbin-Watson tables). Since .62558 is less than 1.41, positive autocorrelation is indicated.

Using Differencing to Correct for Autocorrelation

In order to correct for autocorrelation, one must specify the nature of the relationship among error terms. One of the most straightforward specifications is that the error in one observation is linearly related to the error in the previous observation, or:

$$E_t = \alpha E_{t-1} + R_t. \tag{6.26}$$

R_t is assumed to be a "well-behaved" error. If α can be estimated, then it can be used to difference the CALLY equation, as shown in the text, creating an equation whose error is R_t and that can be estimated with OLS.

One way to estimate α is to use the residuals, the e_t's, from the first (OLS) equation shown in Figure 6.6. The estimated equation would be:

$$e_t = ae_{t-1} + r_t. \tag{6.27}$$

However, since equation (6.27) has no intercept, it is preferable to use a modification of OLS estimation that forces the intercept through zero. Such a modification is possible using SPSS/PC+. The second equation in Figure 6.6 shows the results of the regression of the residuals from the OLS equation on their own lagged values. Note that since lagged values are used, the number of cases declines from 84 to 83. The second equation in Figure 6.6 shows that the estimated value of a is .65416. Of course there is no estimated intercept, because the intercept was forced to zero.

The final step in the correction of autocorrelation using the differencing technique is to take each variable in the original CALLY equation and create a new variable that subtracts from it .65416 times a one quarter lag. For example, the new dependent variable is: $CALLY_t - .65416 \ CALLY_{t-1}$. The third equation in Figure 6.6 shows the regression results of the differenced variables, labelled DIFCALLY. Recall from the test that the slope coefficients from the differenced equation are now substituted directly into the undifferenced, original equation, to obtain estimates that are hopefully free of autocorrelation. The intercept would need some transformation before it could be substituted.

CONCLUSIONS

Multiple regression is a versatile tool for analyzing data. To use the tool intelligently requires knowledge of the assumptions of the model, of the situations when those assumptions are likely not to be met, and of the various solutions to problems that do arise. This chapter has discussed four of the most common problems of the regression model — heteroskedasticity, autocorrelation, error and independent variable correlation, and multicollinearity. The emphasis here has been on identifying situations when these problems will arise and on understanding their consequences. While one or two solutions to each problem have been presented, the analyst will often find that further reading will be required before the most adequate solution can be found and applied. However, knowing when there is a problem is extremely important because that knowledge will prevent the blind and misleading use of the regression model.

The rest of this book assumes that the reader has a solid understanding of the basic multiple regression model. From here, we move forward to discover more sophisticated uses of multivariate statistics, such as dependent variables that are nominal, equations that are parts of systems, and more on times-series analysis.

SUMMARY OF CHAPTER 6

1. While multiple regression is a strong, flexible tool for examining patterns in data, there are problems that can result if the assumptions of the model are not met.

2. Heteroskedasticity, or the presence of error terms whose variances differ across observations, results in standard errors for the regression coefficients that are biased. This problem, in turn, means that the t statistics used to test for significance will not be accurate. The regression coefficients themselves will be unbiased, however.

3. Heteroskedasticity is more likely to occur in cross-section than in time-series data and is often found when the variables are means of a larger group of data.

4. To check for heteroskedasticity, one can plot residuals or use a more formal test, such as the Goldfeld-Quandt. Correcting heteroskedasticity involves making an assumption about how the variances of the error terms differ. This assumption can then be used in techniques such as weighted least squares.

5. Autocorrelation exists when the error terms across observations are correlated. The problem is more likely to occur in time-series rather than cross-section data, and positive autocorrelation is more likely than negative autocorrelation. Autocorrelation results in biased standard errors, and in the case of positive autocorrelation, the expected values of the standard errors are smaller than they should be. This means that t statistics are larger, on average, than they should be, and coefficients are judged to be significant more often than is warranted by the data.

6. Identification of autocorrelation can be done by plotting residuals or by more formal tests, such as the Durbin-Watson. Correction of autocorrelation requires an assumption about how the error terms are correlated. A common, although not usually precisely accurate, assumption is that the errors in neighboring observations are perfectly correlated. In such a case, first differencing is one solution to the problem.

7. If the assumption that the error term and the independent variables are uncorrelated is not met, then the regression coefficients will be biased.

8. There are three common situations when the error term and the independent variables will be correlated. First, a variable may be left out of the model. Second, an independent variable may be measured with error. Third, the regression equation may be part of a simultaneous equation system.

9. Solutions to the bias problem are not easily found. But, in many cases, at least the direction of the bias can be known. For simultaneous equations, some technical solutions are available, and these are discussed in Chapter 8.

10. Multicollinearity, or the existence of troublesomely high correlations between independent variables, neither violates any assumption of the regression model, nor produces bias in the coefficients or the standard errors. Because the independent variables do not have enough independent variation, however, it is difficult to obtain accurate coefficient estimates. The standard errors of the coefficients of highly correlated variables are often large.

11. Detecting multicollinearity is more an art than a science. Signs of the problem may include: (i) a high R^2, with each variable coefficient insignificant one at a time, (ii) an "unstable" equation, where slight changes in the sample or the model produce large changes in the coefficient estimates, (iii) high correlations among independent variables, taken two or more at a time, (iv) larger correlations among independent variables than between independent and dependent variables.

12. Solutions to the multicollinearity problem are difficult to achieve, since basically more information is needed in order to increase the independent variation between variables. But more information is generally not readily available. Poor solutions to the problem are to drop collinear variables from the equation or to form composite variables of the collinear variables. Both of these latter methods will result in misspecified equations, where the danger of biased coefficients is high. Usually, the best that can be done is to identify the problem, be aware of the consequences, and plan a better sample for future research.

7

Qualitative Dependent Variables

Models in which the *dependent* variable involves qualitative choices have become increasingly important in public management and decision making. As examples, decisions may hinge on whether people vote yes or no in a bond referendum election, whether rehabilitated drug addicts relapse or not, whether commuters use public or private transportation, whether families are on welfare or not, and whether or not hospitals provide technically sophisticated services.[1] All of these involve dependent variables that are qualitative, where individuals belong to one group or the other. The dummy variables are now in the dependent instead of the independent variable position. Estimation of such models presents some problems, since the straightforward approach of using ordinary least squares with a dummy dependent variable leads to heteroskedasticity and anomalies in interpretation.

Models involving qualitative choice have always been inherently interesting to public managers. But, it is the increasing availability of appropriate data sets and appropriate computer software that has made their use so popular. Specifically, survey data, where individuals are asked opinions and directed to indicate degrees of agreement or satisfaction along, for example, a 3 or 5 point scale (satisfied, neutral, dissatisfied) are often used to evaluate public services. And, micro data sets that generate large quantities of information about individuals have become more available through better dissemination of census data and increased use of large experimental programs that evaluate such phenomena as peoples' work behavior, medical care choices, or housing choices.[2] Computer software is readily available for mainframe computers and increasingly available for personal computers.[3]

Qualitative choice models can be interpreted as probability models, where one is attempting to determine how the probability of making a choice changes when the value of an independent variable changes. For example, one might wish to know how the probability of attending an art museum changes when the admission charge is raised 10%; or how the probability of paying a medical bill changes with the marital status of an individual; or how the probability of entering a hospital changes with age. There are at least four problems that must be resolved before such models are estimated. First, a good way of obtaining the probability of choice must be obtained. The data will usually contain after-the-fact choices—individuals either did or did not make certain choices. From these after-the-fact data, estimates of probabilities ranging from 0 to 1 must be made.[4] Second, an appropriate functional form must be chosen since, as we will see, the linear form leads to some predictions of probabilities that are greater than 1 and less than 0. Third, the estimation technique must be chosen. Sometimes ordinary least squares is adequate, but usually another technique called maximum likelihood must be used. And, finally, the appropriate way to interpret the results so that they make management and policy, as well as mathematical, sense must be discussed.

This chapter explores alternative ways to estimate qualitative choice models. The first section looks at the straightforward estimation of the qualitative dependent variable model using a linear functional form. The second section considers other, nonlinear, functional forms called logit and probit.[5] The third and fourth sections explain estimation with logit models and with probit models, respectively.

THE LINEAR PROBABILITY MODEL

When the dependent variable is dichotomous, falling into one of two categories, the most straightforward and easiest-to-understand model is the linear probability one.[6] In this model, ordinary least squares is applied to a linear equation, where the dependent variable is valued either zero or one. The estimated equation, with one independent variable, looks as follows (the t subscript is dropped, but the reader should remember that the equation applies to each observation):

$$Y = B_0 + B_1 X + E. \tag{7.1}$$

The dependent variable, Y, in the sample is a dummy variable, with a value of one if an event occurs and zero if it does not (or conversely). The interpretation of this model as a probability model follows when the expected value of each dependent variable is taken:

$$E(Y) = E(B_0 + B_1 X + E) = B_0 + B_1 X. \tag{7.2}$$

Then, since each Y can only take on the values of 1 or 0, the probability distribution of Y can be described as $P(Y = 1) = P$ and $P(Y = 0) = 1 - P$. Therefore, $E(Y) = 1(P) + 0(1 - P) = P$. Thus, $E(Y) = P =$ probability of the event occurring $= B_0 + B_1 X$.

This linear probability model can result in some problems. First, there is no assurance that when various values of X are plugged into the equation that $B_0 + B_1X$ will fall within the range between 0 and 1. If the predicted value of the dependent variable is less than 0 or greater than 1, its interpretation as a probability fails. For that reason, the model is sometimes artificially constrained such that if $B_0 + B_1X$ is greater than one, it is automatically set to one; if it is less than zero, it is automatically set to zero. This is a less than perfect solution because the predictions are sure to have some bias.

A second related problem is that the R^2 will be low, because the sample values can only take on 0 or 1 values, while the regression line will take on all values. A third problem is that the error term is heteroskedastic and, therefore, the standard errors of the coefficients are incorrectly estimated.

Figure 7.1 shows a graph of a hypothetical data set where the regression line is estimated using ordinary least squares. As an example, the regression line might

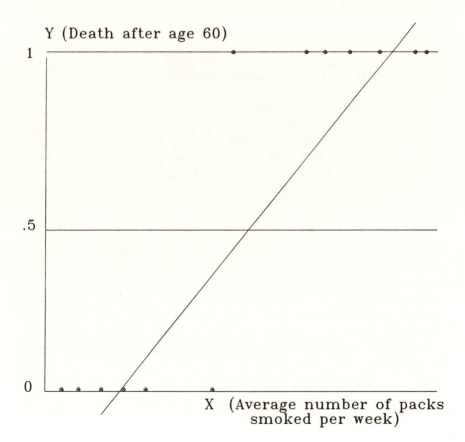

FIG. 7.1. The linear probability model

estimate the relationship between the probability of dying from lung cancer or cardiovascular disease after age 60 and the number of packs of cigarettes smoked per week since age 20. Here, the greater the number of packs smoked (the higher the X value), the more likely is the individual to die from cancer or cardiovascular disease after age 60 (the more values of 1 for the Y variable). Figure 7.1 illustrates some of the problems previously enumerated. Most obviously, the line continues beyond the range of 0 to 1 for the dependent variable, so that the probabilities are not constrained to realistic values. Second, one can see that the R^2 will not be particularly high, since predictions of probabilities in the middle range of .5 will be far from the actual sample values of 0 or 1. Third, the error terms are likely to be larger when the predicted value of the dependent variable is close to .5 than when it is close to 0 or 1. Thus, the variance of the error terms will be higher when the probabilities are around .5 and heteroskedasticity will result.

To see how the linear probability model would be interpreted, suppose the following hypothetical equation relating death from lung cancer or cardiovascular disease to cigarette smoking were estimated (the t subscript is omitted):

$$Y = .02 + .01X. \tag{7.3}$$

($Y = 1$ if an individual died from lung cancer or cardiovascular disease after age 60, otherwise $Y = 0$; and X = average number of packs of cigarettes smoked per week since age 20.)

The interpretation of the equation would be as follows. If an individual never smoked ($X = 0$), then the probability of dying from lung cancer or cardiovascular disease is .02 or 2%. If a person smoked an average of one pack of cigarettes per week from age 20, the probability of death after age 60 would be .03 or 3%. [.02 + .01(1) = .03]. Each additional pack of cigarettes smoked per week raises the probability of death by .01 or one percentage point—the value of the b_1 or slope coefficient in equation (7.3).

While the linear probability model does have a variety of problems, it is still valuable and often-used. It is easy to implement, not very costly, and straightforward to interpret. Whether its defects are critical will depend on how much the results differ from a model with fewer problems; but sometimes the cost of finding out this information will not be worth the effort. This is especially so, if only approproximate results are required.

Example 7.1 illustrates an actual use of the linear probability model. Some of the problems with the linear probability model can be avoided if curved rather than straight (linear) lines are estimated. The next section discusses these curved lines in some detail.

THE LOGIT AND PROBIT FORMS FOR DICHOTOMOUS QUALITATIVE CHOICE MODELS

The problem of having probabilities fall outside the 0 to 1 range can be resolved by changing the estimated functional form from a linear to a curved one. There are many possibilities for curves, but the two most popular are called the logit and the probit.

EXAMPLE 7.1 MEDICAL CARE UTILIZATION, INSURANCE PROGRAMS AND THE LINEAR PROBABILITY MODEL

An opportunity to study hospital and physician utilization patterns when insurance coverage changed arose in 1977 for the United Mine Workers. Richard Scheffler used a sample of United Mine Worker families to see how they responded to a change in their insurance coverage from complete, zero-cost coverage to coverage with a $250 inpatient deductible and a 40% coinsurance rate for physician visits (maximum family liability of $500 per year).[7] He used OLS to estimate a linear probability model of physician visits and of hospital visits before and after introduction of the new insurance program. A dummy variable was included for the time period in which the new coverage was in effect. The author states OLS and probit results showed negligible differences. The OLS results for physicians are shown in Table 7.1.

Questions:

a. The United Mine Workers cost-sharing program was only in effect for five months. How might this have affected the results?
b. What is the effect of cost-sharing on physician visits?
c. What is the effect of patients' age on physician visits?
d. What are the possible problems with using OLS to estimate this model?

Discussion:

a. It might take time for families to adjust to a new program. The results based on five months of measurement might underestimate the effect. Also, some families might have guessed it was temporary, overestimating the effect. However, at least one other researcher has found similar results for a longer-lasting program.
b. *Ceteris paribus,* the new cost-sharing program reduced the probability of a physician visit by .153 or 15.3 percentage points.
c. The effect of an additional year of age on the probability of a visit is $-.0154 + .000464(age)$; that is, the effect is nonlinear and we must know what age individual we are discussing to know the effect of an additional year of age. As an example, at age 20, an additional year of age decreases the probability of a physician visit by .612 percentage points. $[-.0154 + .000464(20) = -.00612 = -.612$ percentage points]. The probability of a visit declines with additional years until age 33 (33.189), at which point the probability of a visit increases with age.
d. A predicted probability of a visit can fall outside the 0 to 1 range and, due to heteroskedasticity, the standard errors are biased such that the t-scores are wrong.

TABLE 7.1
OLS Regression Results for Probability of Physician Visit

Independent Variables	Dependent Variable (Probability of Physician Visit)	
	Coefficient	t-score
Intercept	0.311	1.97
Age (Years)	-0.0154	9.39
Age Squared	0.000232	8.35
Sex (Female = 1)	0.0227	1.31
Hospital Days in 1974	-0.00529	1.62
Hospital Days in 1975	0.0242	8.70
Family Size 2	0.077	2.56
Family Size 3	0.208	7.14
Family Size 4	0.163	5.96
Family Size 5 or More	0.127	4.32
Estimated Price per Visit	-0.000494	0.45
Family Income	0.00000151	0.18
Cost Sharing Dummy (1 for new program)	-0.153	9.88
T	3554	
F	33.39	

Source: Richard M. Scheffler, " The United Mine Workers' Health Plan," *Medical Care* 22 (March 1984), Table 4.

The Logit Form

The logit form is a probability model that looks as follows, when there is one independent variable (again the *t* subscripts are dropped).

$$\text{Prob } (Y = 1) = P = 1/[(1 + e^{-(B_0 + B_1 X)}].\tag{7.4}$$

Figure 7.2 shows a graph of the logit distribution. The relationship between Y and X is nonlinear such that Y never goes above 1 or below 0. (Figure 7.2 also shows the probit curve, to be discussed in the next section.)

After some algebraic and logarithmic manipulations, equation (7.4) can be made a linear one:

Cumulative Probability

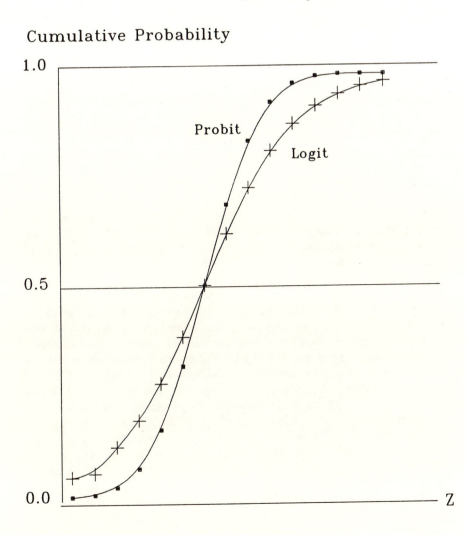

FIG. 7.2. The probit versus logit cumulative distributions

$$\text{Log } [P/(1 - P)] = B_0 + B_1 X. \tag{7.5}$$

$P/(1 - P)$ is the odds of an event occurring (P) relative to it not occurring ($1 - P$). As the probability of the event occurring goes from zero to one, the logarithm of the ratio of the odds goes from minus to plus infinity. While the equation looks like all the other regression equations that have been estimated in previous chapters, it is not quite so, and the interpretation of the equation needs more discussion.

The dependent variable is not a probability, but rather the logarithm of a ratio of probabilities. The relationship between a unit change in an independent variable and the change in the probability itself will depend upon what probability is being evaluated and will look approximately as follows:[8]

$$B_1(P)(1 - P). \tag{7.6}$$

(B_1 is the effect of a change in the independent variable on the change in the logarithm of the ratio of probabilities, and P is the probability of an event occurring).[9]

In order to evaluate the effect of any independent variable on the probability of an event occurring (P), one must choose a specific beginning probability at which to do the evaluation. Equation (7.6), approximating how P changes when an independent variable changes, shows that the effects will be the greatest when beginning probabilities are .5, at the midpoint of the distribution. In contrast, at the tails of the distribution when P is low, the effect of a change in an independent variable will be the least. If the lung cancer and cardiovascular disease example used previously, equation (7.3), were constructed as a logit rather than a linear probability model, there would be some changes in interpretation. Instead of the increase in the probability of death due to an additional pack of cigarettes smoked being equal to B_1 (.01), as it was in the linear model of equation (7.3), the increase would now equal approximately $B_1(P)(1 - P)$. Suppose B_1 in the logit model was estimated to be .06 and the probability of death for an individual was 40%, then the effect of smoking one additional pack of cigarettes per week from age 20 would be approximately (.06)(.4)(.6) or .01444 or a 1.44 percentage point increase in the probability of death. If the initial probability of death were much lower, for example 20%, the effect of an increase in one pack smoked would be lower: (.06)(.2)(.8) = .0096 = .96 percentage points increase in the probability of death. While the probability of death increases with increased smoking, the rate of increase is not constant. Rather the rate is lower when the initial probability of death is low or high, and highest when the probability of death is .5. The slope of the logit line in Figure 7.2 shows this, since that slope is steepest when Y is equal to .5.

Although the logit form is a bit difficult to interpret because it is interactive, it does resolve the problem of probabilities falling outside the 0 to 1 range. In the next section, we will look at how the form can be estimated, but before doing so, an alternative functional form, the probit, will be explored.

The Probit Form

In this model, the probability of an event occurring is the function of an unobservable index, Z. The index is a normally distributed random variable. It has critical cutoffs for individuals such that if an individual is above the critical cutoff, a decision is made in favor of an event, and if an individual is below the critical cutoff, a decision is made against the event. The index itself is a linear function of the independent variables (for one independent variable, with the t subscripts dropped):

$$Z = B_0 + B_1X. \tag{7.7}$$

The idea of the probit model is that values of B_0 and B_1 are estimated such that the Z index gives appropriate cutoff values for individuals in the sample. This is done using the cumulative normal distribution for Z. Once the B_0 and B_1 parameters are estimated, the Z index for an individual with a given value of X can be calculated, and the probability of the event occurring can be determined.

The differences in the shapes of the probit and logit curves are slight and occur in the tails. The effects of unit changes in the independent variables are easier to calculate with logit analysis than with probit analysis. Logit analysis is currently used more often than probit analysis. The next section discusses the logit estimation process and the following section looks briefly at the probit estimation process.

ESTIMATING THE LOGIT MODEL

The estimation procedure for the logit model is no longer the familiar ordinary least squares. Instead, a procedure called maximum likelihood must be used. In this section, the general idea of maximum likelihood estimation is explained, along with the resulting characteristics of the estimators.

Maximum Likelihood Estimation

Maximum likelihood estimators are ones that would generate the observations in a particular sample most often. In order to use maximum likelihood, one must first establish (or assume) the probability function that generates the observations. In the case of logit estimation, the process begins with the original logit probability distribution. Recall, from equation (7.4), with the logit distribution, the probability of an event occurring is:

$$Prob\ (Y = 1) = 1/[1 + e^{-(B_0 + B_1X)}].$$

With some algebraic manipulation, the probability of an event not occurring can be derived as:

$$Prob\ (Y = 0) = 1 - Prob(Y = 1) = 1/[1 + e^{(B_0 + B_1X)}]. \tag{7.8}$$

The sample contains observations of ones and zeros (either the event did or did not occur). If one assumes that each observation is independent of all others, then the probability of observing a particular sample can be represented by the multiplication of the probabilities of occurrences and nonoccurrences. Assume that the observations are ordered with the occurrences (ones) first and the nonoccurrences (zeros) second. The sample size is T. Then the likelihood function is:

$$L = Prob\ (Y_1, Y_2, Y_3, \ldots, Y_T)$$
$$= P_1, P_2, \ldots, P_z, (1 - P_{z+1}), (1 - P_{z+2}), \ldots, (1 - P_T). \qquad (7.9)$$

It is generally the logarithm of the likelihood function that is maximized because the mathematics are easier. This is because the logarithm of a product of probabilities is equal to the sum of the logarithm of the probabilities, and it is easier to perform the maximization procedures with a sum than with a product. Still, when the logit probabilities are substituted into the above equation, and the maximization procedure is performed, the series of simultaneous equations that results is nonlinear. These nonlinear equations are difficult to solve and often must be done iteratively with a computer.

Maximum likelihood estimators have some good characteristics, although these hold for large rather than small samples. They are consistent, meaning that as the sample size increases to infinity, the estimate centers more and more on the true population parameter. In large samples, they are also efficient (have smaller variances compared to other consistent estimators). Practically, these characteristics of maximum likelihood estimators imply that we know how good they are in large samples but we know less about their small sample properties.[10]

Hypothesis Tests

Hypothesis tests follow principles similar to those used with ordinary least squares estimators. The standard errors of the estimated coefficients are used to establish *t* ratios and to test for the significance of individual coefficients. A test that corresponds to the *F* test for the significance of the entire relationship can be executed; it is based on the likelihood function and is generally produced by computer packages. This same test can be used for subsets of variables, such as a set of dummy variables. Unfortunately, there is no good statistic that corresponds to the ordinary least squares R^2. Instead, some analysts use the estimated probabilities to establish whether a predicted observation is closer to 1 or 0. Then, the predicted occurrences (ones) and nonoccurrences (zeros) are compared to the actual occurrences and a ratio of "correct" estimates is found. There is, however, no standard for judging whether the percentage of correct estimates is high or low.

Example 7.2 illustrates the use of the logit model for estimation. Pay particular attention to the way in which the estimated coefficients are interpreted since, as we have seen, some manipulations must take place before the effects of changes in independent variables on probabilities of occurrence can be detected.

EXAMPLE 7.2 HOSPITAL COMPETITION FOR SPECIALIZED SERVICES AND LOGIT ESTIMATION

One theory of hospital behavior assumes that hospitals compete for physicians because physicians refer (admit) patients. If this is true, then in the absence of financial constraints, one expects to see hospitals competing via availability of specialized services, such as mammography units, emergency room services and cardiac catheterization units, because these services are important to physicians. One would expect to see increases in the probability of a hospital having a specialized service when nearby, competitor, hospitals have such services. Harold Luft et al., tested this hypothesis with 1972 sample data for 3,584 hospitals.[11] The authors estimated equations explaining the probability of having a specialized service as a function of the percent of neighbors within a 5-mile radius that have the service, plus several control variables. The equations were logit ones, estimated using maximum likelihood; results for mammography units are presented in Table 7.2.

Questions:

a. What sign on percentage of neighbors within 5 miles with a mammography unit would be consistent with the hypothesis that hospitals compete for doctors with the availability of specialized units?

b. What is the approximate effect of the percentage of neighbors within 5 miles with a mammography unit on the probability of a hospital having a mammography unit itself?

c. What is $-2 \log L$?

Discussion:

a. A positive sign, since this would indicate that when a higher percentage of neighbors have a unit, a hospital is more likely to have one also, presumably so that other hospitals do not compete away the affiliation of doctors who want units available to their patients.

b. The effect is an interactive one and can be determined only with the knowledge of the estimated coefficient and a probability for the dependent variable. The approximate effect of a unit change of an independent variable, such as the percent of neighbors within 5 miles with a unit, on the dependent variable, probability of an individual hospital having a unit, equals: $b(P)(1 - P)$, where b is the estimated coefficient, and P is the chosen probability of having the unit. A common P to choose is the mean of the sample. The effect of a one percentage point change in the percent of neighbors within 5 miles with mammography units on the probability of a given hospital having such a unit, measured at the mean of the percent of hospitals having units in the sample is, approximately: $(.008)(.55)(.45) = .00198$. Thus a hospital with 50% of its neighbors having such units compared to a hospital with none of its neighbors having such units will have a 9.9% higher probability of having a unit. $(.00198)(50) = .099 = 9.9\%$.

TABLE 7.2

Logit Regression Results for Probability of Hospital Having a Mammography Unit

Independent Variables	Dependent Variable (Probability of Hospital Having A Mammography Unit)	
	Coefficient	Standard Error
Percent Neighbors within 5 Miles with Unit	.008	.002
Number of Neighbors within 5 Miles	.252	.215
1 Neighbor	.216	.196
2-4 Neighbors	.075	.184
5-10 Neighbors	-.085	.196
50-99 Beds	1.167	.132
100-199 Beds	2.184	.137
200-299 Beds	2.948	.179
300-399 Beds	3.203	.225
> 400 Beds	4.006	.270
Public Hospital	-.250	.100
For-profit Hospital	.213	.162
Residents per Bed	-1.270	.864
Population per Square Mile	-0.014	.009
Income per Capita	.111	.087
MD's per Capita	191.124	72.096
Inpatient Days per Capita	-.320	.081
Northeast	.364	.138
North Central	.176	.113
West	-.145	.132
Intercept	-2.219	.387
T	3584	
-2 Log L	3,651.46	

Source: Harold S. Luft, James C. Robinson, Deborah W. Garnick, Susan C. Maerki and Stephen J. McPhee, "The Role of Specialized Clinical Services in Competition Among Hospitals," *Inquiry* 23 (1986), Table 2.

c. $-2LogL$ can be converted to a statistic that can be used to test the significance of the entire relationship, analogous to the F statistic in an OLS regression. The new statistic, CS, follows, approximately, the chi-square distribution with K degrees of freedom. The statistic CS is computed as follows: $CS = (-2LogL_0) - (-2LogL)$. Table 7.2 provides the value of $-2LogL$, but the value of $-2LogL_0$ must be calculated as follows: $-2\text{Log}L_0 = N0[\text{Log}\,(N0/T)] + N1[\text{Log}\,(N1/T)]$, where $N0$ is the number of observations where the dependent variable equals zero, $N1$ is the number of observations where the dependent variable equals one, and T is the sample size. If CS is greater than the cutoff chi-square value at a stated significance level with K degrees of freedom, the entire relationship is significant.

ESTIMATING THE PROBIT MODEL

The probability distribution underlying the probit model is the cumulative normal one. As shown in Figure 7.2, using the probit instead of the logit probability distribution leads to slight differences in the tails of the estimated curves. There is generally no way to choose between the probit and logit model a priori. Instead, the choice is made on the basis of the availability of computer packages and perhaps the familiarity of the user with one rather than the other model.

The probit model, like the logit model, is estimated using the maximum likelihood technique. The estimation is more complex because the use of the normal rather than the logit distribution in the likelihood function leads to a series of equations that are more difficult to solve. The equations are solved on the computer, and the resulting parameters define the "Z" index that was described with equation (7.7). Hypothesis testing is the same as for that of the logit model.

As with the logit model, the interpretation of effects of changes in the dependent variables are not straightforward. Instead, the Z index must be manipulated before the effects of independent variables can be interpreted as changes in probabilities of occurrence of the dependent variable. Specifically, the effect of a unit change in an independent variable on the change in the probability of occurrence of the dependent variable is:

$$B_1[f\,(Z)]. \tag{7.10}$$

(B_1) is the coefficient in the probit equation with the Z index as the dependent variable and $f(Z)$ is the value of the standard normal density function for a specified value of the Z index.

Return once again to the lung cancer and cardiovascular disease example—this time suppose the probit model is used and the following hypothetical equation is estimated:

$$Y = -3.0 + .5X. \tag{7.11}$$

Y is the estimated Z index and X is the average number of packs of cigarettes smoked per week since age 20. Suppose we wish to evaluate the effect on the probability of death from lung cancer or cardiovascular disease after age 60 from an increase in one pack of cigarettes smoked per week for an individual who has smoked an average of two packs per week since age 20. The effect will be as indicated in equation (7.10): $b_1[f(Z)]$. Specifically, in this example: $b_1 = .5$; $f(Z) = f[-3.0 + .5(2)] = f(-2.0) = .023$; and $b_1[f(Z)] = .5(.023) = .0115$. That is, smoking an additional pack of cigarettes per week from age 20 increases the probability of death from lung cancer or cardiovascular disease after age 60 by .0115 or 1.15 percentage points.[12]

Example 7.3 shows how the probit model can be used in practice. Pay particular attention to how the effect of a unit change in an independent variable is calculated.

EXAMPLE 7.3 MENTAL HEALTH CARE UTILIZATION, INSURANCE COVERAGE, AND PROBIT ANALYSIS

In an effort to determine how mental health care utilization is influenced by various insurance plan provisions, Randall Ellis and Thomas McGuire used Massachusetts Blue Shield claims data for 1,653 new users to estimate an equation for the probability of exceeding the maximum mental health coverage in the first year of utilization.[13] The probability of exceeding the maximum was estimated as a probit equation using the maximum likelihood technique. The results are presented in Table 7.3.

Questions:

a. Which coefficients are significant at the 10% or better level?
b. How would you interpret the effect of an additional year of age on the probability of exceeding the $475 limit? (ii) How would you interpret the effect of the first month of treatment on the probability of exceeding the limit?
c. What is the log likelihood?

Discussion:

a. The coefficient divided by its standard error yields a z-statistic that is distributed according to the standard normal distribution. The two-tailed cutoff values for the z-statistic at 10%, 5%, and 1% significance are 1.645, 1.960, and 2.567, respectively. Dividing the coefficients by their standard errors, one sees that age ($z = 1.96$), psychologist ($z = 2.20$), informal provider ($z = 2.30$), and month of first treatment ($z = 5.15$) are all significant at the 10% level or better.
b. The effect of a change in an independent variable on the probability of exceeding a limit equals: $b[f(Z)]$, where b is the estimated probit coefficient and $f(Z)$ is the value of the standard normal density function for a specified value of the Z index. The Z index is what is estimated by the probit model. A common value to specify for the Z index is the one that is obtained from the estimated probit equation when the mean of each independent variable is substituted in the equation. That is the method followed here. The Z index calculated at the means of the X variables equals $-.42$. The value of $f(Z)$ is .337. Thus the effects of one-unit

TABLE 7.3
Probit Regression Results for Probability of Exceeding Mental Health Insurance
Coverage Limit

Independent Variables	Dependent Variable (Probability of Exceeding $475 Limit In First Year of Use, 1981-82)		
	Coefficient	Standard Error	Mean
Demographics			
Age	-.0049	.0025	31.397
Sex (1 = Female)	.034	.072	0.578
Individual Coverage	.158	.121	0.135
Numbers of Individuals in Family Making Claims	-.0052	.0263	3.388
Provider Types (Psychiatrist Omitted)			
Psychologist	-.165	.075	0.513
Social Worker	-.060	.203	0.034
Informal Provider	-.336	.146	0.082
Health Status			
Log Previous Medical Visits	.025	.018	2.470
Previous Admissions	-.110	.126	0.139
Mental Health Diagnosis (Adjustment Reaction Omitted)			
Depressive Neurosis	.045	.097	0.186
Psychosis	.124	.172	0.043
Substance Abuse	.262	.543	0.004
Other Mental Health	-.056	.084	0.304
Nonmental health	-.449	.331	0.018
Other			
Time Trend	-.057	.070	2.618
Month of First Treatment	-.067	.013	5.975
Constant	.334	.234	1.000
Sample Size	1,653		
Log Likelihood	-876.23		

Source: Randall P. Ellis and Thomas E. McGuire, "Cost Sharing and Patterns of Mental Health Care Utilization," *The Journal of Human Resources* 21 (1986), Table 3.

changes in the independent variables are—(i) Age: −.0049 (.337) = .0017 or a .17 percentage point decline in the probability of exceeding the limit; (ii) Month of first treatment: −.067 (.337) = −.0226 or a 2.26 percentage point decline in the probability of exceeding the limits.

c. The log likelihood is Log$L$. It can be used to calculate a statistic, CS, which follows, approximately, the chi-square distribution. The statistic, CS, can be used to test for the significance of the entire relationship (similar to the F statistic in an OLS regression). See the discussion in Example 7.2, part c, for details on the calculations.

CONCLUSIONS

This chapter has addressed the problem of estimating models where the dependent variable is qualitative. While ordinary least squares can be used in such circumstances, the results produce heteroskedasticity and inconsistency and the coefficients do not necessarily fall within the 0 to 1 range. The logit and probit models are alternatives that yield results that are better statistically but are somewhat more difficult to interpret. It is particularly important to note that the estimated coefficients of the various models have different meanings. The coefficients of the linear probability model are the most straightforward: a unit change in the independent variable is associated directly with a change in the probability of the dependent variable and the size of that change is equal to the estimated coefficient. In the logit model, the coefficient shows the change in the logarithm of the odds of an occurrence. And in the probit model, the coefficient shows how the probability changes when a cumulative normal index changes by one unit.

Sometimes, qualitative choice models will involve dependent variables that are polytomous—where there are three or more choices. Extensions of the logit model can be used in estimation.

Models with discrete dependent variables are becoming more common as micro data sets and public opinion surveys become more available for analysis and as computer software is more available. Sometimes the simpler ordinary least squares technique will be satisfactory for estimation. Many analysts use it as a first approximation. When more precise results are needed, logit and probit analysis are called upon.

SUMMARY OF CHAPTER 7

1. Qualitative choice models, where the *dependent* variable is categorical, have become increasingly important in public management and decision making.

2. Qualitative choice models can be interpreted as probability models, where one

is attempting to determine how the probability of making a choice changes when the value of an independent variable changes.

3. When the dependent variable is dichotomous, the most straightforward model is the linear probability one. OLS is used to estimate an equation with a 0 or 1 dependent variable. The interpretation of the slope coefficient shows the change in the probability of the dependent variable when the independent variable changesby one unit. The problems with the model are that the predicted dependent variable can fall outside the 0 to 1 range and the error term is heteroskedastic, causing the standard errors to be biased.

4. Two functional forms that remedy the linear probability model's problem of having predictions fall outside the 0 to 1 range are the logit and the probit forms. Both are S shaped, such that they fall within the 0 to 1 range.

5. The logit form estimates the logarithm of the odds of an event occurring relative to it not occurring. The equation is estimated with a maximum likelihood technique. The resulting equation is an interactive (nonadditive) one, so the interpretation of the effect of a unit change in an independent variable on the dependent variable requires specification of a beginning probability for the dependent variable.

6. The probit model uses a slightly different functional form than the logit model. It differs in the tails, near Y values of 0 and 1. It is also estimated using a maximum likelihood technique and again the interpretation of the effect of a unit change of an independent variable on the probability of the dependent variable requires both the estimated slope coefficient, and in this case, the value of the cumulative standard normal distribution for an estimated Z index.

8

Some Advanced Topics: Pooled Time-Series and Cross-Section Analysis, Lagged Variables, Missing Data, Time-Series Analysis, and Multiequation Systems

The first seven chapters covered single equation estimation. The data were implicitly complete and uncomplicated and the models underlying the regression equations were causal. In this chapter, we look at some of the complications that arise when these implicit assumptions are not met.

The first section discusses how to use data sets that contain both cross-section and time-series observations. These data sets potentially provide a rich amount of information, but sometimes adjustments in estimation techniques need to be made. The second section looks at models where some of the independent variables are lagged one or more time periods. The third section discusses various ways to use data sets where some observations for some of the variables are missing. The fourth section outlines what is meant by time-series analysis and how it differs from, and is similar to, regression analysis. In this section, some of the more common techniques used in time-series analysis are described intuitively. The final section explains multiequation systems — why they are important in causal modeling, what problems they present for regression estimation, and some of the simpler techniques for overcoming the estimation problems. The study of time-series analysis and multiequation estimation have filled books on their own. Here, the purpose is to introduce you to what they are, to explain the reasons for their use, and to provide an intuitive understanding of some of the technical aspects involved in estimating their parameters. For all the topics, the primary goal in this chapter is to explain what and why problems can develop and to point a direction to solutions.

USING POOLED CROSS-SECTION AND TIME-SERIES DATA

Occasionally one will have available data on states, cities, individuals, organizations, and so forth, that include observations over time as well as across units. These data can be valuable if the observations in the time-series alone or the cross-section alone would be too small to yield reliable results. Even if one set, time-series or cross-section, would be large enough, the efficiency of the estimators can be increased with yet more data. As an example of a possible model where cross-section and time-series data would be available, think about the determinants of a city's "financial health." Financial analysts have spent considerable time trying to define financial health, and although one single measure is considered insufficient, such variables as the ratio of debt to tax base, expenditures per capita, percent of people in poverty, and measures of the use of available revenue capacity are commonly proposed.[1] Independent variables that might influence how these measures of financial health move include such data as income, property wealth, education, health of population, and unemployment. Regression analyses that use one or more of the above dependent variables would need as data either a time-series on one city or a cross-section of several cities. If both of these were available, then one could combine the data into a pooled cross-section, time-series set.

Other possible examples where pooled cross-section, time-series data would be useful are in modeling the determinants of various types of governmental expenditures (such as medicaid, education, or transportation) in the states; or looking at earnings, consumption patterns, or child rearing behavior of individuals. In these examples, data might be available both over time and across units (states or individuals).

If the use of a pooled data set seems appropriate, then the analyst must determine the best way to use the data. The simplest procedure is to use ordinary least squares on the expanded data set. This is unlikely to take into account some important things happening with the model. For example, over time, the cross-section intercept may change, or across units the time-series intercept may differ, or both may happen. More serious, from the point of view of correction, autocorrelation and/or heteroskedasticity in the time-series or cross-section data may be present. Let's look briefly at how to accommodate some of the less straightforward presentations of the pooled data.[2]

Shifting Intercepts

Consider a two variable model with both cross-section (subscript i) and times-series (subscript t) dimensions, where $i = 1, \ldots, N$, and $t = 1, \ldots, T$:

$$Y_{it} = B_0 + B_1 X_{it} + E_{it}. \tag{8.1}$$

Now suppose one thinks that the intercept shifts both across observations (cross-section) and over time (time-series). This can be accommodated by adding a series of dummy variables, so that the equation looks as follows:[3]

$$Y_{it} = B_0 + B_1 X_{it} + R_2 C_{2t} + R_3 C_{3t} + \cdots + R_N C_{Nt}$$
$$+ Z_2 S_{i2} + Z_3 S_{i3} + \cdots + Z_T S_{iT} + E_{it}, \qquad (8.2)$$

where $C_{it} = 1$ for the ith individual, 0 otherwise, and $S_{it} = 1$ for the tth time period, 0 otherwise. C_{1t} and S_{i1} are omitted to permit the equation to be estimated, as discussed in Chapter 5. This method of estimation, called the fixed effect model, allows the intercept to differ for each observation. One can test to see if the dummies as a group are signficant using the F test described in Chapter 3. The test can be done for the cross-section and time-series dummies separately, or for both groups together.

It is possible that the slopes as well as the intercepts shift over time and/or across units. One could add a series of multiplicative variables (dummies times each independent variable) for every individual or time period to account for the slope differences, but degrees of freedom would start to decline quickly. If a great many intercepts and slopes differ, then several separate models should be run.

It is also possible to imagine a model where the intercepts differ, but in a stochastic way, so that each intercept has a random element attached to it. This is called a random effects model. It is possible to estimate a random effects model using an error term that combines the randomness for the entire model with randomness for the cross-section and the time-series elements as well.

Example 8.1 discusses the use of dummy variables versus random errors in a pooled time-series, cross-section estimation of children's literacy rates in Alabama schools.

EXAMPLE 8.1 ANALYZING SEGREGATED SCHOOLS WITH REGRESSION ANALYSIS

Robert Margo used regression analysis to show that had Alabama schools been separate but truly equal, from 1920 through 1940, literacy rates for black children relative to white children would have been significantly improved.[4] Margo collected pooled cross-section, time-series data by Alabama counties for three census years (1920, 1930, and 1940) for blacks and for whites and estimated a model of the following general form:

Achievement = f (student motivation, school inputs, socioeconomic variables).

Achievement was measured as the literacy rate of children and young adults, aged 7 to 20; it was transformed to a logarithm in the regression analysis. Separate

TABLE 8.1

Random Effects and Fixed Effects Regression Results for Black Children's Literacy Rates

	Dependent Variable			
	(Logaritm of Literacy Rate for Black Children)			
	Random Effects		Fixed Effects	
Independent Variables	Coefficient	t-score	Coefficient	t-score
Student Motivation				
Log Average Daily Attendance, Grades 1 through 6	0.15	2.93	0.13	2.09
School Inputs				
Log. Length of School Year, In Days	0.25	6.62	0.18	3.54
Log. per Pupil Expenditure on Teachers' Salaries per School Day	0.48	2.32	0.12	0.40
Log. per Pupil Value of School Capital	-0.04	0.38	-0.16	1.53
Percent One-Teacher Schools	-0.03	0.74	0.03	0.52
Socioeconomic Inputs				
Log. per Capita Income	0.05	2.10	0.03	0.40
Percent Owning Home	0.30	3.05	0.26	0.76
Constant	-1.29	6.17	-1.23	5.03
T	180		180	

Source: Robert A. Margo, "Educational Achievement in Segregated School Systems: The Effects of Separate-but-Equal," *American Economic Review* 76 (1986), Table 2.

equations for blacks and whites were estimated. Also, a fixed effects equation with dummy variables for counties and for census years was contrasted with a random effects equation, where there were county, year, and general error terms. A random effects equation and a fixed effects equation for blacks are shown in Table 8.1.

Questions:

a. (i) What is the unit of analysis in these regressions? (ii) What is the difference, in concept, between the fixed effects and the random effects model? (iii) In the regressions reported in Table 8.1, does the model seem to make a difference?

b. For the random effects model, interpret the coefficients on length of school year, expenditures, and per capita income.

c. Can you think of ways the numbers in these regressions could be used to quantify the effects of separate, but unequal schools?

Discussion:

a. (i) The unit of analysis is the county in a particular year. (ii) The fixed effects model assumes the intercepts vary by a constant nonrandom amount depending on the year and county. The random effects model assumes the intercepts vary by a stochastic amount, or intuitively by a fixed amount plus a random error. (iii) The fixed effects model has fewer significant variables, two versus five, excluding the constant. Of the significant variables in both equations, none differs in sign, and only length of school year seems to differ much in magnitude (.25 versus .18).
b. Holding constant changes in other variables, a one-percent increase in the number of days in the school year, would result in one-fourth of a percent (.25) increase in the literacy rate. Holding all else constant, a one percent change in per pupil teacher salaries would result in a half percent (.48) increase in the literacy rate. *Ceteris paribus,* a one percent change in county per capita income would result in a 5/100 of a percent (105) increase in the literacy rate.
c. One could take the difference in the school inputs for white and black pupils ($X_w - X_b$, where X is the input and w and b represent whites and blacks, respectively) and multiply this difference by the regression coefficient for black children. The resulting number would show how an increase in inputs from the black to the white level would influence black children's literacy. If this resultant number were divided by the difference in the literacy rates for whites and blacks ($L_w - L_b$), then the percentage change in the literacy gap due to a change in the inputs would result. The author performed calculations such as these for each census year and for a number of inputs and sociological factors. Some of his results, using the random effects model are shown in Table 8.2. While the increase in total school inputs to

TABLE 8.2
Percentage Changes in Literacy Gap for Black Children

Variable (From Black Level to White Level)	EFFECT (Percentage Change in Literacy Gap)		
	1920	1930	1940
Length of School Year	30.7	31.3	13.0
Teachers' Salaries	17.0	20.5	41.6
Total School Inputs	47.7	51.8	54.6
Per Capita Income and Home Ownership	40.6	57.3	106.4

Source: Robert A. Margo, "Educational Achievement in Segregated School Systems: The Effects of Separate-but-Equal," *American Economic Review* 76 (1986), Table 3.

black separate schools would have increased literacy by between 48% (47.7) and 55% (54.6), depending on the year, the equalization of per capita income and home ownership would have helped immensely as well (between 41% and 106%, depending on the year). School inputs can be more quickly changed than per capita income and home ownership, but as in all school outcome research, these results show that schools alone will be hard pressed to completely redress the problems of the general society.

LAGGED VARIABLES

The logic of a causal model will often indicate that an independent variable should be "lagged" one or more time periods. This means that the value of the independent variable is specified one or more periods previous to when the dependent variable is specified. For example, models of governmental budgeting that use spending on individual functions (such as police, education, health) as the dependent variables often include appropriate environmental variables (such as crime rates, income levels, high school dropout rates, age of population) as independent variables. Logically, these independent variables will only have an influence on *future* years' expenditures, since it takes a while for governments to perceive and document trends in the environmental variables.

An example of how a model with a one-year lag might be specified is:

$$Y_t = B_0 + B_1 X_t + B_2 X_{t-1} + E_t. \tag{8.3}$$

The independent variable, X, is included both for the current year (t) and the previous year ($t - 1$). If Y were police expenditures per capita in 1988 and X were the crime rate, the crime rate would be included for both 1988 and 1987.

Sometimes, a priori logic indicates that the effect of the lagged variable occurs gradually over time. In such a model, a series of lagged variables would be included and, in the extreme, an infinite number of lags would be included:

$$Y_t = B_0 + B_1 X_t + B_2 X_{t-1} + \ldots + B_\infty X_{t-\infty} + E_t. \tag{8.4}$$

While models with lags often make conceptual sense, they can present estimation problems. First, if there are many lags, then the degrees of freedom lost from estimating additonal coefficients can be large. Second, since all of the lagged variables are the same except for the time period of their occurrence, troublesome multicollinearity can occur. The solution to both of these problems is to reduce the number of lags by making a priori specifications on how they behave. Two of these specifications are briefly described.

Specifications of Lags

One specification is the *geometric distributed lag*, where the lagged variables are weighted such that the weights decline as the lags become more distant in the past. This means that the largest influence on the dependent variable will be the independent variable that is most recent in time. The geometric lag specification allows the calculation of the permanent effect of a unit change in the lagged independent variable on the dependent variable. It also allows one to identify the number of time periods before half of the total effect of a unit change in the independent variable on the dependent variable will occur.

A second common specification that is more general than the geometric is the *polynomial distributed lag*. Again, the lagged variables are weighted, but now the weights are described by continuous polynomial equations. This formulation, as contrasted with the geometric distributed lag, permits more flexibility. Specifically, on the rare occasion when an analyst wishes to allow lags that are farther away in time to have greater impacts than lags that are more recent in time, the polynomial distributed lag can do this. The polynomial distributed lag can also allow more recent lags to have larger impacts.

Using Lags To Test for Causality

Lags can sometimes be used to test for causality in time-series models. For example, it could be postulated that the school dropout rate, lagged, would influence public spending on education. However, one would also expect (or at least hope) that educational spending would influence the dropout rate. Thus, the causality between spending and dropout rates might go in both directions. To test the direction of the causality, one could regress educational spending on dropout rates that are lagged into the past and "lagged" into the future. The model, in general, would look as follows:

$$Y_t = B_0 + B_1 X_t + B_2 X_{t-1} + \cdots + A_1 X_{t+1} + \cdots + E_t. \qquad (8.5)$$

The Y variable is educational spending and the X variable is the dropout rate. An F test on the B coefficients, as a group, would indicate if dropout rates, in the past, influenced spending in the future. An F test on the A coefficients, as a group, would indicate if dropout rates, in the future, influenced educational spending in the past. If the B coefficients were significant, this would imply that changes in dropout rates affect changes in spending. If the A coefficients were significant, this would imply that the causality runs from spending to dropout rates, since, of course, future dropout rates cannot affect past spending. Such a finding would imply the need for a simultaneous model, where spending and dropout rates influence each other.

MISSING DATA

At times, values for some of the variables for selected observations will be missing. The.e are a number of ways to resolve this missing data problem, and the most desirable will depend on the particular circumstances. The easiest solution is to drop the observations where any piece of data is missing and to run the regression with the remaining observations. The problem with this solution is that the dropped observations may not be random, and, thus, the regression estimates will be biased. In addition, even if the dropped observations are random, the sample size will be reduced when observations are dropped, and this will increase the standard error of the estimated coefficients.[5]

A second solution is to use the mean value for the variable in observations where there are data in order to replace the values of variables that are missing. While in a two variable model this will produce a result identical to dropping the observations altogether, in the three or more variable model the results can differ so that standard errors are estimated more efficiently.

Unfortunately, if the dropped observations with missing data are not random, then using the mean of the variables for existing observations will cause bias. And usually missing data will not be random, but rather will follow some pattern. For example, in a survey of child care expenditures by working parents, accurate observations for high income parents may be missing because these parents are reluctant to reveal their income. In such a case, using average income from nonmissing observations will mitigate the positive correlation between expenditures and income.

A solution to the missing data problem when randomness cannot be assumed is to look for proxy variables that are correlated with the one that is missing, but uncorrelated with the error term in the equation. A popular way of doing this is to use what are called *instrumental variables*. Instrumental variables can be obtained by regressing the available observations of a variable on other independent variables that are correlated with it, but not with the error term in the equation.

A simple example of the instrumental variable approach uses time-series data. Assume the following two variable model:

$$Y_t = B_0 + B_1 X_t + E_t. \tag{8.6}$$

If the observations on Y and X are yearly, and some of the observations for the X variable are missing, it is possible to regress the existing observations for X on time, and then to use the estimated equation to predict values of X that are missing. Thus, the estimated equation for the X variable would look as follows:

$$X_t = A_0 + A_1 t + U_t, \tag{8.7}$$

where t equals time and U_t is a random variable. Equation (8.7) would then be used to predict missing values of X by plugging in the appropriate time period for the missing values as an independent variable and using the estimated A coefficients.[6]

TIME-SERIES ANALYSIS

Time-series analysis is used to forecast the values of a dependent variable into the future. The analysis is based on the patterns of the past behavior of the dependent variable, rather than on a causal relationship between the dependent variable and a group of independent variables. Time-series analysis is a sophisticated way to extrapolate a series of data; it differs in concept from regression analysis because there is no causality assumed.

Why Choose Time-Series Models

Intuitively a causal model seems superior to the reproduction of a past pattern of data. Why, then, would one choose time-series analysis over regression analysis? First, an appropriate causal model may be unavailable—that is, perhaps little is known about the causes of movements in the dependent variable. Second, even if a causal model is available, the data to estimate it may not be. Or, if the data are available, the estimation may not work. The standard errors of the coefficients may be so large that all the variables are insignificant. Finally, even a well-estimated model can cause problems if the independent variables cannot themselves be forecasted. After all, to use a regression model for forecasting into the future, the independent variables must take on their future values. In most cases, this will require that those independent variables be forecasted themselves, and this is seldom an easy task.

Two Classes of Time-Series Models

There are two general classes of time-series models—those that are deterministic and those that are stochastic. Every series of data will contain some element of randomness, but deterministic models do not take this into account. Instead, the deterministic models use *relatively* simple methods of extrapolating and smoothing the data. Many of these methods have been around for a long time and their relative ease of computation makes them useful in a wide variety of situations. Stochastic models, on the other hand, attempt to describe the random nature of the process that generated the sample data. These are more difficult to construct and use than the models that extrapolate and smooth, but there are some advantages. In particular, confidence intervals can be formed around the forecasts so that users can obtain some sense of how much faith to put in a particular projection. In the following sections a brief overview is presented of some of the better known deterministic and stochastic models.

Deterministic Time-Series Models

For purposes of explaining various types of time-series models, assume that the variable to be forecasted is Y_t, that there are T observations, that the first observation is Y_1, the second is Y_2, and the last is Y_T. Thus, the object is to forecast Y_t into future values such as Y_{T+1} and Y_{T+2}.

One simple kind of extrapolation model is a regression of Y_t on either time (t) or on itself (Y_{t-1}), as shown by the following equations.

(Y_t regressed on time)

$$Y_t = B_0 + B_1 t + E_t \qquad (8.8)$$

(Y_t regressed on itself)

$$Y_t = B_0 + B_1 Y_{t-1} + E_t. \qquad (8.9)$$

There are variations of these models, especially the one involving time, where instead of linear relationships, there can be exponential and other curved relationships. These models are simple to execute, but they often provide inaccurate predictions.

Another type of extrapolation model is one that uses what is called a moving average. For example, if the data are monthly and one wishes to forecast one month into the future, one can take the average of the previous twelve months as the forecast:

$$Y_{T+1} = \tfrac{1}{12} (Y_T + Y_{T-1} + Y_{T-2} + \ldots + Y_{T-11}).$$

Each subsequent forecast, then, eliminates the earliest data point (Y_{T-11}) and substitutes the most recent data point (Y_{T+1}). More sophisticated versions of this model weight differently the twelve data points that are averaged, for example weighting more recent points more heavily than less recent ones. Finally, seasonal, secular, and cyclical adjustments can be added to the moving average in order to adjust for predictable blips or trends that occur over the time period.

Example 8.2 illustrates the use of a simple moving average model and a regression model to forecast health care placement for the elderly.

Stochastic Time-Series Models

Stochastic models are more difficult to construct and more difficult to estimate. In turn, they often yield more accurate predictions and, at a minimum, they allow the construction of confidence intervals around the forecasts. There are two basic classes of stochastic models, ones that are stationary and ones that are nonstationary. The underlying random process that generates the variable does not change with time in the stationary model. This means that the equation depicting the time-series can be assumed to have fixed coefficients. If the series is nonstationary, then the coefficients change with time and model construction is very difficult. In practice, nonstationary processes can sometimes be transformed into stationary models. The popular stochastic time-series models are ones that apply to stationary processes.

Currently, the most popular time-series models are those that combine autoregressive and moving average components (ARMA) and, in the case of nonstationary series, that can be transformed, produce integrated autoregressive moving average models (ARIMA). The autoregressive component is where the dependent variable, Y_t, is related to itself, lagged various numbers (p) of periods. The moving average component is where the dependent variable is related to a random disturbance that goes back various numbers (q) of periods. Thus, the autoregressive, moving average model, of order (p, q) and abbreviated ARMA, looks as follows:

$$Y_t = \alpha_1 Y_{t-1} + \alpha_2 Y_{t-2} + \ldots + \alpha_p Y_{t-p} + \ldots + \delta + E_t$$
$$+ \gamma_1 E_{t-1} + \gamma_2 E_{t-2} + \ldots + \gamma_q E_{t-q}. \quad (8.10)$$

If a series is nonstationary, it can sometimes be transformed by differencing it (subtracting the value of one time period from the value of an earlier time period). The number of time periods the model must be differenced (*d*), along with the autoregressive (*p*) and moving average (*q*) order, define the ARIMA (*p,d,q,*) model.

EXAMPLE 8.2 FORECASTING DEMAND FOR LONG-TERM HEALTH CARE SERVICES FOR THE ELDERLY

An interdisciplinary group of Canadian researchers were interested in forecasting the kinds of care that a group of elderly would receive over time.[7] The ability to do this accurately would be extremely valuable to managers of long-term care programs, as well as to policy analysts concerned with ways to provide appropriate care for the elderly. The data were from a sample of elderly admitted to a newly established program of long-term care in British Columbia. Individuals were tracked over a 5-year period. There were eight possible options for care in the program—four levels of care, each possible at home or in a facility. The goal of the research was to compare alternative methods of predicting how many individuals would be in each type of care at the beginning of each year. Two of the three methods tried by the researchers are reported here—a simple version of the moving average method and a linear regression equation.[8]

The moving average method looked at each kind of care separately, and applied the previous year's growth rate in that kind of care to predict the next year's number of patients. For example, home care at the least level of care had 759 elderly people at the beginning of the 5 years (time 0) and 476 people at the end of the first year (time 1). The rate of growth (or decline in this case) over the year was −.373 or −37.3%. The prediction for time 2 (end of second year) would be 298.5 or [(1 − .373)(476)]. Each year a new growth rate, using actual numbers of elderly, was calculated and used for forecasting.

The regression model also looked at each kind of care separately. A regression equation of the following form was estimated, using four years of data. (One year was left out so that the prediction could be compared to the actual.) Log Number of Patients = $b_0 + b_1 t$, where t is the time period, 0 to 4. The regression equation using the home care patients at the least level of care was: Log Number of Patients = $6.6099 - 0.4265t$.

Questions:

a. What are the possible problems with using these two methods, as described here, for forecasting in this context?

b. What are some conceptual problems with forecasting at all in this context?

Discussion:

a. Neither the moving average nor the regression are based on enough years of data to be totally reliable. The moving average would be better if it were averaged over several years and, in this case, adjusted for clear trends. The regression would be more accurate with more than four data points. In addition, neither method takes account of the interaction between types of care. That is patients move from one type of care to another and this information should be useful and used in forecasting. Nevertheless both methods provide some information and are easy to execute. (The preferred method of the researchers, which was not reported here because it is not relevant to this text, does take account of interactions between types of care.)

b. From a management and policy viewpoint, the movement of patients must have a lot to do with policy and administrative decisions. That is, it is not a purely objective decision whether someone is placed in level 1, 2, 3, or 4 care at home or in a facility. Thus, the movements that are being forecasted mirror the particular policy and administrative decisions that were made.

Specifying the parameters of ARMA and ARIMA models is complicated. The first step involves a determination of $p, q,$ and d. This first step is an art and is often based on patterns shown by the *autocorrelation functions*. Autocorrelation functions show how data points, with various lags, are correlated. Once the degrees of differencing (d) and the number of lags (p and q) have been determined, the model's parameters are derived by minimizing an error function, similar to the one minimized in regression anlaysis. The estimation process is often nonlinear and therefore iterative. Once estimated, the ARMA or ARIMA models can be used to forecast recursively. That is, first a forecast is made one period ahead, then that forecast is used to make a forecast two periods ahead, and so on.

Stochastic time-series modeling is more difficult than deterministic time-series modeling. This brief introduction is meant to allow you to understand the basic ideas of stochastic time-series models. To use such models, more advanced texts obviously must be consulted. Example 8.3 illustrates a simple example of an ARIMA model.

EXAMPLE 8.3 HOSPITAL BEHAVIOR, FINANCIAL INCENTIVES AND A SIMPLE ARIMA MODEL

The literature on health care management presents at least two alternative models of hospital behavior. One model postulates that hospital behavior reflects physician practice patterns, or is "physician-driven"; the other model hypothesizes that hospital behavior responds directly to environmental and financial incentives, or is "hospital-driven." David Smith and Robert Pickard studied the response of Philadelphia hospitals to the introduction of new financial incentives (new prospective payment procedures or DRG's, and new tax laws, that is, TEFRA) to see which of the two models was more plausible.[9] The authors reasoned that if measures of hospital utilization changed when the financial incentives changed, then the hospital-driven model was correct. The authors looked at a number of hospital utilization measures (such as average length of stay, occupancy rates, and admission rates) from the first quarter of 1978 through the second quarter of 1985. The measures were differenced four quarters to remove seasonal variations. Then they were regressed on themselves lagged one period, and on dummy variables for the introduction of DRG payment procedures and for tax law changes. The model was an ARIMA (1, 4, 0), where the variable was differenced four quarters (4) and then lagged one quarter (1). There was no moving average component (0). For the average length of stay variable (ALOS), the equation looked as follows:

$$(\text{ALOS}_t - \text{ALOS}_{t-4}) = b_0 + b_1(\text{ALOS}_{t-1} - \text{ALOS}_{t-5})$$
$$+ b_2(\text{DRG dummy}_t) + b_3(\text{TEFRA dummy}_t).$$

The results for the average length of stay measure (ALOS) is shown below, $R^2 = .822$; (t statistics in parentheses):

$$\text{ALOS}_t = .024 + .118(\text{ALOS}_{t-1}) - .766 \text{ (DRG Dummy)}$$
$$(.584) \quad (.564) \qquad\qquad (3.706)$$
$$- .383 \text{ (TEFRA Dummy)}.$$
$$(3.296)$$

Questions:

a. Data from the first quarter of 1978 through the second quarter of 1985 provide 30 observations. The degrees of freedom $[T - (K + 1)]$ for the *t*-scores was 21. What accounts for the difference in these numbers?

b. How would you interpret the coefficient on the DRG dummy?

c. Looking at the equation presented above, would you conclude that the Philadelphia hospitals responded to the financial incentives?

Discussion:

a. The dependent variable is differenced four quarters, which means that the first four data points cannot be used. Then the first independent variable is lagged one quarter, eliminating one more data point. Thus, beginning with 30 observations and subtracting 5, leaves 25. Then, the degrees of freedom equals the 25 observations minus $(K + 1)$ or 4, or 21.

b. The introduction of the DRG payment procedures resulted in a downward shift in the average length of stay of .766 days and the coefficient was significant at the 5% level.

c. According to this equation, the hospitals did respond to financial incentives since the coefficients on both the DRG and the TEFRA dummies were negative and significant at the 5% level.

MULTIEQUATION MODELS

Multiequation models differ from single equation ones because there are two or more equations that are related, either through the dependent variables and/or through the error terms. Here, the term multiequation will be used broadly to describe three different types of models—simultaneous, recursive, and "seemingly unrelated." First, each type of model will be described. Then, some of the estimation techniques that can be used when ordinary least squares fails to provide unbiased or consistent estimators will be presented.

Types of Multiequation Models

Simultaneous Models. A simultaneous model is one in which the dependent variable in one equation is an independent variable in another equation. In other words, the dependent variables in at least two equations are determined at the same time. In such models, the dependent variables are called endogenous. The other variables are either called exogenous, or if they are lagged versions of the dependent (endogenous) variables, they are called predetermined. The spending-dropout rate example developed earlier in this chapter could be construed as a simultaneous model.[10] In order to do so, one would have to assume that the variables are measured over rather long time periods, such as a few years, and that adjustments that take place in smaller time periods are not revealed by the data. If this were not the case, then one would expect spending to be causally related to last period's dropout rates and dropout rates to be related to last period's spending. In such a case the model would not be simultaneous but rather it would be two single equation lagged variable models. There is a lesson in this explanation. Simultaneity will often result because of the time period over which data are gathered, and the existence of simultaneity can change if the time periods over which the data are collected change.

Let's develop further the spending-dropout model in its simultaneous form in order to illustrate terminology as well as estimation techniques. Suppose that the following is an expanded version of the spending-dropout model:

$$Y_{1t} = B_0 + B_1Y_{2t} + B_2X_{1t} + E_{1t} \tag{8.11}$$
$$Y_{2t} = A_0 + A_1Y_{1t} + A_2X_{2t} + A_3X_{3t} + E_{2t}. \tag{8.12}$$

Y_1 is spending per pupil; Y_2 is the dropout rate; X_1 is the community income level; X_2 is the community unemployment rate; and X_3 is the average wage rate in the community. One would expect higher spending, all else constant, if community income is higher; and a higher dropout rate if the average wage rate is higher. A higher unemployment rate might result in a lower dropout rate since the opportunity cost of school is lower. In this model, Y_1 and Y_2 are endogenous; X_1, X_2, and X_3 are exogenous; and there are no predetermined variables.

Recursive Models. A recursive model is a group of equations related hierarchically, such that the dependent variable in the first equation is an independent variable in the second equation, but not vice versa.[11] For example, analysts have tried for years to find a link between spending on schooling and earnings of individuals. If such a relationship exists, it is probably an indirect one where, for example, spending influences achievement, achievement influences years of schooling, and years of schooling influences earnings.

The following equations illustrate how the recursive model might look:

$$ACH_t = B_0 + B_1SE_t + B_2X_{1t} + B_2X_{2t} + \ldots + E_{1t} \tag{8.13}$$
$$YE_t = A_0 + A_1ACH_t + A_2X_{3t} + A_3X_{4t} + \ldots + E_{2t} \tag{8.14}$$
$$AE_t = C_0 + C_1YE_t + C_2X_{5t} + C_3X_{6t} + \ldots + E_{3t}. \tag{8.15}$$

ACH is the individual's achievement level; *SE* is the expenditures per pupil on schooling; *YE* is the individual's years of schooling; *AE* is the individual's average earnings; and the X variables are various exogenous explanatory factors. Thus, in this multiequation system, the effect of school expenditures (*SE*) on earnings (*AE*) is indirect; it works through achievement (*ACH*), and then years of schooling (*YE*).

There are no purely simultaneous effects here, and yet the equations are related to one another "recursively."

Seemingly Unrelated Models. A seemingly unrelated model is one in which the independent variables in one equation do not enter another equation and yet the equations are tied together via constraints on the error terms. A common example is the estimation of the determinants of shares of an organization's budget that are devoted to various functions. The shares must add up to 100%, and thus the error terms in the equations must sum to zero. Because the errors must sum to zero, they cannot be independently generated and the equation system is related. For example, suppose one wished to determine the shares of a state's budget devoted to three functional areas, broadly defined. The model might be represented as follows:

$$S_{1t} = B_0 + B_1 X_{1t} + B_2 X_{2t} + \cdots + E_{1t} \tag{8.16}$$

$$S_{2t} = A_0 + A_1 X_{3t} + A_2 X_{4t} + \cdots + E_{2t} \tag{8.17}$$

$$S_{3t} = C_0 + C_1 X_{5t} + C_2 X_{6t} + \cdots + E_{3t}. \tag{8.18}$$

S_1, S_2, and S_3 represent the shares of the budget for three functional areas (such as health and human resources, criminal justice, and general administration); the X's represent other exogenous variables. Since S_1, S_2, and S_3 must total to 100% (assuming all budget areas are covered), the sum of the error terms must sum to zero. This constraint on the sum of the error terms makes the equations related to one another and requires modified estimation techniques.

Estimation Problems in Multiequation Systems

If ordinary least squares is used on each equation of a multiequation system, then the coefficients may be biased and inconsistent. Recall that consistency is the large sample counterpart of unbiasedness. It says that as the sample size approaches infinity, the distribution of sample coefficient estimates collapses onto the population value of the coefficient. Consistency is a less desirable property than unbiasedness because most samples are small not large. When even consistency is missing from an estimation technique, then it is wise to consider alternative procedures.

In the simultaneous equation system, the bias occurs because the independent variables and the error terms are not independent. Refer back to equations (8.11) and (8.12). Y_1 is related to the error term E_1 in equation (8.11). Y_2 is related to Y_1 in equation (8.12) and is therefore also related to E_1. But, Y_2 is an independent variable in equation (8.11) and since it is related to the error term in that equation, its coefficient (and perhaps others as well) will be biased (and inconsistent).

In the recursive system, ordinary least squares estimators need not be biased. In fact, they will not be so, unless the error terms *across* equations are related.

Unfortunately, there are a number of reasons to suppose that the error terms will be related. For example, similar factors may be omitted from each of the equations of the recursive system and thus included in all of the error terms. Or, similar measurement errors may be present if, for example, many of the endogenous variables are derived from scaled questionnaires. While recursive systems are often estimated equation by equation using ordinary least squares, it is wise to think about whether the errors across equations really are independent of one another. Example 8.4 illustrates the estimation of a recursive model relating school spending to earnings.

In the seemingly unrelated system, as we have already noted, the error terms across equations are not independently determined. To avoid inconsistency and to improve the efficiency of the estimators, estimation techniques other than ordinary least squares are needed.

EXAMPLE 8.4 SCHOOL EXPENDITURES, EARNINGS, AND RECURSIVE MODEL ESTIMATION

While a number of analysts have studied the effects of elementary and secondary school expenditures on the achievement levels of students, few have gone further to see if there are any effects on earnings. Using survey data, John Akin and Irwin Garfinkel constructed a recursive model relating achievement orientation, verbal ability, years of schooling, school expenditures and earnings.[12] Their goals were to estimate the direct and indirect effects of school expenditures on earnings and to calculate the rates of return for blacks versus whites of additional school expenditures. The complete model is an expanded version of the one presented in equations (8.13) through (8.15). It is presented in an abbreviated form below, with the equation for earnings fully represented.

Achievement Orientation = f_1 (school expenditures, father's income, father's education, parents in lower or middle or upper income group, number of siblings, father a farmer or not).

Verbal Ability = f_2 (school expenditures, achievement orientation, father's income, father's education, parents in lower or middle or upper income group, number of siblings, father a farmer or not, age).

Years of Education = f_3 (school expenditures, achievement orientation, verbal ability, father's income, father's education, parents in lower or middle or upper income group, number of siblings, father a farmer or not, grew up in city or not, age).

Log of 5-Year Average Annual Earnings = $b_0 + b_1$(log school expenditures) + b_2 (verbal ability) + b_3 (achievement orientation) + b_4 (years of education) + b_5 (father's income) + b_6 (father's education) + b_7 (middle income dummy) + b_8 (upper income dummy) + b_9 (dummy for father a farmer) + b_{10} (dummy for grew up in city) + b_{11} (potential years of labor force experience) + b_{12} (experience squared) + b_{13} [(experience)(years of education)] + b_{14} (average annual weeks work missed).

The data used to estimate the model were obtained from a survey of 1,049 males between the ages of 30 and 55 as well as from Census and Survey of Education data from 1930, 1940, 1950, and 1960.

The estimated coefficients and t-values are shown in Table 8.3 for one independent variable (logarithm of per pupil school expenditures for blacks) on every dependent variable. The entire earnings equation for blacks is shown. All the equations in the model were estimated using ordinary least squares. Since the sample included males only, the results apply only to males.

Questions:

a. What is the direct effect of school expenditures on the earnings of blacks?
b. Could there be any simultaneity in these equations and, if so, how would the estimates be affected?
c. Why would one expect school expenditures to have a direct effect on earnings?
d. Do you think the variables should be corrected (deflated) for price changes over time or across communities?
e. How could the results be used to calculate rates of return to additional spending on education?

Discussion:

a. *Ceteris paribus,* a 1% increase in the school expenditures results in a .2129% increase in average annual earnings; or a 100% increase in school expenditures results in a 21.29% increase in average annual earnings.
b. Yes. For example, years of education may influence achievement orientation as well as vice versa. If there is this kind of simultaneity, then the model's coefficients will be biased when they are estimated using OLS.
c. The authors worried about why school expenditures should appear directly in the last equation. In theory one would expect these expenditures to work *only* indirectly, through what they are supposed to produce, such as verbal ability. One reason for including the spending directly in the earnings equation is that it may capture left-out variables, such as math ability and self-confidence, or even the per capita income of the community in which the child grew up. This per capita income variable was tested by including a proxy for that income in the earnings equation. The results changed more for whites than for blacks. In the end, the authors left as an open question why spending would and did have a direct effect.
d. The data are for different time periods; for example, the dependent variable on average annual earnings is for the 5-year period from 1968 through 1972, while the per pupil school expenditures are for the year in which the respondent was 12 years old. The data are also from different states, depending on where the respondent lived as an adult (dependent earnings variable) and where he grew up

TABLE 8.3
OLS Regression Results for per Pupil School Expenditures and Average
Annual Earnings

Dependent Variable	Independent Variable (Log. Per Pupil School Expenditures Blacks)	
	Coefficient	t-score
Achievement Orientation	.2215	1.25
Verbal Ability	.5614	2.70
Years of Education	.8096	2.61
Log. Average Annual Earnings	.2129	4.70

Independent Variable	Dependent Variable (Average Annual Earnings Blacks)	
	Coefficient	t-score
Father's Income	.00003	0.45
Father's Education	.0063	0.70
Upper Income Dummy	.1566	1.75
Middle Income Dummy	.0238	0.28
Father Farmer Dummy	.0919	1.15
Grew Up in City Dummy	-.0102	0.14
Log. School Expenditures	.2129	4.70
Achievement Orientation	.0261	2.29
Verbal Ability	.0423	3.46
Years of Education	.1109	2.69
Experience	.0698	1.73
Experience Squared	-.0007	1.23
Years of Education x Experience	-.0018	1.35
Average Weeks Worked Missed	-.0898	5.82
R^2	.36	
Sample Size	333	

Source: John S. Akin and Irwin Garfinkel, "Social Expenditures and the Economic Returns to Schooling," *Journal of Human Resources* 12 (1977), Tables 1 and A-1.

(independent variables on school expenditures, father's income, state per capita income, and so forth). The authors did deflate the variables for differences in time and for differences across communities and found that the biggest differences occurred for whites.

e. One could use the equations to predict how changes in educational spending would influence earnings. Then a rate of return could be calculated, with the additional costs being the additional school expenditures plus any lost earnings associated with more years spent in school and the additional returns being the additional earnings. This was done for whites and blacks, using all the equations (direct and indirect effects of schooling expenditures on earnings), and using just the earnings equation (direct effect only). The results were as follows:

Rate of Return to Increased School Expenditures

	Whites	Blacks
Total Effect	14%	18%
Direct Effect	14%	20%

The indirect (total) effect for blacks is lower than the direct effect because, for blacks, increased school expenditures leads to increased years of schooling, which raises costs by keeping the men out of the labor market for more years.

Reduced Form Equations

There is one way to obtain unbiased coefficient estimates from a simultaneous equation system using ordinary least squares. That way involves estimation of what are called the *reduced form* equations. Referring again to equations (8.11) and (8.12), where there are two equations and two endogenous variables, it is possible to solve for Y_1 and Y_2 in terms of exogenous variables only—that is, in terms of X_1, X_2, and X_3. The specific solutions are not shown.[13] What is important here is that two new equations that are functions of exogenous variables alone are created. These two equations can be estimated individually, using ordinary least squares, because the exogenous variables are not related to the error terms.

There are advantages and disadvantages to estimating reduced form equations. The major disadvantage is that it is generally not possible to get back to the coefficients of the structural equations.[14] Thus, one is left with the total effect of the exogenous variables on the endogenous variables, without any information on the structure that generated that effect. This is fine, if one's objective is to forecast final effects. If one wishes, however, to understand how the final changes occur and to describe the behavioral processes that generate those changes, the coefficients of the structural equations will be needed.

Estimation Techniques for Multiequation Systems

Identification of Multiequation Systems. A nonstatistical property of the equation systems must be ascertained before any estimation techniques are attempted. In particular, one must know if there is inherently enough information in the equations to obtain any estimates of the coefficients. This is called identification. A system can be under-, exactly, or over-identified. An under-identified system does not have enough information for estimation, while exactly and over-identified systems do. The exactly identified system will yield the same coefficients no matter what multiequation estimation technique is used, while the over-identified system will be sensitive to the estimation technique. As one might suspect, most equations are over-identified.

Identification depends upon the amount of information in other equations that can be used to identify the equation of interest. Perhaps it is easiest understood with the aid of a diagram. Going back to the spending-dropout rate example and assuming at first that spending is a function of a dropout rates alone and dropout rates are a function of spending alone, Figure 8.1 represents the following equations:

$$Y_{1t} = B_0 + B_1 Y_{2t} + E_{1t} \tag{8.19}$$

$$Y_{2t} = A_0 + A_1 Y_{1t} + E_{2t}. \tag{8.20}$$

Y_1 is spending per pupil and Y_2 is the dropout rate.

Spending Per Pupil

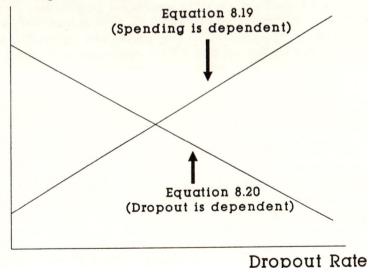

Equation 8.19
(Spending is dependent)

Equation 8.20
(Dropout is dependent)

Dropout Rate

FIG. 8.1. Spending per pupil and dropout rates

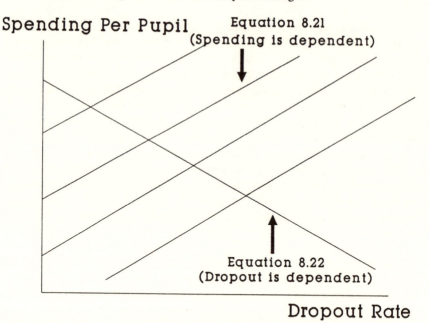

FIG. 8.2. Spending per pupil and dropout rates with exogenous variable

The data will trace out the simultaneous solution, or intersection, of the two equations, and it will be impossible to separate one equation from the other. However, if an exogenous variable is added to the spending equation (8.19), and the data provide some variation in that exogenous variable, the variation will, in essence, shift the spending curve and trace out the dropout curve. Figure 8.2 shows this process and the following depict the equations:

$$Y_{1t} = B_0 + B_1Y_{2t} + B_2X_{1t} + E_{1t} \tag{8.21}$$
$$Y_{2t} = A_0 + A_1Y_{1t} + E_{2t}. \tag{8.22}$$

What this example demonstrates is that exogenous variables, excluded from one equation but present in another, will help in identification. A rule of thumb is that in order for an equation to be identified, the number of exogenous (or predetermined) variables excluded from the equation must be greater than or equal to the number of endogenous variables included in the equation minus one. This is a necessary but not sufficient rule. Equation (8.22), but not equation (8.21), has the necessary information to be identified. In equation (8.22), the one excluded exogenous variable (X_{1t}) is equal to the two endogenous variables minus one (Y_{2t} and Y_{1t} are endogenous). Equation (8.21) cannot be identified because there are no excluded exogenous variables and two included endogenous variables (Y_{1t} and Y_{2t}).

Estimation Techniques. There are two broad classes of estimation techniques, limited information and full information. Limited information estimators are based on each equation singly, using some of the information from the other equations. Full information methods use all of the equations together to estimate all of the parameters at one time. Full information estimators are more efficient, but they are also more sensitive to how each equation is specified. An error in specification becomes magnified with full information methods. Here we discuss two limited information techniques—indirect least squares and two-stage least squares—and the general idea of full information methods.

Indirect least squares works only when an equation is exactly identified. The method takes the coefficient estimates from the reduced form equation and solves for the structural coefficients.[15] Coefficients obtained from indirect least squares are consistent, but biased. The exactly identified equation is rare, so methods other than indirect least squares are necessary.

A popular method for estimation of overidentified equations is two-stage least squares (2SLS). The first stage involves the creation of an *instrument* that correlates highly with each endogenous variable, but does not correlate with the error terms in the structural equations. The most common way to obtain such an instrument is from the reduced form equations. Recall that the reduced form equations have each endogenous variable as a function of all of the exogenous and predetermined variables, only. These exogenous and predetermined variables should not be correlated with the error terms in the structural equations. Therefore, the estimates of the endogenous variable values that are obtained from the reduced form equations should likewise be uncorrelated with the error terms. The two-stage method estimates the reduced form equations using ordinary least squares. Estimates of the endogenous variables are obtained from these reduced form equations by plugging in the values of the exogenous variables for each observation. The estimates of the endogenous variables are then used as observations in the structural equations, and ordinary least squares is used to estimate these structural equations. Thus, ordinary least squares is used twice; once to estimate the reduced form equations, and once to estimate the structural equations with the values of the instruments substituted for the endogenous variables. The resulting structural coefficient estimates are consistent, but biased. See Example 8.5 for a comparison of ordinary least squares and two-stage least squares estimation.

Two-stage least squares is probably the most popular multiequation estimation technique. Its main problem is that it does not estimate all the coefficients from all of the equations at one time. As a consequence, some information is lost, and the estimators have higher standard errors than if a full information technique is used. The full information techniques use knowledge of the error terms across equations, and this is especially valuable if the error terms are correlated. The knowledge of the cross-equation error terms is often gained from estimates of residuals in the two-stage technique. Thus, one full information system is called three-stage least squares. These methods are advanced and will not be discussed further here.

CONCLUSIONS

Multiequation systems potentially provide a wealth of information about how the world works. Most equations that one wishes to estimate are probably part of multiequation systems, and the structural coefficients of such models give basic information about causes and effects. Naturally, this information does not come cheap. The estimation techniques are more complicated and more prone to sensitivity about how the equations are specified. Using ordinary least squares on the structural equations is possible, but the coefficients will be biased and inconsistent. Two-stage least squares is a way to obtain consistent estimators, but the standard errors will often exceed those of ordinary least squares. A third alternative, a full information method, reduces the standard errors of the estimators, but is more sensitive to how the model is specified than two-stage estimators. All and all, two-stage estimation is currently a more popular estimation technique.

EXAMPLE 8.5 PHYSICIAN VISITS, USUAL SOURCES OF MEDICAL CARE, AND OLS VERSUS 2SLS ESTIMATION

Analysts have found that having a usual source of medical care is correlated with the number of visits made to a physician. It is unclear whether having a usual source (*US*) is a cause of increased visits, a consequence of increased visits, or both. John Kuder and Gary Levitz explored alternative models of determinants of physician visits to see what differences there were in the estimated coefficient on *US*.[16] Using survey data on 820 adults, they constructed several models of demand for illness-related visits to a physician. One model had *US* as an independent variable only and was estimated with OLS. Another, simultaneous model had physician visits and *US* both endogenous and was estimated with 2SLS. The instrument for *US* was estimated using a probit model, where *US* was defined dichotomously as having a regular medical source or not having one. Both models included variables for health status/need factors, predisposing factors (age, education), and enabling factors (insurance, income, and time). Results of the single equation model and of the simultaneous model are shown in Table 8.4.

Questions:

a. (i) How do the two models compare? (ii) Does the model seem to be important in determining the effect of *US* on physician visits?
b. Why do managers and analysts care about the influence of *US* on physician visits?

Discussion:

a. (i) How to compare the models depends upon the purpose for which the results will be used. For explaining variation and possibly forecasting, the R^2's are

TABLE 8.4
OLS and 2SLS Regression Results for Number of Visits to Physician

	Dependent Variable			
	(Log. Illness-Related Visits to the Physician)			
	OLS		2SLS	
Independent Variables	Coefficient	t-score	Coefficient	t-score
Perceived Need of Health Care	-.197	5.25	-.191	4.89
Number of Chronic Conditions	.179	5.41	.177	5.30
Injury Dummy	.098	1.61	.099	1.61
Hospitalization Dummy	.692	7.17	.693	7.15
Number of Disability Days	.013	6.01	.013	5.79
Age	.009	1.07	.008	0.95
Age Squared	-.0001	1.46	-.0001	1.37
Sex Dummy	.166	3.50	.168	3.50
College Dummy	-.059	-1.19	-.064	-1.29
Income per Family Member	.00001	2.55	.00001	2.55
Travel Time Plus Office Waiting	-.056	2.68	-.059	2.77
Time Between Making Appointment and Seeing Provider	.001	1.35	.0009	1.11
Ambulatory Insurance, No Deductible Dummy	.200	2.14	.215	2.29
Ambulatory Insurance, Deductible Dummy	.207	2.17	.211	2.21
Hospitalization Insurance Only Dummy	.190	1.95	.207	2.11
Usual Source, Dummy (OLS) or Instrument (2SLS)	.193	3.30	.047	2.20
Constant	.216	1.04	.288	1.39
R^2	.32		.32	
$\bar{R}^2$	.31		.30	
T	820		820	

Source: John M. Kuder and Gary S. Levitz, "Visits to the Physician: An Evaluation of the Usual-Source Effect," *Health Services Research* 20 (1985), Table 5.

important. For determining the effect of individual variables, the coefficient values, their consistency and their *t*-ratios are important. These two models have similar R^2's. Also, except for the *US* coefficient, the size of the coefficients are remarkably similar. (ii) The *US* coefficient does differ in magnitude; it is more than four times larger in the single-equation OLS model.

b. There are many reasons why people are interested in promoting ambulatory care visits, including that they can prevent more serious and costly hospitalizations and that they can help to equalize access to medical care. In addition, managers of organizations such as HMO's are interested to know the determinants of their clients' usage. If visits are influenced by having a regular source of medical care, then analysts and managers will want to know the magnitude of that effect. What this research indicates is that there is a statistically significant, positive influence of *US* on physician visits, but the magnitude of that effect may have been overestimated in the past, when two-way causation was ignored. That is, single equation models produce upwardly biased estimates of the effect of *US* on physician visits.

SUMMARY OF CHAPTER 8

1. Estimation using pooled cross-section and time-series data will often require modification of ordinary least squares estimation techniques. For example, there may be a need to add dummy variables or to correct for heteroskedasticity and/or autocorrelation.

2. Models that contain lagged variables can result in inefficient estimators and/or serious multicollinearity. Correction generally involves a priori restrictions on how the lags are specified. Two popular restrictions are geometric distributed lags and polynomial distributed lags.

3. Missing values of variables create problems when they are not random. If they are not, then it is often necessary to use some type of proxy or instrumental variable technique to estimate the values of the missing variables.

4. Time-series analysis differs from regression analysis because it eschews cause and effect relationships. Instead, it relies on replication of past patterns of the data.

5. There are two general types of time-series models—deterministic and stochastic. Typical deterministic models are moving average and simple regression. The most popular stochastic model is the ARIMA (integrated, auto-regressive, moving average) model.

6. Multiequation systems are important because they reveal the structure of cause and effect relationships. They are often difficult to estimate, because ordinary least squares, equation by equation, leads to biased and inconsistent estimators. Instead of using ordinary least squares on the structural equations, the analyst will often need to settle for reduced form coefficient estimates or use two-stage least squares.

9

An Overview

This book carries three messages. First, multivariate statistics are most meaningful when a good theoretical model precedes their use. The statistics alone cannot prove causation, and even associations will be of little help to public managers and analysts if there is no theory to explain the associations. Second, appropriate use of multivariate statistics requires a good understanding of what the assumptions behind those statistics are. If assumptions are clearly violated, then at a minimum the user should know in what directions the statistics will error. Better yet, adjustments may be possible to make the model consistent with the statistical assumptions. Third, multivariate models can be extremely helpful in the practical world of public management and analysis. It is the third point that is reemphasized in this rather brief concluding chapter.

Chapter 1 discussed three uses for multivariate statistics—for forecasting, for hypothesis testing, and for policy and program evaluation. There are several alternative ways to classify the uses, and here we emphasize the currently popular dichotomy between management-relevant and policy-relevant tools. Management-relevant generally refers to those techniques helpful in administering the *internal* workings of a particular organization—the budget, personnel, maintenance, and long-range planning functions. Policy-relevant uses refer to decisions by *outside*-bodies, such as legislatures, courts, or governmental executive agencies, that will affect whole groups of organizations. For example, the institution of a cash management system that maximizes the amount of interest earned on idle cash, while still maintaining adequate balances to pay creditors, would be a typical financial *management* decision. On the other hand, a law by a state legislature that disallowed local governments within the state from investing cash in extra-ordinarily risky instruments (specifically defined, of course) would be a *policy* decision. It is not difficult to find examples of distinctions between internal and external decisions. Nevertheless, part of the purpose of these conclusions is to demonstrate that multivariate equations estimated with one type of decision in mind will often be equally useful for the other type of decision.

How, then, can multivariate statistics, and particularly multiple regression, aid managers and policymakers? Here are a few examples.

A MANAGEMENT USE OF MULTIPLE REGRESSION: ADJUSTED PRODUCTIVITY MEASURES

Public managers are often called upon to measure the productivity of various programs they administer. Job training programs are supposed to increase the employability of trainees; how effective are they? Programs to locate absentee fathers are supposed to increase the collection rates for child support; how well do they do this? In both of these examples, the use of simple productivity figures, such as the placement rate of trainees, or the dollars of child support collected per case pursued, would be misleading if looked at over time or across organizations. This is because productivity may be directly influenced by factors outside the control of managers. Productivity figures corrected for these uncontrollable factors would provide more meaningful comparison figures. And corrected productivity figures are not simply an "academic" game, for if a legislative body decides to tie funding to productivity, managers will be quick to worry about reasons why their program may not have the highest productivity numbers.

How can productivity figures be corrected for uncontrollable factors? They can be corrected by use of multiple regression, where the productivity number is the dependent variable, and the uncontrollable as well as the controllable factors are the independent variables. Staying with the job training example, if one of the measures of productivity is the placement rate (the percentage of trainees who find jobs upon termination from the program), there are a number of factors that might influence this number. These factors are listed below as controllable and uncontrollable; the particular designation depends on the context of the program, and these particular divisions are only illustrative. Also only a few factors are mentioned in order to keep the example a simple one.

Possibly Controllable:
   Hours of Training

Possibly Uncontrollable:
   Some Beginning Characteristics of
   Enrollees Such as Sex

Suppose a regression were estimated, using data from a cross section of local training agencies, with the dependent variable "placement rate" and the independent variables "hours of training" and "sex of enrollee."[1] Suppose the results were as follows:

Placement Rate = 63.0 + 1.0 (average hours of training per enrollee)
– 0.5 (percent male enrollees).

The estimated equation could then be used to evaluate productivity across organizations by *predicting* the productivity of each program, where the organization's own values are used for uncontrollable independent variables, and the average values for all organizations are used for controllable independent variables. This predicted value could be compared to the organization's actual productivity number. If the predicted value is lower than the actual, the organization is doing better than one would expect, given the average behavior of all other organizations *and* its own uncontrollable factors. On the other hand, if the organization's predicted value is higher than its actual, then the organization is not meeting its potential. Organizations could be ranked on the basis of the differences between actual and predicted values, with high positive differences showing the best adjusted productivities.

As a hypothetical example, suppose a training organization had a placement rate of 60%. Suppose also that the value of its uncontrollable factor and the average for all organizations of the controllable factor are given below.

Uncontrollable Factor	*Actual Value for One Organization*
Percent Males	44%
Controllable Factor	*Average Value for All Organizations*
Hours of Training	30 hours

The predicted productivity rate for the one organization would be 71%, computed by plugging the values listed above into the hypothetical regression equation shown previously. [71 = 63 + 1.0(30) – 0.5(44)]. Compared to the actual rate of 60%, this organization would be underperforming.

While the regression equation methodology helps adjust productivity rates, the method is not without problems. These problems are highlighted in the next policy example, which uses actual data.

A POLICY USE OF MULTIPLE REGRESSION: ADJUSTED HOSPITAL MORTALITY RATES

In an effort to reduce the rate of growth of federally funded health insurance programs such as Medicare, the government has tried to control hospital health care costs. This effort has led many individuals to be concerned that the quality of care might erode to unacceptable levels. While it is difficult to measure quality of hospital care, one relevant indicator would be the number of deaths that occur. If hospitals were ranked on the basis of mortalities, one could see which hospitals were high and which were low. But, mortality is to some extent out of the control of any individual hospital; deaths are also due to "risk factors" of individual patients. To be meaningful, mortalities need to be risk-adjusted. One way to attempt such an adjustment is with a multivariate statistical model.

An Ideal Risk-Adjusted Mortality Model

An ideal model would be based on individual patient data.[2] The independent variables would include relevant risk factors, such as demographic characteristics (for example, sex and age) and medical indicators (for example, diagnosis and stage of progression of disease at entry to hospital), as well as hospital indicators (for example, hospital service characteristics such as staffing ratios).[3] The resulting equation would be used to predict risk-adjusted mortality probabilities, where the values of patient's actual risk factors were used and the sample average values for hospital characteristics were used. The predicted probability for each type of patient (possibly each patient, if patients are all unique) could be multiplied by the number of patients of that type entering a particular hospital. Then, the resultant numbers of deaths for each type of patient would be summed to obtain a hospital's risk-adjusted predicted number of deaths. This number could then be compared to actual deaths to see if the hospital were doing better or worse than expected.

An Actual Risk-Adjusted Mortality Model

In March of 1986, the Health Care Financing Administration, which is part of the U.S. Department of Health and Human Services, released a list of hospitals that were doing better or worse than expected in terms of mortality rates of patients covered by Medicare.[4] The list was generated from a multiple regression equation that will be described shortly. The Department did not expect to use the regression analysis to publish the list of hospitals, but was forced to do so when consumer groups requested the information under the Freedom of Information Act.[5] The analysis was, instead, intended to be used by regional Peer Review Organizations to check further into the quality of care of the listed hospitals.

The regression study was based on Medicare bills for all inpatient stays in acute-care hospitals for calendar year 1984. The unit of analysis was the hospital, although the regressions were weighted by the number of Medicare discharges. The dependent variable was "deaths per Medicare discharge." The independent variables were: average age of discharged Medicare patients, percent of all patients who were black, percent of all patients who were minority other than black, percent of all patients who were male, average length of stay for hospitals in the state, percent of cases falling into 81 specific DRG's (Diagnostic Related Groups), percent of cases in cancer-related DRG's not included in the previous 81 groups.

The regressions were also run separately for nine DRG categories. Only the regression using all the DRG categories is discussed here. Thirty-nine of the coefficients were significant at the 10% or lower level. Of these significant coefficients, 37 were DRG groups. The DRG coefficients are not shown, but the other two significant coefficients are. $R^2 = .5888$; $\bar{R}^2 = .5825$; coefficients on 37 DRG's not shown.

Deaths per Medicare discharge = .003312967 (ALOS)

$$- .000218884 \text{ (Average Age Medicare Patient)}.$$

This model of mortality rates was then used to predict the mortality rate for each hospital in the sample, using the hospital's individual values for each independent variable. The predicted rate was compared to the actual rate, and outliers, both positive and negative, were identified for further study (as well as for publication in national newspapers). There followed abundant complaints from hospitals and hospital associations, and various scholarly critiques.[6] In addition, there are statistical problems with the method of using residuals, including that some variation in death rates among hospitals is stochastic and cannot be explained by any model and that the coefficients differ from the true population coefficients because they are estimates.[7]

Do all the problems mean that this method should not be used? One expert puts the answer this way:

> Some steadfastly deny that it is possible to adjust adequately for variations in inpatient condition and to make meaningful comparisons of outcomes of care in different settings. That viewpoint comes close to denying any scientific basis to the practice of medicine, since it is based on the assumption that variations among patients make every case unique. In contrast, I believe that one can place persons into groups with similar prognoses by logical and objective use of patient attributes present on admission. This is the essence of risk-adjusting outcomes of care.[8]

In other words, the method is valid, but one must be extremely careful in its implementation. At the very least, it is difficult to argue that the use of residuals from a carefully estimated equation would move the system in the wrong direction.

MANY USES, NOT SO MANY DISTINCTIONS

One could go on for a very long time enumerating uses of multiple regressions and trying to organize those uses by their policy or management emphasis. In the end, however, the categories of uses are not so important. A productivity study can be helpful to managers, but it can also be used by policymakers in allocating resources among competing agencies. A mortality study can be used by policymakers, but managers of individual hospitals could also review the results to help determine the controllable factors in their own hospital that decrease mortality. The worlds of policy and management weave in and out of each other; multiple regression and other multivariate techniques are useful supplements for decision makers in either world.

Appendix A

Simple Summation Operators and Expected Values

ALGEBRA OF SUMMATIONS

Expressions involving sums are often abbreviated in statistics using a summation operator (Σ). The summation operator is used in conjunction with a variable or variables that take on different values. The variable (for example, X) is subscripted (for example, X_t), with the values of the subscript representing different observations or actual values of the X variable. Thus, if there are three possible values of a variable, X_t, then the sum of these three values would be written as follows.

$$\sum_{t=1}^{3} X_t = X_1 + X_2 + X_3.$$

If there are T possible values, the sum would be written:

$$\sum_{t=1}^{T} X_t = X_1 + X_2 + \cdots + X_T$$

There are a number of rules that the summation operator follows, and a few of the more useful ones are shown here.
a) The sum of a constant:

$$\sum_{t=1}^{3} 4 = 4 + 4 + 4 = (3)(4).$$

$$\sum_{t=1}^{T} b = (T)(b).$$

b) The sum of a constant times a variable:

$$\sum_{t=1}^{3} 5X_t = 5X_1 + 5X_2 + 5X_3 = 5(X_1 + X_2 + X_3) = 5\sum_{t=1}^{3} X_t.$$

$$\sum_{t=1}^{T} bX_t = b\sum_{t=1}^{T} X_t.$$

c) The sum of the sum of two variables.

$$\sum_{t=1}^{3}(X_t + Y_t) = X_1 + Y_1 + X_2 + Y_2 + X_3 + Y_3 = \sum_{t=1}^{3} X_t + \sum_{t=1}^{3} Y_t.$$

$$\sum_{t=1}^{T}(X_t + Y_t) = \sum_{t=1}^{T} X_t + \sum_{t=1}^{T} Y_t.$$

d) The sum of a product of two variables.

$$\sum_{t=1}^{3} X_t Y_t = X_1 Y_1 + X_2 Y_2 + X_3 Y_3 \neq \sum_{t=1}^{3} X_t \sum_{t=1}^{3} Y_t.$$

$$\sum_{t=1}^{T} X_t Y_t \neq \sum_{t=1}^{T} X_t \sum_{t=1}^{T} Y_t.$$

EXPECTED VALUES

When studying population values of random variables, one is often interested in particular characteristics of their distribution. Specifically, the mean (called expected value in the population) and the variance (called variance in the population) are emphasized. In this section, which is meant as a brief introduction to the topic of expected value, discrete random variables are used to demonstrate how to represent the mean and the variance and to show a few rules of the expected value operator.

Mean = Expected Value = $E(X) = \sum_{t=1}^{T} X_t f(X_t)$,

where X_t = a (discrete) random variable, T = the total number of values of X_t, and $f(X_t)$ = probability of X_t occurring.

The expected value is, then, the sum of all values of X_t, weighted by the probability of occurrence of each value of the variable.

Variance = $E[X_t - E(X)]^2 = \sum_{t=1}^{T} [X_t - E(X)]^2 f(X_t)$.

The variance is, then, the expected value of the variable minus its mean, squared. Alternatively put, it is the sum of the variable minus its mean, squared and weighted by the probability of each value of the variable occurring.

A few rules of the expected value operator are as follows.

Where a and b are constants and X is a random variable:

$E(a + bX) = a + bE(X).$

Where X and Y are random variables:

$E(X + Y) = E(X) + E(Y).$

Where X and Y are random variables that are not independent:

$E(XY) \neq E(X)E(Y).$

Appendix B

The Pearson Correlation Coefficient

One of the simplest bivariate statistics that can be calculated is the linear correlation coefficient. It is sometimes called the Pearson correlation coefficient to distinguish it from nonparametric (no probability distribution assumed) correlation coefficients such as the Spearman coefficient. The Pearson coefficient describes the strength of the linear relationship between two variables. In particular, it answers the question, Is the variable Y linearly related to the variable X, and if it is, how closely is it related?

Figure B.1 graphically represents scattergrams for several possible correlation coefficients. Each point on a graph shows a specific value (or case or observation) of the Y variable (Y_i) and the X variable (X_i). For example, if Y represents yearly earnings and X represents years of education, Figure B.1.(d) is the most likely scatter, and the correlation coefficient is likely to be positive but less than 1.0. Figures B.1.(a) and B.1.(b) show the extreme cases of perfectly negative and perfectly positive correlations. Figures B.1.(c) and B.1.(d) show the more usual cases of negative and positive correlations that are greater than minus one and less than plus one. Figure B.1.(e) illustrates a nonlinear relationship. It is a perfect nonlinear relationship in that all the points lie on a curve. The Pearson correlation coefficient, however, will not be a perfect plus or minus one, because the Pearson correlation coefficient measures only the linear relationship between two variables.

A seemingly perfect statistic to measure the extent of the relationship between two variables would be the covariance between them (the sum of the product of X deviations and Y deviations, divided by the sample size minus one). The problem with the covariance, however, is that it is sensitive to the units in which the X and Y variables are measured. Thus, the covariance would become larger if the measurement of one of the variables were changed from years to months. To avoid

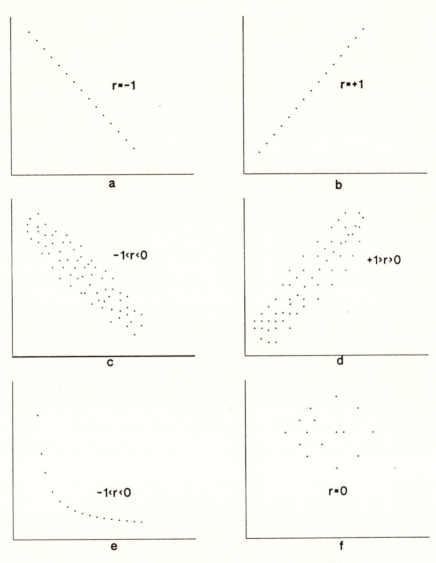

FIG. B.1. Scattergrams for several possible Pearson correlation coefficients

the problem with units of measure, the correlation is standardized: the covariance is divided by the standard deviations of X and Y. This results in a statistic that always falls between plus and minus one.

Algebra can be used to represent the estimator (formula) for the sample correlation coefficient. In general, the sample correlation coefficient equals the sample covariance between X and Y, divided by the product of the sample standard deviation of X times the sample standard deviation of Y.

$$r = \frac{\sum_{t=1}^{T}[(X_t - \bar{X})(Y_t - \bar{Y})]/(T - 1)}{\{[\sum_{t=1}^{T}(X_t - \bar{X})^2/(T - 1)][\sum_{t=1}^{T}(Y_t - \bar{Y})^2/(T - 1)]\}^{1/2}} \; .$$

The estimator is more easily represented in deviation form where $x_t = X_t - \bar{X}$, and $y_t = Y_t - \bar{Y}$. Then if we cancel the $T - 1$ terms and drop the t's:

$$r = (\Sigma xy)/(\Sigma x^2 \Sigma y^2)^{1/2}.$$

The sample correlation coefficient is always less than or equal to one and greater than or equal to minus one.

A few closing remarks on the interpretation of the correlation coefficient are in order. A correlation coefficient different from zero does not prove causation. In fact, no statistic alone can prove causation. An extreme example in the case of the correlation coefficient demonstrates the point. Suppose that the X variable is the shoe size of a young child each September and the Y variable is the Consumer Price Index (CPI) each September. There will indeed be a positive correlation but no causation. It is easy to see that there is no causation in this example. But when an analyst is using statistics to test a theory, the point may be less obvious, yet more crucial, to remember.

Correlation coefficients, while easy to calculate and interpret, are inadequate for many social science purposes. First, they do not indicate the magnitude of the effect of one variable on another. Second, unless the more complicated and less well-known multiple correlation coefficients are used, they do not control for other factors that may influence a relationship. And they do not allow specification of a dependent and independent variable. The regression model addresses all of these shortcomings and is often a necessary adjunct to the correlation coefficient.

Appendix C

Review of Hypothesis Testing for the Sample Mean

FORMING THE NULL AND ALTERNATIVE HYPOTHESES

Let's use as an example the problem of testing a hypothesis about the mean number of almonds in chocolate almond candy bars in October. Suppose you have a random sample of 27 chocolate almond bars from grocery shelves in the month of October and, as a lover of nuts, you are passionately interested in the average number of almonds in such bars. The first step in testing a hypothesis about these nuts is to state a guess about how many nuts you think each bar will contain, on average. If you are very cynical or have very little knowledge about candy bars, you might hypothesize that there is an average of zero nuts in each bar. This would be your null hypothesis. On the other hand, a little bit of experience with the world of junk food might lead you to suppose that there are somewhere around 5 almonds, on average, in each bar, in which case your null hypothesis would be 5. The null hypothesis, then, is either what you really expect or hope for (that is, an average of 5 in the candy bar case), or sometimes what you hope to reject (that is, zero). The context of the problem will usually help you decide on an appropriate null hypothesis.

The alternative to the null hypothesis can then be formulated in a variety of ways. In the candy bar example, if the null hypothesis is that there are, on average, 5 nuts per candy bar, the alternative could be that the average is not equal 5, or that the average is greater or less than 5. The alternative hypothesis will depend on how much you already know about the problem. If you have no idea whether there will be more or fewer than 5 nuts, then the alternative of "not equal to 5" will be appropriate. It is this latter hypothesis that will be used for this example. The null and alternative hypotheses would be written as follows.

> Null Hypothesis H_0: mean = 5
> Alternative Hypothesis H_A: mean $\neq$ 5.

THE LOGIC OF HYPOTHESIS TESTING

Before looking at the specifics of hypothesis testing for the mean, let's first discuss the logic of the testing. Suppose the sample of 27 bars results in a sample mean of 5.78 whole equivalent almonds. The hypothesis testing procedure will help decide if this sample mean of 5.78 is close enough to 5 to accept the null hypothesis or, alternatively, if 5.78 is far enough away from 5 so that the null hypothesis should be rejected. The answer depends on the variance of the sampling distribution of means in samples of size 27. That is, the estimated mean of 5.78 is from one sample out of an infinite number of samples of size 27. Other samples would sometimes result in different sample means. The variance of the sampling distribution of means refers to the variance of all the possible means that one could obtain from sample sizes of 27 chocolate almond bars. If the variance of the sample means in this case is small, then 5.78 is a more accurate estimate of the true population mean, and the null hypothesis that the mean of 5 is more likely to be rejected.

THE TEST STATISTIC

Let us now get more specific about testing the hypothesis that there are 5 nuts, on average, in chocolate almond bars in October. First, we need to establish a test statistic whose probability of exhibiting specific values when the null hypothesis is true can be determined. This test statistic must follow an established distribution so that the probability of specific values occurring can be determined, generally by using already published statistical tables. In the case of the sample mean, when the population variance is unknown and must be estimated from the sample, the test statistic is the standardized value of the mean. The mean is standardized to a variable with a mean of zero and a standard deviation of one by taking the sample mean, subtracting the population mean, and dividing by the sample standard deviation. This test statistic can be represented as follows:

Test statistic = (sample mean − population mean)/(sample standard deviation of the mean).

The distribution of this test statistic depends on the distribution of the sample mean ($\bar{X}$) and of the sample standard deviation. We could assume that X is normally distributed, in which case $\bar{X}$ is also normally distributed, and the sample standard deviation of the mean is distributed according to the chi-square distribution. Alternatively, the central limit theorem can be invoked to say that however X is distributed, as the sample size increases, $\bar{X}$ will be normally distributed (and, as before, the sample standard deviation of the mean will be chi-square distributed). In either case, the standardized test statistic will be distributed according to Student's t distribution—a distribution that, in the case of tests on the sample mean, will be almost identical to the normal distribution after sample sizes of around 120.

The test statistic just described is one that we can calculate except that the population mean is unknown (it is the subject of the hypothesis test). In its place, we use the population mean in the null hypothesis. Returning to the example of the chocolate almond candy bars, a sample of 27 bars resulted in a sample mean of 5.78. Suppose the sample standard deviation of the mean is .33. The test statistic, given a null hypothesis of 5 as the population mean, is then: $(5.78-5.00)/.33 = 2.36$.

SETTING SIGNIFICANCE LEVELS AND DETERMINING CUTOFF POINTS

Two last steps before the hypothesis test is complete are (i) the setting of a significance level and (ii) the determination and interpretation of cutoff points. Setting a significance level involves a determination of the chance one is willing to take that the null hypothesis will be rejected when it is actually true. There are a number of ways to think about how to establish a significance level, including the use of the costs of being wrong, or the use of traditional standards in a given area of inquiry. Here, we will settle on one of the more common choices, that is 5%. Chapter 3 contains more discussion of ways to choose levels. A significance level of 5% means that if we obtained all possible samples of size 27 from a population where the true number of almonds per chocolate bar was 5, then in 5% of those samples, the testing procedure would reject the null hypothesis of 5 nuts per bar. Rejecting the null hypothesis when it is true is called a type I error. A type II error, where the null hypothesis is accepted when it is false, it also possible, but in all but the simplest statements of alternative hypotheses, the probabilities of type II errors are impossible to state precisely. We can say, however, that reducing the probability of type I errors will increase the probability of type II errors. The only way to reduce both types of errors is to increase the sample size.

Student's t probability distribution, along with the established significance level of 5%, are used to set cutoff points. One looks at the statistical table of Student's t distribution, under the significance level and appropriate degrees of freedom, for the values of the test statistic that cut off 2.5% of the probability distribution on the positive and negative side of the mean of the test statistic (which is zero because it has been standardized). The test statistic is calculated as follows—in a sample of 27, where the significance level is 5%. The degrees of freedom, which are obtained by taking the sample size and subtracting one, are 26 in this case, and the cutoff points are plus and minus 2.056. These cutoff points mean that there is a probability of 5% that our test statistic will fall outside the boundaries of plus and minus 2.056 and, conversely, a probability of 95% that our test statistic will fall within the boundaries, when the true population mean is 5. Thus, we reject the null hypothesis of a mean of 5 if the test statistic is above plus 2.056 or below minus 2.056. In our candy bar example, the test statistic is 2.36 and so the null hypothesis is rejected. However, there is a 5% probability that we have made a type I error and rejected the null hypothesis when it is true. Also, the best we can say about the population mean at this point is that it is not equal to 5 at a 5% significance level. The way the alternative hypothesis was stated does not permit a more specific conclusion.

CONFIDENCE INTERVALS

Significance tests can be alternatively stated as confidence intervals. Instead of using the cutoff points to establish boundaries outside of which the test statistic must fall, the cutoff points are used to set boundaries that will include the true population mean with a 95% probability. After several algebraic manipulations, the confidence interval is then constructed as:

sample mean +/– sample standard deviation times cutoff point.

(A more thorough derivation of the confidence interval construction is shown in Chapter 3.)

In the candy bar example, the 95% confidence interval would be 5.78 +/– (.33)(2.056) or 5.10 to 6.46. In 95% of all possible samples of size 27, these limits would include the true population mean for almonds in chocolate bars in the month of October. Since 5 is outside the limits, the null hypothesis of a population mean of 5 almonds is rejected.

THE ALTERNATIVE HYPOTHESIS AGAIN

One final point concerns the alternative hypothesis. It is possible to specify a one-sided test where the alternative is, for example, that the mean is greater than 5 almonds. In such a case, the cutoff changes, since all 5% of the *t* distribution must fall above the cutoff point. As an example, the new cutoff point would be 1.076 and again the null would be rejected since our test statistic of 2.36 falls outside the cutoff point. It should be emphasized that only one significance test exactly as described here can legitimately be performed for any sample. The statistical characteristics of the test are not retained if one hypothesis is tested, and then on the basis of its results, another one of exactly the same form is performed.

Appendix D

Statistical Tables

TABLE D.1

Percentage Points of Student's t Distribution

	Level of significance for one-tailed test					
	.10	.05	.025	.01	.005	.0005
	Level of significance for two-tailed test					
df	.20	.10	.05	.02	.01	.001
1	3.078	6.314	12.706	31.821	63.657	636.619
2	1.886	2.920	4.303	6.965	9.925	31.598
3	1.638	2.353	3.182	4.541	5.841	12.941
4	1.533	2.132	2.776	3.747	4.604	8.610
5	1.476	2.015	2.571	3.365	4.032	6.859
6	1.440	1.943	2.447	3.143	3.707	5.959
7	1.415	1.895	2.365	2.998	3.499	5.405
8	1.397	1.860	2.306	2.896	3.355	5.041
9	1.383	1.833	2.262	2.821	3.250	4.781
10	1.372	1.812	2.228	2.764	3.169	4.587
11	1.363	1.796	2.201	2.718	3.106	4.437
12	1.356	1.782	2.179	2.681	3.055	4.318
13	1.350	1.771	2.160	2.650	3.012	4.221
14	1.345	1.761	2.145	2.624	2.977	4.140
15	1.341	1.753	2.131	2.602	2.947	4.073
16	1.337	1.746	2.120	2.583	2.921	4.015
17	1.333	1.740	2.110	2.567	2.898	3.965
18	1.330	1.734	2.101	2.552	2.878	3.922
19	1.328	1.729	2.093	2.539	2.861	3.883
20	1.325	1.725	2.086	2.528	2.845	3.850
21	1.323	1.721	2.080	2.518	2.831	3.819
22	1.321	1.717	2.074	2.508	2.819	3.792
23	1.319	1.714	2.069	2.500	2.807	3.767
24	1.318	1.711	2.064	2.492	2.797	3.745
25	1.316	1.708	2.060	2.485	2.787	3.725
26	1.315	1.706	2.056	2.479	2.779	3.707
27	1.314	1.703	2.052	2.473	2.771	3.690
28	1.313	1.701	2.048	2.467	2.763	3.674
29	1.311	1.699	2.045	2.462	2.756	3.659
30	1.310	1.697	2.042	2.457	2.750	3.646
40	1.303	1.684	2.021	2.423	2.704	3.551
60	1.296	1.671	2.000	2.390	2.660	3.460
120	1.289	1.658	1.980	2.358	2.617	3.373
∞	1.282	1.645	1.960	3.326	2.576	3.291

Source: Table is an abridged version of Table III taken from R. A. Fisher an∴ F. Yates, *Statistical Tables for Biological, Agricultural, and Medical Research*, 6th ed. published by Longman Group UK Ltd. (previously published by Oliver and Boyd Ltd, Edinburgh), by permission of the authors and publishers.

F Distribution, 5 Percent Significance

Degrees of freedom for numerator

	1	2	3	4	5	6	7	8	9
1	161	200	216	225	230	234	237	239	241
2	18.5	19.0	19.2	19.2	19.3	19.3	19.4	19.4	19.4
3	10.1	9.55	9.28	9.12	9.01	8.94	8.89	8.85	8.81
4	7.71	6.94	6.59	6.39	6.26	6.16	6.09	6.04	6.00
5	6.61	5.79	5.41	5.19	5.05	4.95	4.88	4.82	4.77
6	5.99	5.14	4.76	4.53	4.39	4.28	4.21	4.15	4.10
7	5.59	4.74	4.35	4.12	3.97	3.87	3.79	3.73	3.68
8	5.32	4.46	4.07	3.84	3.69	3.58	3.50	3.44	3.39
9	5.12	4.26	3.86	3.63	3.48	3.37	3.29	3.23	3.18
10	4.96	4.10	3.71	3.48	3.33	3.22	3.14	3.07	3.02
11	4.84	3.98	3.59	3.36	3.20	3.09	3.01	2.95	2.90
12	4.75	3.89	3.49	3.26	3.11	3.00	2.91	2.85	2.80
13	4.67	3.81	3.41	3.18	3.03	2.92	2.83	2.77	2.71
14	4.60	3.74	3.34	3.11	2.96	2.85	2.76	2.70	2.65
15	4.54	3.68	3.29	3.06	2.90	2.79	2.71	2.64	2.59
16	4.49	3.63	3.24	3.01	2.85	2.74	2.66	2.59	2.54
17	4.45	3.59	3.20	2.96	2.81	2.70	2.61	2.55	2.48
18	4.41	3.55	3.16	2.93	2.77	2.66	2.58	2.51	2.46
19	4.38	3.52	3.13	2.90	2.74	2.63	2.54	2.48	2.42
20	4.35	3.49	3.10	2.87	2.71	2.60	2.51	2.45	2.39
21	4.32	3.47	3.07	2.84	2.68	2.57	2.49	2.42	2.37
22	4.30	3.44	3.05	2.82	2.66	2.55	2.46	2.40	2.34
23	4.28	3.42	3.03	2.80	2.64	2.53	2.44	2.37	2.32
24	4.26	3.40	3.01	2.78	2.62	2.51	2.42	2.36	2.30
25	4.24	3.39	2.99	2.76	2.60	2.49	2.40	2.34	2.28
30	4.17	3.32	2.92	2.69	2.53	2.42	2.33	2.27	2.21
40	4.08	3.23	2.84	2.61	2.45	2.34	2.25	2.18	2.12
60	4.00	3.15	2.76	2.53	2.37	2.25	2.17	2.10	2.04
120	3.92	3.07	2.68	2.45	2.29	2.18	2.09	2.02	1.96
∞	3.84	3.00	2.60	2.37	2.21	2.10	2.01	1.94	1.88

	10	12	15	20	24	30	40	60	120	∞
1	242	244	246	248	249	250	251	252	253	254
2	19.4	19.4	19.4	19.5	19.5	19.5	19.5	19.5	19.5	19.5
3	8.79	8.74	8.70	8.66	8.64	8.62	8.59	8.57	8.55	8.53
4	5.96	5.91	5.86	5.80	5.77	5.75	5.72	5.69	5.66	5.63
5	4.74	4.68	4.62	4.56	4.53	4.50	4.46	4.43	4.40	4.37
6	4.06	4.00	3.94	3.87	3.84	3.81	3.77	3.74	3.70	3.67
7	3.64	3.57	3.51	3.44	3.41	3.38	3.34	3.30	3.27	3.23
8	3.35	3.28	3.22	3.15	3.12	3.08	3.04	3.01	2.97	2.93
9	3.14	3.07	3.01	2.94	2.90	2.86	2.83	2.79	2.75	2.71
10	2.98	2.91	2.85	2.77	2.74	2.70	2.66	2.62	2.58	2.54
11	2.85	2.79	2.72	2.65	2.61	2.57	2.53	2.49	2.45	2.40
12	2.75	2.69	2.62	2.54	2.51	2.47	2.43	2.38	2.34	2.30
13	2.67	2.60	2.53	2.46	2.42	2.38	2.34	2.30	2.25	2.21
14	2.60	2.53	2.46	2.39	2.35	2.31	2.27	2.22	2.18	2.13
15	2.54	2.48	2.40	2.33	2.29	2.25	2.20	2.16	2.11	2.07
16	2.49	2.42	2.35	2.28	2.24	2.19	2.15	2.11	2.06	2.01
17	2.45	2.38	2.31	2.23	2.19	2.15	2.10	2.06	2.01	1.96
18	2.41	2.34	2.27	2.19	2.15	2.11	2.06	2.02	1.97	1.92
19	2.39	2.31	2.23	2.16	2.11	2.07	2.03	1.98	1.93	1.88
20	2.35	2.28	2.20	2.12	2.08	2.04	1.99	1.95	1.90	1.84
21	2.32	2.25	2.18	2.10	2.05	2.01	1.96	1.92	1.87	1.81
22	2.30	2.23	2.15	2.07	2.03	1.98	1.94	1.89	1.84	1.78
23	2.27	2.20	2.13	2.05	2.01	1.96	1.91	1.86	1.81	1.76
24	2.25	2.18	2.11	2.03	1.98	1.84	1.89	1.84	1.79	1.73
25	2.24	2.16	2.09	2.01	1.96	1.92	1.87	1.82	1.77	1.71
30	2.16	2.09	2.01	1.93	1.89	1.84	1.79	1.74	1.68	1.62
40	2.08	2.00	1.92	1.84	1.79	1.74	1.69	1.64	1.58	1.51
60	1.99	1.92	1.84	1.75	1.70	1.65	1.59	1.53	1.47	1.39
120	1.91	1.83	1.75	1.66	1.61	1.55	1.50	1.43	1.35	1.25
∞	1.83	1.75	1.67	1.57	1.52	1.46	1.39	1.32	1.22	1.00

Source: Reproduced with permission of the Biometrika Trustees from M. Merrington, C. M. Thompson, "Tables of percentage points of the inverted beta (F) distribution," *Biometrika,* vol. 33 (1943), p. 73.

TABLE D.3
Critical Points of the Durbin-Watson Test, 5 Percent Significance (d_1 and d_u)

n	$k = 1$		$k = 2$		$k = 3$		$k = 4$		$k = 5$	
	d_l	d_u	d_l	d_u	d_l	d_u	d_l	d_u	d_l	d_u
15	0.95	1.23	0.83	1.40	0.71	1.61	0.59	1.84	0.48	2.09
16	0.98	1.24	0.86	1.40	0.75	1.59	0.64	1.80	0.53	2.03
17	1.01	1.25	0.90	1.40	0.79	1.58	0.68	1.77	0.57	1.98
18	1.03	1.26	0.93	1.40	0.82	1.56	0.72	1.74	0.62	1.93
19	1.06	1.28	0.96	1.41	0.86	1.55	0.76	1.73	0.66	1.90
20	1.08	1.28	0.99	1.41	0.89	1.55	0.79	1.72	0.70	1.87
21	1.10	1.30	1.01	1.41	0.92	1.54	0.83	1.69	0.73	1.84
22	1.12	1.31	1.04	1.42	0.95	1.54	0.86	1.68	0.77	1.82
23	1.14	1.32	1.06	1.42	0.97	1.54	0.89	1.67	0.80	1.80
24	1.16	1.33	1.08	1.43	1.00	1.54	0.91	1.66	0.83	1.79
25	1.18	1.34	1.10	1.43	1.02	1.54	0.94	1.65	0.86	1.77
26	1.19	1.35	1.12	1.44	1.04	1.54	0.96	1.65	0.88	1.76
27	1.21	1.36	1.13	1.44	1.06	1.54	0.99	1.64	0.91	1.75
28	1.22	1.37	1.15	1.45	1.08	1.54	1.01	1.64	0.93	1.74
29	1.24	1.38	1.17	1.45	1.10	1.54	1.03	1.63	0.96	1.73
30	1.25	1.38	1.18	1.46	1.12	1.54	1.05	1.63	0.98	1.73
31	1.26	1.39	1.20	1.47	1.13	1.55	1.07	1.63	1.00	1.72
32	1.27	1.40	1.21	1.47	1.15	1.55	1.08	1.63	1.02	1.71
33	1.28	1.41	1.22	1.48	1.16	1.55	1.10	1.63	1.04	1.71
34	1.29	1.41	1.24	1.48	1.17	1.55	1.12	1.63	1.06	1.70
35	1.30	1.42	1.25	1.48	1.19	1.55	1.13	1.63	1.07	1.70
36	1.31	1.43	1.26	1.49	1.20	1.56	1.15	1.63	1.09	1.70
37	1.32	1.43	1.27	1.49	1.21	1.56	1.16	1.62	1.10	1.70
38	1.33	1.44	1.28	1.50	1.23	1.56	1.17	1.62	1.12	1.70
39	1.34	1.44	1.29	1.50	1.24	1.56	1.19	1.63	1.13	1.69
40	1.35	1.45	1.30	1.51	1.25	1.57	1.20	1.63	1.15	1.69
45	1.39	1.48	1.34	1.53	1.30	1.58	1.25	1.63	1.21	1.69
50	1.42	1.50	1.38	1.54	1.34	1.59	1.30	1.64	1.26	1.69
55	1.45	1.52	1.41	1.56	1.37	1.60	1.33	1.64	1.30	1.69
60	1.47	1.54	1.44	1.57	1.40	1.61	1.37	1.65	1.33	1.69
65	1.49	1.55	1.46	1.59	1.43	1.63	1.40	1.66	1.36	1.69
70	1.51	1.57	1.48	1.60	1.45	1.63	1.42	1.66	1.39	1.70
75	1.53	1.58	1.50	1.61	1.47	1.64	1.45	1.67	1.42	1.70
80	1.54	1.59	1.52	1.63	1.49	1.65	1.47	1.67	1.44	1.70
85	1.56	1.60	1.53	1.63	1.51	1.66	1.49	1.68	1.46	1.71
90	1.57	1.61	1.55	1.64	1.53	1.66	1.50	1.69	1.48	1.71
95	1.58	1.62	1.56	1.65	1.54	1.67	1.52	1.69	1.50	1.71
100	1.59	1.63	1.57	1.65	1.55	1.67	1.53	1.70	1.51	1.72

Source: Reproduced with the permission of The Biometrika Trustees from J. Durbin and G. S. Watson, "Testing for Serial Correlation in Least Squares Regression," *Biometrika*, vol. 38 (1951), pp. 159–177.

Notes

Chapter 1

1. The book is for public managers. The term public includes both governmental and nonprofit organizations (as contrasted to for-profit organizations). To streamline the terminology, frequently the term not-for-profits will be used instead of governmental and nonprofit organizations.

2. The *Cleveland Plain Dealer,* August 1984, reports the research of two University of Delaware researchers, Robert E. Davis and Roger S. Ulrich, on work attendance patterns of federal employees. Davis and Ulrich found that hot weather, especially on a sustained basis at night, reduces work attendance in Northern cities. They hypothesized that lack of air conditioning was responsible, since people had trouble sleeping in the heat. They also found that rain during the daytime hours on weekends cut attendance on Mondays, probably because the rain interfered with weekend leisure, reducing the recuperative power of the weekend, and causing more people to feel ill on Monday.

3. Over the last decade, social scientists have conducted a number of large-scale experiments that have used random assignment. A literature comparing various experimental designs (experimental, quasi-experimental, and nonexperimental) has developed. For a classic work, see D. Campbell and J. Stanley, *Experimental and Quasi-Experimental Design for Research* (Chicago: Rand McNally, 1963).

4. Chapter 7 will elaborate on this issue.

5. There are more sophisticated techniques to use with nominal data, such as logit and probit analysis. These will be explained in Chapter 7.

6. It is important to know if the groups being compared have been randomly assigned or not. See Robert J. LaLonde, "Evaluating the Econometric Evaluations

of Training Programs with Experimental Data," *American Economic Review* 49 (1986): 604-620, for a comparison of results using randomly assigned (experimental) data and nonrandomly assigned data.

Chapter 2

1. Anita Summers and Barbara Wolfe, "Intradistrict Distribution of School Inputs to the Disadvantaged: Evidence for the Courts," *Journal of Human Resources* 11 (1976): 328-342.

2. The intercept coefficient for the regressions was not reported in the article. It was estimated from other statistics given in the article.

3. The first derivatives, with respect to b_0 and b_1, are set equal to zero, and the second derivatives are checked to make sure they are positive. The first derivatives and their solutions, up until the normal equations, are shown here. Recall that, dropping the t's:

$$\Sigma e^2 = \Sigma(Y - b_0 - b_1 X)^2.$$

Then, the first derivatives are:

$$\partial\Sigma e^2/\partial b_0 = -2\Sigma(Y - b_0 - b_1 X) = 0.$$

Dividing through by -2:

$\Sigma(Y - b_0 - b_1 X) = 0$, or the first normal equation.

$$\partial\Sigma e^2/\partial b_1 = -2\Sigma(Y - b_0 - b_1 X)(X) = 0.$$

Dividing through by -2:

$\Sigma(Y - b_0 - b_1 X)(X) = 0$, or the second normal equation.

4. This definition is for the sample R^2. There is a corresponding population R^2 that indicates how well the population regression line fits the population data.

Chapter 3

1. A.G. Holtmann and E. Odgers Olsen, "The Demand for Dental Care: A Study of Consumption and Household Production," *Journal of Human Resources,* 11 (1976): 546-560.

2. It is important to note that bestness for least squares estimators refers only to estimates that are unbiased. If we expanded our options to consider estimators

that were biased as well as unbiased, we could find estimators whose variance was smaller.

3. Although the BLUE qualities of the least squares estimators are desirable, it should be remembered that it is possible to use formulas that result in smaller variance estimators, if one is willing to accept some bias. Least squares estimators are best only among all linear *unbiased* estimators. In addition, it is also possible to construct nonlinear estimators with smaller variances (and possibly no bias as well). Nonlinear estimators will be more difficult to use in the sense that solving for the estimated values of the coefficients may be very time consuming, even on a computer, and therefore expensive. Nonlinear regression refers to the use of estimators that are not linear in the coefficients (the slopes and intercepts) and therefore are not linear in the Y's. For a good part of this text, only the least squares estimators will be discussed. Some of the last chapters will deal with nonlinear estimators that are particularly useful for public management and analysis problems.

4. This is strictly true only if several of the assumptions of the least squares model are met (the error term must have zero mean, constant variance, and zero covariance and the X's must be fixed). These assumptions are discussed in Chapter 6.

5. In the bivariate case, the formulas for the variances of the slope and intercept are as follows, with the t subscripts dropped:

$$\text{Variance } b_1 = S^2_b = (S^2_e)/\Sigma(X - \bar{X})^2 =$$
$$(S^2_e)/[(T - 1)\Sigma(X - \bar{X})^2/(T - 1)] = S^2_e/[(T - 1)S^2_x].$$
$$\text{Variance } b_0 = S^2_{b_0} = (S^2_e \Sigma X^2)/(T\Sigma(X - \bar{X})^2 =$$
$$[S^2_e \Sigma X^2]/[(T - 1)(T)\Sigma(X - \bar{X})^2]/(T - 1) = [S^2_e X^2]/[(T - 1)(T)S^2_x]$$

where

S^2_e = the estimated variance of the error term =
$$\Sigma(e - \bar{e})^2/[T - (K + 1)] = \Sigma e^2/[T - (K + 1)],$$

K = the number of independent variables,

$[T - (K + 1)]$ = the degrees of freedom, and

S^2_x = estimated variance of $X = \Sigma(X - \bar{X})^2/(T - 1)$.

6. Intuitively, this makes sense because the variance of the slopes depends on the variance of the error term, and the error term is assumed to have a normal distribution.

7. The idea for this example was suggested by Kathleen Faughnan, a doctoral student at New York University's Graduate School of Public Administration in 1985.

8. One would expect that if the null hypothesis of $R^2 = 0$ is rejected at a given

significance level, then at least one of the regression slope coefficients would be significant at the same significance level. While this expectation is generally confirmed, it occasionally happens that the null hypothesis of zero effect for each slope coefficient cannot be rejected, but still the entire relationship is significant. Conceptually, this phenomenon occurs because, in combination, all the variables explain some of the variation in the dependent variable, but the individual effects cannot be separated. Statistically, the result often occurs when some of the independent variables are very highly correlated with one another, making it statistically impossible to separate their effects.

Likewise, when the null hypothesis of $R^2 = 0$ is not rejected, we would expect all the slope coefficients to be insignificant. In some cases, one or more slope coefficients will be significant even though the entire relationship is not. Technically, this is because the degrees of freedom used for the F and t tests differ. Conceptually, there is little sense one can attach to such results.

9. Joseph L. C. Cheng and William McKinley, "Toward an Integration of Organization Research and Practice: A Contingency Study of Bureaucratic Control and Performance in Scientific Settings," *Administrative Science Quarterly* 28, 1 (1983): 85-100, by permission of *Administrative Science Quarterly*, copyright © 1983 Cornell University.

10. Ibid. 86.

11. Ibid. 86.

12. SPSS/PC+ is a trademark of SPSS Inc. of Chicago, Illinois, for its proprietary computer software. For detailed instruction on entering data and requesting statistics, see *SPSS/PC+ V2.0 Base Manual* (Chicago, Illinois: SPSS Inc., 1988).

13. Matthew P. Drennan, *Modeling Metropolitan Economies for Forecasting and Policy Analysis,* (New York: New York University Press, 1985).

Chapter 4

1. Ideally, the regression equation would be reestimated using independent variables that were cost-adjusted. Then, the cost-effectiveness of each controllable variable could be ascertained directly from its coefficient. See Dennis J. Aigner, *Basic Econometrics* (New Jersey: Prentice-Hall, Inc., 1971): 105-106.

2. Stuart J. Greenfield, "Audit Productivity: A Cross-Sectional Analysis," *National Tax Journal* 15 (1982): 501-506.

3. Stepwise regression can be performed in other ways as well. Instead of automatically retaining all variables already entered, those that do not meet a specific criterion on the F test can be eliminated at each step. Or all the variables can be entered into the equation in the first step, and then variables can be eliminated one by one. See *SPSS^X User's Guide* (Chicago, Illinois: SPSS Inc., 1986): 666, for an explanation of how one popular preprogrammed computer regression package handles stepwise regression.

4. Charles A. Lave, "Appendix C, Speeding and Highway Fatalities," in *55: A Decade of Experience,* study chairman Alan Altshuler (Washington, D.C.: Transportation Research Board, Special Report 204, National Research Council, 1984): 200-208. Also see the regression results reported in Charles A. Lave, "Speeding, Coordination, and the 55 MPH Limit," *American Economic Review* 75 (1985): 1159-1164. A follow-up on the National Research Council study that looks at costs and benefits of various speed limits on rural and urban highways is available in: Dana Kamerud, "Benefits and Costs of the 55 MPH Speed Limit: New Estimates and Their Implications," *Journal of Policy Analysis and Management* 7 (1988): 341-352.

5. Time-series data are ones whose values are generated across time (quarters, months, years). Cross-section data are generated among cases at one point in time (for example, large cities in 1985, hospitals in each state in 1980).

Chapter 5

1. If females were left out (coded 0), while males were coded 1, then the estimated equation would be as follows:

Earnings per year = 2000 + 1000 education + 3000 sex.
The regression equation automatically adjusts to the left-out variable and the end result is the same.

2. There is a test, called the Chow test, for the difference between coefficients in two equations; however, it applies only under limited circumstances. See Gregory C. Chow, "Test of Equality Between Sets of Coefficients in Two Linear Regressions," *Econometrica* 28 (1960): 591-605.

3. Two other ways to understand the interpretation of seasonal dummies are (i) by writing four equations, one for each season; and (ii) by graphing the estimated equation as four different lines.

4. Luk J. Cannoodt and James R. Knickman, "The Effect of Hospital Characteristics and Organizational Factors on Pre- and Postoperative Lengths of Hospital Stay," *Health Services Research* (1984): 561-585.

5. In addition, one can represent continuous compounding using "*e,*" the base of the natural logarithm:

$$Y = 100e^{rt}.$$

This says that the one hundred dollars will grow continuously at r interest rate for t periods. The r and t must be stated in similar units; for example, .03 per day (r = .0003 and t = days).

6. Logarithm$_{10}$1 = 0 because 10^0 = 1. The logarithm of one is equal to zero for any base because one is obtained when any number is raised to the zero power.

7. In order for the traditional hypothesis tests for the coefficients to be valid, we must assume that the logarithm of the error term ($Log_{10}E$) is distributed normally, not that E itself is so distributed.

8. The base of the logarithm can also be the natural *e*.

9. Ralph A. Pope, "Economies of Scale in Large State and Municipal Retirement Systems," *Public Budgeting and Finance,* 6 (1986): 70-80.

10. If the reader knows calculus, finding the effect of an interactive variable is not difficult. If

$$Y = b_0 + b_1X_1 + b_2X_1X_2,$$

then the effect on *Y* of a change in X_1 is found by taking the partial first derivative:

$$\frac{\partial Y}{\partial X_1} = b_1 + b_2X_2.$$

11. Reprinted from Joseph L. C. Cheng and William McKinley, "Toward an Integration of Organization Research and Practice: A Contingency Study of Bureaucratic Control and Performance in Scientific Settings," *Administrative Science Quarterly* 28, 1 (1983): 85-100, by permission of *Administrative Science Quarterly,* copyright © 1983 Cornell University.

12. Matthew P. Drennan, *Modeling Metropolitan Economies for Forecasting and Policy Analysis,* (New York: New York University Press, 1985).

13. Masamori Hashimoto and John Raisian, "Employment Tenure and Earnings Profiles in Japan and the United States," *American Economic Review* 77 (1985): 721-735.

Chapter 6

1. See S.M. Goldfeld and R.E. Quant, "Some tests for Homoskedasticity," *Journal of the American Statistical Society* 60 (1965): 539-547. Other texts, such as Robert S. Pindyck and Daniel L. Rubinfeld's *Econometric Models and Economic Forecasts,* 2nd ed. (New York: McGraw-Hill Book Company, 1981), explain other tests.

2. See J. Durbin and G.S. Watson, "Testing for Serial Correlation in Least Squares Regression," *Biometrika* 38 (1951): 159-171, or any standard regression text.

3. Matthew P. Drennan, *Modeling Metropolitan Economies for Forecasting and Policy Analysis* (New York: New York University Press, 1985), Chapter 6.

4. The direction of the impact depends on how home and school variables are defined. It is assumed that both are defined so that a positive coefficient is expected in an equation that regresses school and home inputs on achievement.

5. Specification bias also occurs when too many variables are included in the equation. In such a case, the problem is that the standard error of the estimates is increased, and it is more difficult to identify significant variables. However, no bias results.

6. Charles Brecher and Susan Nesbitt, "Factors Associated with Variation in Financial Condition Among Voluntary Hospitals," *Health Services Research* 3 (1985): 267-300.

7. Drennan, *Modeling Metropolitan Economies.*

Chapter 7

1. Further examples include whether individuals are employed or not, whether college students live on or off campus, whether high school students drop out or not, whether workers join unions or not, and whether the public is satisfied or not with the provision of governmental services.

2. See the work on the negative income tax, much of it published by the Institute for Research on Poverty, University of Wisconsin-Madison; the work on the demand for health insurance by the Rand Corporation, Santa Monica, California; and the 1/1000 samples provided by the decennial censuses of the United States, the United States Department of Commerce.

3. SPSS provides programs for mainframes and for personal computers. See Maria J. Norusis, *Advanced Statistics Guide, SPSS^X* (Chicago, Illinois: McGraw-Hill Book Co., 1985). Many other personal computer packages are available as well. See, for example, Jeffrey A. Dubin and Douglas Rivers, "Statistical Software Tools," Dubin/Rivers Research, 1510 Ontario Avenue, Pasadena, California 91103; or William Greene, "E.T.–The Econometrics Toolkit," Econometric Software, Church Street Stations, Box 3526, New York, New York 10008-3526.

4. The range of probabilities from 0 to 1 can also be represented as a range from 0% to 100%. In this chapter, 0 and 1 rather than 0% and 100% will be used.

5. This model is also called the cumulative normal because it is based on a function of a normally distributed variable.

6. Discriminant analysis can give the same results as the linear probability model when the dependent variable is a dichotomy.

7. Richard M. Scheffler, "The United Mine Workers' Health Plan," *Medical Care* 22 (March 1984): 247-254.

8. Computer programs used to estimate logit models often provide exact calculations for the user.

9. Since each P is a function of all of the independent variables (all of the X's), this means that the model is an interactive one, where the effect of any one independent variable will depend on the value of other independent varaiables.

10. There is a technique called Monte Carlo experiments that uses computer-generated random samples that conform to certain assumptions about the population model and the distribution of the error term to provide small sample "data" on maximum likelihood estimators.

11. Harold S. Luft, James C. Robinson, Deborah W. Garnick, Susan C. Maerki, and Stephen J. McPhee, "The Role of Specialized Clinical Services in Competition Among Hospitals," *Inquiry* 23 (1986): 83-94.

12. This is actually a rather high amount since if zero packs are smoked, the probability of death after age 60 is approximately zero. If $X = 0$, $Y = -3$; then $f(Z) = f(-3) = .001$ and $b_1 f(Z) = .5 (.001) = .0005$ or .05 percentage points (close to zero).

13. Randall P. Ellis and Thomas G. McGuire, "Cost Sharing and Patterns of Mental Health Care Utilization," *The Journal of Human Resources* 21 (1986): 359-379.

Chapter 8

1. For an excellent analysis of the meaning and measurement of financial condition, see Robert Berne and Richard Schramm, *The Financial Analysis of Governments* (Englewood Cliffs, New Jersey: Prentice-Hall, 1986).

2. As in any other model, a pooled one may exhibit autocorrelation and/or heteroskedasticity. The solutions for these problems are not harder (or easier!) than for any other model. A version of differencing can be done, if autocorrelation is present. And, a version of weighted least squares can be performed to correct for heteroskedasticity.

3. This formulation estimated using OLS will often lead to inconsistent estimates. Methods other than OLS need to be used for estimation in such a case.

4. Robert A. Margo, "Educational Achievement in Segregated School Systems: The Effects of "Separate-but-Equal," *American Economic Review* 76 (1986): 794-801.

5. The only time when the standard error will not be increased by dropping observations is when all of the values of the X variable that are missing are exactly equal to the sample mean of the observed values of X.

6. The instrumental variable approach only provides an approximation to the actual values for the missing data. When all is said and done, missing data still represent missing information.

7. D. Lane, D. Uyeno, A. Stark, E. Kliever, and G. Gutman, "Forecasting Demand for Long-Term Care Services," *Health Services Research* 20 (1985): 435-460.

8. The preferred method of the researchers was the Markov method. It is not explained here because the method, while not difficult, is beyond the scope of this book. Nevertheless, the other two methods are interesting examples of methods explained in this book.

9. David Barton Smith and Robert Pickard, "Evaluation of the Impact of Medicare and Medicaid Prospective Payment on Utilization of Philadelphia Area Hospitals," *Health Services Research* 21 (1986): 529-546.

10. The most common example of a simultaneous equation system is the economic model of supply and demand, where price and quantity are determined jointly.

11. The relationship of the error terms across equations is important to how the equations are estimated. Estimation methods are discussed later in this chapter.

12. John S. Akin and Irwin Garfinkel, "School Expenditures and the Economic Returns to Schooling," *Journal of Human Resources* 12 (1977): 460-481.

13. Footnote 15 shows two similar equations and their reduced form solutions.

14. If an equation is "exactly identified," it is possible to obtain the structural coefficients from the reduced form ones. The next section will discuss what is meant by exactly identified.

15. The second equation in the following system is exactly identified.

$$Y_1 = B_0 + B_1Y_2 + B_2X_1 + E_1 \text{ and } Y_2 = A_0 + A_1Y_1 + E_2.$$

The reduced form equations look as follows:

$$Y_1 (B_0 + B_1A_0)/(1 - A_1B_1) + [B_2/(1 - B_1A_1)]X_1$$
$$+ [B_1/1 - A_1B_1)E_2 + [1/(1 - A_1B_1)]E_1$$

and

$$Y_1 = (A_0 + A_1B_0)/(1 - A_1B_1 + A_1B_2)/(1 - A_1B_1)]X_2$$
$$+ [A_1/(1 - A_1B_1)]E_1 + [1/(1 - A_1B_1)]E_2.$$

or:

$$Y_1 = \pi_{11} + \pi_{21} + U_1$$

and

$$Y_2 = \pi_{12} + \pi_{22} + U_2.$$

Using the reduced form coefficients, one can solve for the structural coefficients as follows:

$$A_1 = \pi_{22}/\pi_{21}$$
$$A_0 = \pi_{12} - A_1\pi_{11}.$$

16. John M. Kuder and Gary S. Levitz, "Visits to the Physician: An Evaluation of the Usual-Source Effect," *Health Services Research* 20 (1985): 579-596.

Chapter 9

1. Note two things about this productivity regression. First, there is no effort to assess if the program works. There is no control group of nontrainees; it is possible that a higher percentage of nontrainees are employed. What is assessed here is the comparative productivity of this program. Naturally, one would hope that it had already been determined that the program "worked." Second, the measure of productivity is purely illustrative. In reality, a number of different measures would probably be used; the one described here might not even be among the most useful

to a particular program. The choice of the productivity measure would depend on the goals of the program and, to some extent, the "politics" of who chooses.

2. The data base would include procedures where significant numbers of preventable deaths could theoretically occur. Patients with risk factors that were extraordinarily high, such as ones with secondary malignancies, would possibly be excluded altogether. Likewise, hospitals that are hospices or in other ways served primarily dying patients would be omitted. A logistic model, with the dependent variable describing whether a patient died or not, would be appropriate.

3. Not everyone agrees that hospital characteristics should be included in the regression. Some authors think only patient risk factors should be included. See Mark S. Blumberg, "Comments on HCFA Hospital Death Rate Statistical Outliers," *Health Services Research* 21 (1977): 715-739.

4. "U.S. Lists 27 New York Hospitals in Medicare Deaths," *New York Times,* 12 March 1986.

5. See Harry M. Rosen and Barbara A. Green, "The HCFA Excess Mortality Lists: A Methodological Critique," *Hospital and Health Services Administration* (1987).

6. There are a number of legitimate criticisms of the way the Health Care Financing Administration's study was done. First, the data were not as accurate as one would wish. For example, hospitals in some states apparently underreport their death rates. Second, the included variables were not precisely the desired ones. DRG's upon discharge were meant to capture severity of cases, but there is much variation within these groupings, they do not adequately control for severity upon admission, and some are tautological (for example, DRG 123 is all acute myocardial infarcts *resulting in death*). Average length of stay was meant to measure the amount of time in the hospital, since patients who stay longer have more days to die. But this variable is highly correlated with region of the country. Average patient stays are longer in the Northeast than in the West, and one would not want to control for region. What is needed here is death within a certain period, including time after discharge. The independent variable for percent of minority patients is problematic. While it was intended to capture patient risk, it might also represent degree of hospital care, and one would not want to reward hospitals that uniformly giver poorer care to minorities. Third, some small hospitals had such small numbers of reported deaths that it was difficult for their actual death rate to be lower than would be predicted from an average regression relationship. Fourth, there were difficulties involved in the choice of which residuals were high enough to warrant special attention.

7. There are four possible reasons for a sample residual (a difference between predicted and actual death rates):

i. some variables that are controllable by the hospital are omitted from the model,

ii. some variables that are uncontrollable by the hospital (patient risk factors) are omitted,

iii. some of the variation in death rates among hospitals is truly stochastic and cannot be explained by any model, and

iv. the coefficients differ from the true population coefficients because they are estimates.

Of these four reasons, only numbers one (i) and four (iv) would be acceptable when using a residual to imply something about care within a hospital. If number three (iii) results in a model with a low R^2, then one needs to be relatively sure that one thinks this is because controllable factors, which presumably cannot be measured with available data, have been omitted and account for the unexplained variation. Otherwise some hospitals will be unfairly singled out, simply because they are by chance high or low on death rates, or because there are unmeasured risk factors beyond their control. If one uses statistics at all, one must learn to live with estimations as listed in number four (iv).

8. Mark S. Blumberg, "Comments on HCFA Hospital Death Rate Statistical Outliers," 732.

Bibliographical Essay

Several traditional textbooks cover material similar to what is discussed in this book. These traditional texts use more advanced mathematics, including calculus and matrix algebra, but parts can be read even without an understanding of the mathematics. For readers who want to go on to do their own statistical analyses, two texts in particular are highly recommended. These are Robert S. Pindyk and Daniel Rubinfeld, *Econometric Models and Economic Forecasts,* 2nd ed. (New York: McGraw-Hill Book Company, 1981) and Eric Hanushek and John E. Jackson, *Statistical Methods for Social Scientists* (New York: Academic Press, 1977).

Some of the paperbacks written in the Sage Publications series in Quantitative Applications in the Social Sciences are particularly readable. For example, I recommend John H. Aldrich and Forrest D. Nelson, *Linear Probability, Logit, and Probit Models* (Beverly Hills: Sage University Paper series on Quantitative Applications in the Social Sciences, series no. 07-045, Sage Publications, 1984); and Larry Schroeder, David L. Sjoquist, and Paula E. Stephan, *Understanding Regression Analysis* (Beverly Hills: Sage University Paper series on Quantitative Applications in the Social Sciences, series no. 07-057, Sage Publications, 1986).

One book provided a model and data for computer examples in Chapters 3 through 6. This book is an excellent illustration of how multiple regression can be used to enlighten public decision-making and I recommend it to those who wish to see how a skillful analyst applies multiple regression to a public management problem. See Matthew Drennan, *Modeling Metropolitan Economies for Forecasting and Policy Analysis* (New York: New York University Press, 1985).

The manuals and guides that accompany the SPSS products also cover the essentials of many statistical techniques. For those who want to perform their own analyses, these manuals serve the dual purpose of explaining the statistics and documenting how to use the computer program. See in particular the following two books: Maria J. Norusis, *SPSS/PC+ V2.0 Base Manual* (Chicago: SPSS Inc., 1988) and *Advanced Statistics Guide, SPSS^x* (New York, McGraw-Hill Book Company, 1985).

Finally, there are journals in each management specialty that often report results of projects and research using the statistical methods discussed in this book. A few of these in a variety of management areas are listed here and may serve as both a source of further statistical applications and a helpful reference in your own work. In the general management area, *Administrative Science Quarterly;* in health care management, *Health Services Research, Inquiry,* and *Medical Care;* in human resources management, *Journal of Human Resources;* in financial management, *Public Budgeting and Finance* and *National Tax Journal;* in education management, *Journal of Education Finance;* and in policy management, *Evaluation Review* and *Journal of Policy Analysis and Management.*

Index

About the Author

Leanna Stiefel, associate professor of Economics at New York University's Robert F. Wagner Graduate School of Public Service, teaches courses in statistical methods, public finance, accounting, financial management, and microeconomics. She was previously on the faculties of Michigan State University and Sarah Lawrence College. Her research has focused on the incentive structures and distributional impacts of different methods of financing kindergarten through twelfth grade education and on the effect of in-kind transfers on the distribution of income. She is coauthor (with Robert Berne) of *The Measurement of Equity in School Finance,* and her work has appeared in *Policy Analysis, Policy Sciences, Public Administration Review, Journal of Education Finance, Journal of Economic Issues, American Behavioral Scientist, Educational Evaluation and Policy Analysis* and several edited books.

Leanna Stiefel received her B.A. in French from the University of Michigan, her M.A. and Ph.D. in Economics from the University of Wisconsin-Madison, and an Advanced Professional Certificate in Finance from the Stern School of Business at New York University.